THE EVERYTHING

MONEY BOOK

Learn how to manage,
budget, save, and invest
your money so there's plenty left over

Rich Mintzer with Kathi Mintzer, C.P.A.

Adams Media Corporation
Holbrook, Massachusetts

An Everything Series Book.
The Everything Series is a trademark of Adams Media Corporation.

Published by Adams Media Corporation
260 Center Street, Holbrook, MA 02343

ISBN: 1-58062-145-7

Printed in the United States of America.

J I H G F E D C B

Library of Congress Cataloging-in-Publication Data
Mintzer, Richard.
The everything money book / Richard Mintzer with Kathi Mintzer.— 1st ed.
p.   cm.
ISBN 1-58062-145-7
Includes index.
1. Finance, Personal. 2. Investments. I. Mintzer, Kathi. II. Title.
HG179.M528   1999
332.024—dc21   98-50877
CIP

The information contained in this book is general in nature and is provided for
informational purposes only. It should not be construed as the provision of tax,
legal, or investment advice. For specific guidance as to how this information affects
your personal circumstances, consult your tax, legal, or financial advisor.

Illustrations by Barry Littmann

This book is available at quantity discounts for bulk purchases.
For information, call 1-800-872-5627
(in Massachusetts, call 781-767-8100).

Visit our home page at http://www.adamsmedia.com

CONTENTS

ACKNOWLEDGMENTS

In an effort to select and present the most significant information in an easy-to-follow, concise book, a lot of very knowledgeable people in the financial field were consulted, and we appreciate their contributions.

First and foremost we thank our father, Jerome Mintzer, for guidance, wisdom, and a lot of late-night editing and assistance in putting this book together. His years as a CPA have served us well and taught us a great deal. Also, we thank our mom for utilizing her skills as a proofreader. And thank you to our respective spouses: Carol Mintzer for all your editorial and research help and Dave Lipschitz for your patience and computer assistance.

Pam Liflander, thank you for getting this project off the ground and all your efforts to bring this book to fruition.

Among the many others we thank are Fritz Elmendorff of the Consumer Bankers Association; Marge McGowan of the Bank of New York; Margerie Wasserman of Personal Financial Advisors; Kate Stonehouse, Fiona Adams, and Luma Murad at Sallie Mae; Maxine Sweet of Experian Information Services in Chatsworth, California; Eileen Dorsey, MBA, MS, CFP at Money Consultants Inc. in St. Louis; Lou Stanasolovich, CFP at Legend Financial Advisors Inc. in Pittsburgh; Robert H. Moody II, MS, CFP, and CLU of Tombs, Moody and Clontz Llp. in Atlanta; Sid Blum, CFP, CPA/PFS at Successful Financial Solutions, Inc. in Northbrook, Illinois; Barry Kilzer, JD, MBA of the Kilzer Financial Group in Carmel, California; *Frugal Luxuries* author Tracey McBride; Ron Michelman, attorney at Michelman & Michelman Inc. in Los Angeles; Linda Cicillini of Alan T. Nahoum in New York; Esther Berger, managing director at Berger & Associates, Llc., Beverly Hills; Cheryl Rowling and Chris Phelps at Rowling, Dold and Associates in San Diego; Stan Chadsey of Capitol Planning Associates in New York City; James Battaglia, CFP of Battaglia Financial Planning in New York City; Warren King, a very helpful real estate broker and consultant from the King Group in New York City; Michael Joyce, CFA at Michael Joyce & Assoc. in Richmond, Virginia; David Frisch, CPA at Joel Issacson & Co. in

New York City; Jack Joyce at College Board in New York City; Gary H. Schatsky, chairman of the National Association of Personal Financial Advisors; Greg Horton, CFP; Roger Volz; Jennifer Goffman of American Illustrators Gallery in New York City; the Bond Investor Association; the FDIC; and a special thank you to Lou Spiazzi of Phoenix Home Mutual and Ron and Bonnie Rafaloff; and to others too numerous to mention here, thank you all.

INTRODUCTION

We are all (or almost all) chasing the all-mighty dollar to some degree. Trying to succeed, to earn more money, to fulfill a dream, to support a family, or to simply have a better life are just a few of the reasons why money matters. From a psychological perspective, money can be a positive or a negative driving force. It can motivate people to work hard or cause people to use poor judgment out of greed or a need for power. Money can do strange things to people, so it's important to handle it wisely and keep its importance in perspective. Don't let money run your life, or you could be in big trouble.

This book is written to help you handle, manage, and, possibly, earn money through investments. It can provide some suggestions to help you achieve your goals, from saving to pay for college tuition to setting up your retirement plan. It is designed to guide and assist you in matters of personal finance and point you in the right direction to acquire more information when necessary. There are plenty of warnings to help keep you on track and some suggestions to help steer you along the financial highway.

One of the main purposes of this book is to introduce you to the world of investing. Investing does not have to be intimidating. You need not be a "shrewd Wall Street type" to put money into a college or retirement fund, or to buy stocks or mutual funds, or invest in real estate. You need only to plan ahead, consider your future goals, and determine how you can best achieve them. Many people enjoy living for today, which is a marvelous concept when you're young and carefree. However, once you've graduated from high school and perhaps college, it may be time to start thinking about your financial future. As you get older and your responsibilities increase, it's important to formulate a game plan. As your life changes, you may have to re-evaluate and even alter your plans, but it's worth your while to set up a realistic financial plan to start off with.

From budgeting to teaching your children about money to saving for college to making major purchases to retirement and estate plan-

ning, we try to touch upon all the areas that involve you and your hard-earned money. We don't discuss where you earn your money (except through investments); we simply mention various ways to let your money work for you. After all, if your money works well for you, you'll be able to retire.

LOVE AND MONEY

Study after study has shown that money is the number one cause of discord and fighting in marriage. It is at the root of fights over where to go on vacation or when to start a family, or even the classic "we never go anyplace" spats. It's important, therefore, that couples are able to settle their differences and stay on common ground when it comes to money.

Good communication is at the root of any good relationship, and that is especially true where money is concerned. First, a couple should discuss their goals and priorities openly and honestly. If one person has a spend now, worry later attitude while the other is hell bent on a secure lifelong savings plan for a comfortable retirement, there will be trouble in paradise unless compromises are made.

People come into a relationship with different spending philosophies. Therefore, it's important to find common ground and create a plan in which both of you can enjoy some flexibility. Often, for example, one person is the keeper of *the book*, the checkbook, that is, and he or she pays the bills. This is fine if both of you are comfortable with that arrangement. Money should not be used in your relationship as a source of power. That's worth repeating: Money should not be used in your relationship as a source of power! Be sure to establish each person's role regarding money management.

DO WHAT YOU DO BEST

It's also important that each person let the other do what he or she does best. If one is better at making investments, then let that person take the lead role in that area. If your spouse or significant other is better at making sure bills are paid on time and records are kept properly, then that person should utilize his or her skills in that area. Most important, you both should be aware of where you stand financially.

It's also important to make contingency plans. Then, for example, if one of you should lose your job, rather than feel resentment toward that person for "blowing" the strategy, you would have a plan ready to rectify the situation. Say a couple is each putting $500 a month into a retirement fund and she loses her job. Then he may be able to put $750 into the fund for a short time, or they may have to accept that for a while they will put less in their retirement plan. Or, perhaps, they could cut back (together) and save money in another area. It's a matter of choosing options.

WHOSE MONEY IS THIS ANYWAY?

Will you be pooling your money or keeping separate accounts? Whose name will be on the credit cards? Discuss such matters ahead of time. Many couples pool some resources while maintaining separate accounts. They do this to maintain a sense of individuality—which is perfectly fine. This arrangement also works well if they are from different spending backgrounds, as mentioned previously. However, there still should be a common account or ledger in which joint household expenses are shared.

COMPROMISES

If he wants to invest in the market and she is reluctant to take risks, perhaps a safer investment might be a good compromise, maybe a bond or balanced fund, which allows him to own stocks through the fund but offers her a low-risk investment. (For more on saving and investing, see Part II.)

PRIORITIES

If you and your significant other have similar priorities and a similar mind-set, then you are in a good position to avoid money fights. Discuss what you both value most and respect each other's differences. See which priorities you have in common. Do you both value family and want to put money aside for your children? Are you both on lucrative career paths and want to hold off on starting your family until you are both where you want to be in your careers? Where do you rate money on

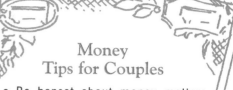

Money Tips for Couples

- Be honest about money matters (as well as other things).
- Keep each other posted on all significant expenditures and investments. Discuss them, unless you've agreed ahead of time that one of you can handle investments on your own.
- Establish in advance how you will keep your money—separate, shared, or some of each.
- Have your own roles established—he pays the bills, she balances the checkbook, or visa versa.
- Don't get petty. Save the serious money talks for the bigger issues.
- Keep money issues between the two of you; they are not for public consumption.
- Be ready to put all else aside when there is a crisis.
- Seek a trained marriage counselor if money matters are pulling your relationship apart.

your list of what is important to you? How much money do you need to feel comfortable? We hope that money won't be your first and foremost priority. After all, it's only one of the many aspects of life.

TEACHING KIDS ABOUT MONEY

Children need to learn the value of money from their parents. It's a good idea to start teaching them at an early age. Starting as preschoolers, children can be given small amounts of money to spend on candy or a small toy. Thus, they will learn early that money can be exchanged for other things. You can show them that their quarter can buy a gum ball or a piece of chocolate, but not both. From such simple examples, children can learn to appreciate that money means making choices.

As children reach school age, they can learn that money is used not only to buy toys and candy but also to buy food, clothing, and household items, as well as pay for goods and services. You can show a child at the market, or in any type of store, how you pay for things and even how you get change back. As children see you spending money and making choices about where you spend it, they will begin to understand its many uses.

It's also a good idea to bring your children with you to the bank to show them how money is kept safely. Be careful, however, that you explain the ATM machine as a place that is giving you your own money, much like a Pez dispenser gives you the candy you put into it. Otherwise your children will think the ATM is an endless source of money for you.

It's also important to explain how you obtain money by doing something to earn it. Bring Your Daughter to Work Day has been very popular. It shows girls where their moms work and earn money. Obviously, this idea works equally well with father and sons, mothers and sons, or fathers and daughters. To further reinforce the lesson of doing something to earn money, you can reward children with small amounts of money for doing certain chores, such as cleaning up their rooms or helping with household chores. An allowance can teach kids how to save and make choices about spending their money, but one that varies slightly, depending on a couple of chores, also shows them that they can work harder and earn a little bit more.

Parents can also help develop a child's attitude toward money by including them in discussions and decisions regarding money matters. If you explain to a child that a vacation and a new computer cost the same but that you only have enough money to pay for one, they can help the family decide. While details of the family economic picture are not for young children or even teens to evaluate, they can be part of the decision-making process when it comes to money spent on family matters.

As children grow up they can take on a part-time job—deliver newspapers or become a lifeguard, for example. Children who've learned that money means making decisions will most likely spend their money wisely; those who believe there's an endless supply of money out there will likely learn the hard way.

As hard as you try, you won't be the only one shaping your child's attitudes about money (or anything else for that matter). Friends, teachers, other relatives, and the media will have their impact as well. Thus, if you can instill in your child a good foundation for saving and spending money at an early age, he or she will be better off as they grow up.

Here are some basics:

1. Let children make a few mistakes. If you scold them every time they spend money in a way you don't approve of, they may develop a bad attitude toward money. What adult hasn't made a spending mistake or two?

2. Let them enjoy buying things and saving money. The first part is easy; the second may require a "game" approach. If they can enjoy both sides of the

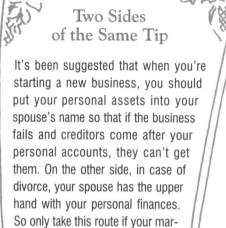

Two Sides of the Same Tip

It's been suggested that when you're starting a new business, you should put your personal assets into your spouse's name so that if the business fails and creditors come after your personal accounts, they can't get them. On the other side, in case of divorce, your spouse has the upper hand with your personal finances. So only take this route if your marriage is strong.

Pay Yourself First

You'll see this piece of advice in almost every book and article relating to personal finance. What it means is that you should set aside money for your own needs first. For some people, this means paying a personal debt; for others, it means putting money into personal investments. Whatever the case may be, set aside money for your own personal finances at the start of the month, rather than at the end when there may not be any left.

equation, they'll be more easily able to develop a sense of confidence in their money-related decision making.

3. Let children's gift money belong to them. Put it in a safe place for them. You don't want them squandering it, but on the other hand, they should have some say in spending it, unless it's been given to them for an express purpose, such as for a college account opened by their grandparents. And parents should not use their children's money for themselves. One woman recalls: "I could have gone to college but when my parents divorced my dad took all my money."

4. Understand that children lose things, including money. If a small child loses a nickel or an older child loses a five dollar bill, you might replace it the first time. If it happens often, you may need to let them learn the hard way that lost money is just that. However, if your child complains of losing lunch money every day, even when you're certain it's in a secure place, find out whether he or she is losing it or being bullied into giving it to another child. This is a more common scenario than you may think.

5. Teach children at an early age not to take money from (or give money to) strangers.

6. Don't get children involved in money fights at home. Money, as we all know, has a great deal of power attached to it. Children need not have *all* the responsibilities attached to money. They need not see money as power.

7. Let children also learn that money does not buy everything. When the opportunity presents itself, show them that something for free, perhaps a day at the beach or a day at the park, can be better than something that requires spending money. It's a valuable lesson for all of us.

PERSONAL BORROWING AND LENDING

Besides borrowing money from the bank against the equity of your home or retirement account, you can also borrow from friends and family. Naturally, there are no set guidelines and no Web sites designed to give you the best interest rates among family members. Only you will be able to determine from whom you feel comfortable borrowing money. Below are a few friendly pointers.

Here are some important considerations when borrowing from family and friends:

1. Look to borrow from people who are financially sound. Thus, you can avoid the awkward situation in which someone says, "I'd love to lend you the money, but I don't have it myself."
2. Borrow money only for specific needs.
3. Write up an agreement, no matter how basic, detailing how much you're borrowing and when you anticipate paying it back.
4. From time to time, remind the lender that you are aware of the loan.
5. Pay off the loan as soon as you can.

Money has come between many friends. The best intentions have led to feuding even among the closest pals. Money has a strange effect on people. If you feel that someone has a very different outlook regarding money than you do, this may not be the person to borrow from. Personalities vary and so do outlooks regarding money. Many people will lend money without interest due; in fact, they'll often say, "Don't worry; pay it back whenever you can." These same people may then, in a subtle, often unconscious manner, become controlling. Money lent with emotional strings attached can be harder to pay off than money lent with interest due. Once again, know your lender.

LENDING MONEY

There are two simple rules of thumb when lending money. First, if you cannot afford to lend it, don't. Second, if you do lend money, treat it like an investment; you may or may not recoup it. If you go into the lending process with that attitude, you won't be disappointed if you don't see it again. Even when a lending company lends money, they know there is a risk involved. For this reason they look for collateral. It's more difficult for most people, however, to say to a friend, "Give me your watch, and if you pay back the money, I'll return it to you."

If you ask for interest, spell out in writing exactly what interest rate you are seeking. Be reasonable.

You may also help someone out by paying off a debt for them, rather than handing them the money directly. You can then set up an arrangement for them to pay you back. This works well when you are helping someone who is in credit trouble or having a hard time managing money.

It's often recommended that you base both lending and borrowing on standard business operating procedures. This means, you look at what banks and other lending institutions are doing and, in a simplified manner, follow some of their procedures. For example, you could follow their procedure in regard to a term loan or an installment loan. With a term loan, you pay the loan back in one lump sum at a lower interest rate. With an installment loan, you pay it off gradually, usually at a higher interest rate. Or you could simply agree on the going interest rate and then collect the money in monthly, weekly, or biweekly installments.

Part I

Spending

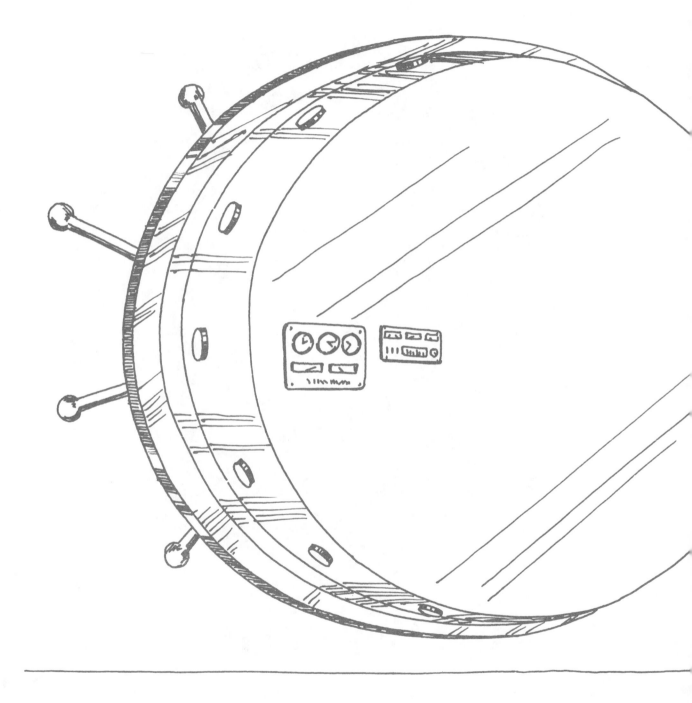

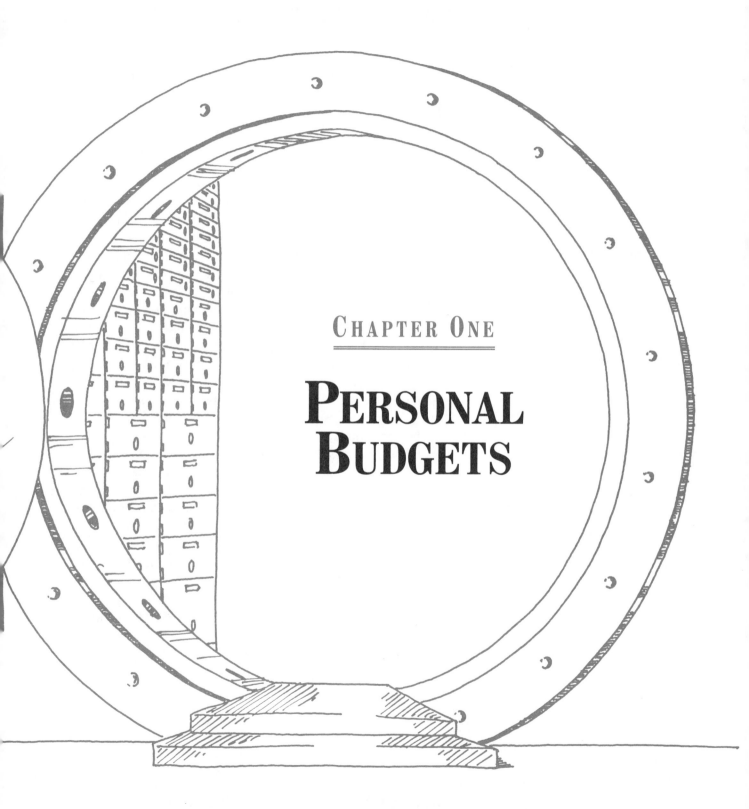

CHAPTER ONE

PERSONAL BUDGETS

How Much You Earn Isn't What Matters!

What really matters in accumulating wealth is how much you save and how well you invest it! And what also is crucial is how early you start saving and investing! If you start while you are still in your twenty's, investing just $2,000 a year in a retirement account with a market average rate of return, you will have a nest egg of over $500,000 by the time you retire! This is because of the power of compounding. Not only are you adding to your investment each year—but every year your investment grows and grows!

If you are already well past that tender young age—don't despair—it's never too late to start saving and investing. But remember, the sooner you start— the better off you'll be!

The premise behind this book is not necessarily to make you rich (although that certainly wouldn't hurt) but to help you manage, maintain, and increase the money you have. The first step is to establish a system of record keeping so that you can assess your net worth and create a budget that gives you a solid indicator of where you stand financially at any given time.

Before you work out a budget, it is always a good idea to take stock of your overall financial picture. In the ongoing battle between assets and liabilities, which is winning? It is hoped that if you list all of your assets and liabilities, the difference between the two will be a positive amount, which means you are in the black and not in debt.

Assets include all of your current bank accounts, mutual funds, money market accounts, securities, bonds, and treasury bills. Also included are life insurance policies, retirement accounts, and personal property, including your home—all of which fall into the "other assets" pool. On the other side of the ledger are the liabilities, including all outstanding debts, those annoying small bills you need to pay, mortgage payments, all long-term loans, and unpaid taxes. Your net worth is the difference between the liabilities and the assets. Once you've determined your net worth, it is time to start a budget.

A personal budget is a tool that can help you achieve your financial goals. A workable budget can keep you out of debt and help you avoid a last-minute rush to pull together money when it's time to file your tax return. It can also help you avoid the hassle of bounced checks or difficulties associated with trying to negate a bad credit rating. Besides keeping you out of financial trouble, a budget allows you to gauge how much you have available to invest. Thus, you can plan ahead and set money aside for college tuition, retirement, or other significant life events.

In short, a budget can help you stay in control of your money and keep you on track, allowing you to organize your income and expenditures during a set period of time (e.g., weekly, monthly, or quarterly). Following are the keys to effective money management:

1. Know your current financial picture at any given time.
2. Keep good records in a simple filing system.
3. Be aware of your spending habits.
4. Know your financial priorities and goals.

FINDING THE BUDGET THAT WORKS FOR YOU

It is important to first find a budget that you are comfortable with. Many people try to create a budget using a system—perhaps a computer program that someone else swears by—that does not suit them. Somewhere between an elaborate home computing system and "winging it" is the budget and record keeping system for you. With this in mind, use sample budgets as a guide, then tailor them to suit your needs. And leave room for expansion (or for items you forgot to include on the initial go round).

WHY YOU NEED A BUDGET

No matter how good you think you are at "watching your money," life's little surprises and catastrophes can throw your best intentions into a tailspin. Although some people always seem to land on their feet, others always seem to struggle. Between 1987 and 1997, the rate of personal bankruptcy in America nearly doubled. Therefore, the need to budget your spending—which does not necessarily mean "restrict" yourself—is more imperative today than ever before. For some, it's just reinforcing what they already know. For the vast majority of Americans, however, who worry about spending, a budget can be an eye-opening experience.

Here are some more reasons for budgeting:

1. *"In your face" advertising.* Today, there is a compulsion to buy the newest, the latest, and the most "trendy" item. Often it's not necessary or within your best financial interests to do so. A budget helps you take a more practical look at your spending and curb impulsive buying. You'll also be able to avoid debt from overspending.
2. *A rainy day.* The motto "Save for a rainy day" should not be taken to mean it's time to become a tightwad or a penny-pincher. A budget will help you keep a certain amount of money in place for when

Don't Hold Me Back!

Frequently, people complain that budgets are too limiting. In actuality, though, a budget supplies a system of priorities so that you can best determine where to spend your money. You can budget a certain amount to dine out every week or for vacations twice a year. It's entirely your choice. Or you can forego the dinners in fine restaurants to save for a home in a lavish retirement golfing community. Again, the choice is yours. A budget is simply a tool that helps you determine how to get to wherever it is you choose to be financially.

Therefore, don't look at a budget as something to hold you back. Instead, see it as something to steer you in the right directions.

you *need* to spend on an emergency or for something that is important for you or your family.

3. *Values and priorities.* Once you have learned to maintain a budget, you'll establish a set of priorities. You will begin to make determinations. Do I need a big screen TV? Would a second car serve the family well and make everyone's life easier? Your priorities will change depending on your current stage of life. There is nothing wrong with including entertainment and recreational purchases in your budget. However, with a budget to guide you, you will have a sense of value and make better determinations about when to splurge on something "fun" and when to hold back.

4. *Major events.* From a wedding to a vacation to buying your "dream house," a budget will help you prepare in advance for significant expenditures.

5. *Teaching family members about money.* No, YOU might not be the big spender in the household, but someone else may be spending money like it's "going out of style."

    Most teenagers enjoy spending money at an exaggerated rate. And those adults who haven't yet outgrown their adolescence also might fit into the category. A budget can help teach others the simple notion of living within the means of the family or household, regardless of how many people are bringing home paychecks.

6. *Tax time.* Not that doing taxes is ever easy, but a budget can give you a place to refer to when looking for those deductions. Also, good record keeping will help if you are audited.

7. *"Peace of mind."* If you aren't awake at night worrying about the bills coming in tomorrow's mail, you will feel— and sleep—much better.

One of the most interesting aspects of a personal budget is that it will grow and change along with you. A college student starting a budget will have a set of priorities different from someone who is about to retire after twenty-five years of employment. Those who are single will have budgets different from those who are married or, particularly, those who have children. As your life changes, so will your income and expenses; therefore, your budget must be flexible. A budget is a financial indicator that can actually tell you how you have changed and matured as a person. The $500 you once budgeted for a wild fraternity party may later be used for a down payment on a wedding ring or to purchase a new crib, or for your child's college fund.

FINANCIAL GOALS AND SAVINGS

Establishing what your financial goals are and setting up your strategies to meet those goals are important when planning your financial future (and, subsequently, when setting up your budget). Besides keeping tabs on your daily, weekly, monthly, and yearly spending, you will, if you budget properly, be able to determine how much money you can set aside for long-term savings or investments. Reflected in your budget will be different times in your life when your ability to save or invest may change.

For example, a single individual who is working will probably be able to put aside some money if he or she is not overspending. But a two-income family with young children may be paying off a mortgage on a new home and paying for child care and a host of other family-related expenses and may not be able to save much money, until their children are in public school and they are further along in their own careers. And neither a single individual nor a two-income family may be able to save during a career change. In fact, this may be a time for using the budget to monitor one's lifestyle more closely.

As you begin to make up an annual budget, consider a few budget tips:

1. *Be patient.* You do not need to set up your annual budget in one sitting. Give yourself a few days, then go back and look it over.
2. *Round up to whole numbers.* This invariably leads to a little more extra cash at the end of the month.

Build Your Own Budget

A well-structured budget has these characteristics:

1. It's easy to follow.
2. It fits into your lifestyle.
3. It covers all your expenses and sources of income.
4. There's room for expansion.
5. It suits your needs.
6. It helps you meet your financial goals.

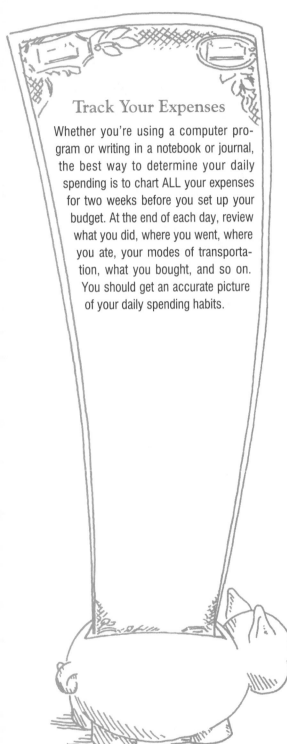

Track Your Expenses

Whether you're using a computer program or writing in a notebook or journal, the best way to determine your daily spending is to chart ALL your expenses for two weeks before you set up your budget. At the end of each day, review what you did, where you went, where you ate, your modes of transportation, what you bought, and so on. You should get an accurate picture of your daily spending habits.

3. *Expect the unexpected.* Allow for rising costs and emergencies. Give yourself some room in case you have to spend more.
4. *Start with a weekly plan.* For example, it's hard to answer the question, How much money do we spend on food in a year? However, if you determine how much you spend on your one, two, or three trips to the supermarket in the average week, you will be able to figure it out.
5. *Discuss the budget items with others in the family.* Budgeting is not a solo operation when it impacts others.
6. *Be realistic.* Sure the budget would get a lot easier to manage if you won the lottery, but don't count on it. Don't assume found money or that an expense could disappear. Don't speculate too much; try to work with "what is" and "what is likely" in the future.

Once you can effectively keep track of how much money is coming in and going out each week, you will know where you stand financially at any given time should any item on either list change or should any emergency arise.

ATM VISITS AND CREDIT CARDS

When you establish your spending habits to create your budget, make a note of how many times you used the ATM and your credit card. It's not uncommon for people to routinely take $200 out of the bank every two or three days. Then they wonder why their account is so low. Credit cards and ATMs make it very easy to spend, but by keeping track of your charges and withdrawals, especially from these two sources, you'll be able to better curtail your spending, if and when necessary.

Often, one less trip to the cash machine, one less dinner in a restaurant, and two less magazines per week is all it takes to keep you on track. When people look at their budgets, they often worry over the large items. However, it is commonly the smaller ones that add up and can wreak havoc with a budget.

KEEPING TRACK

If your annual budget is broken down into months, you'll have an ongoing statement of how you are doing financially at a given time. This allows you to compare how much you are earning with how much you are spending in a particular area and adjust before the year ends. Naturally, certain expenses, like heating costs, will be higher in certain months. Therefore, you may have to look at the whole picture, knowing seasonal expenses will come into play at different times of the year.

At the end of the year, you will be able to adjust for the following year by placing a plus or a minus sign next to the annual totals in comparison to your budgeted amounts.

BUDGET CATEGORIES

INCOME

Income includes your net paycheck (your take-home pay) after withholding taxes and social security. If, however, your primary source of income is derived from freelancing or any other means of self-employment, list your total income, then subtract estimated self-employment taxes in your expense column.

Other sources of income include bonuses, tips, royalties, stock dividends, interest, trust funds, disability benefits, veterans benefits, inheritance, alimony, child support, and even gifts and gambling winnings. There are also a host of investments that provide interest dividends or capital gains (these will be discussed later). Those that are defined and will be coming in during the year can be included (don't guess that a stock will go up and pay $10,000). Any definite income source should be included. This is for your eyes only, so be honest. When you are through listing your sources of income, compile your total.

EXPENSES

This part is never as much fun as the income section, but it will define your expenditures and give you an idea of where you stand financially, for better or worse. Your budget should have a column for everything you will routinely spend money on, extra columns for specific areas you might add, and a miscellaneous category for unforeseen expenses.

There are two categories of expenses: fixed and variable expenses. First, list your fixed expenses. These are the ones that don't change from month to month, such as rent or any other steady payment. They can also be once-a-year payments that are predetermined.

Although the variable expenses fluctuate from month to month, they are a constant for most people. Because they are necessary and ongoing, we do not refer to them as "discretionary." (*Discretionary* implies that such expenses are elective—although you may hear others refer to all nonfixed expenses as "discretionary expenses.")

Medical expenses

In this day of limited medical plans and HMOs, you may end up paying for a variety of uncovered medical expenses, including medical premiums. You can include any medications, medical related equipment (including glasses), and doctor's fees that aren't covered in your plan or the portion for which you are not reimbursed. Dental expenses can run extremely high, and most health plans do not include this coverage. Also include travel expenses to and from a doctor or dentist. And do not forget therapists, psychologists, psychiatrists, or marriage counselors.

Accounting and legal expenses

The more complex your financial picture, the more advantageous it may be to have a professional help with your taxes. As for attorneys, in this day of lawsuit abuse, you should limit your need to hire an attorney to when it is absolutely necessary.

Travel expenses

Travel expenses include all of the tolls you pay getting to and from work and wherever else you routinely travel. Any travel-related expenses that your business does not cover should be included.

Power Over Money!

Once you start tracking each of your expenditures, you will be on your path to really gaining control of your money . . . and your financial life!

Once you know how your money is getting spent, then you can decide if you want to re-allocate it. Is there some expense that you can do without? Do you want to start saving and investing? Is there some big purchase item that you really want to buy that you realize you can now afford by cutting back on some other area?

Once you know where your money is going, you are on the path to controlling your financial life!

Weekly living expenses

These include food from the grocery store, meals out, snacks, and sundry goods including toiletries and the multitude of items that fill your medicine and linen closets.

Utilities

Gas, telephone, electric, heating, water, and cable bills that vary monthly fall into this category. Some of these bills may have a basic monthly rate, but most will differ depending on usage. The fierce competition of phone companies should allow you to research and find the cheapest long-distance rate.

Auto expenses

Your car loan is a fixed cost; the maintenance and upkeep varies depending on usage. If you keep the car well maintained (remember to put in little things like oil), you'll be less likely to run up major repair shop expenses. Include gas expenses.

Business- and work-related expenses

If you run your own business, you will need a separate business budget. This book focuses on personal finance; thus, this category relates to the money that you spend personally on items that relate to your job, including appropriate magazines or books, computer programs, resume-writing services, associations you may join, or any other expenses that relate to your job. Commuting to and from work, however, can either be left under transportation or included in this column.

Home-related expenses

Besides the fixed cost of rent or a mortgage, you need to consider the cost of furniture and home improvements, such as aluminum siding, wood paneling, your finished basement, or that room you added on last spring. Some of this will be "discretionary" spending, but a lot of the upkeep of a house is ongoing and necessary, such as preparation for winter in certain areas or repainting. Any money you spend on improving your home (although it may raise the value in the long run) is currently an expense. You should also include in home maintenance a weekly cleaning person or gardener if you have one.

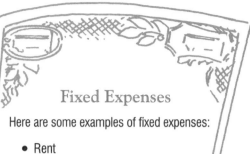

Fixed Expenses

Here are some examples of fixed expenses:

- Rent
- Loan payments
- Auto financing or leasing plus insurance (and monthly garage payments)
- Child support or alimony
- Mortgage payments
- Certain monthly bills (e.g., cable TV bill)
- Real estate taxes
- Insurance premium payments

Income taxes

Often the deductions from your paycheck don't fully satisfy Uncle Sam, so you'll be paying more. Also, if you have other sources of income or work as a freelancer, you must set aside money for taxes. Freelancers must also remember to pay social security taxes regularly. (For more on taxes, see Chapter 16.)

Clothing expenses (including shoes and accessories)

Your clothing expenditure will depend largely on where you work, your lifestyle, and the impression you need to make. Don't forget to include laundry and dry-cleaning expenses.

Entertainment and recreation

CD players, VCRs, that new big-screen TV, and trips to the movies, the theater, the ballet, and the ballpark all count as entertainment. This is where many people believe they have to deprive themselves to maintain a budget. Don't feel that this is a reward or punishment category. However, if you learn to budget more carefully in other areas, you'll be able to enjoy yourself. For example, turning off lights every time you leave the house and shutting off the air conditioner when you're away for a few days will buy you a night out at the movies.

Gifts and charitable contributions

List whatever you give. This category adds up, especially around the holidays. Include donations as well as personal gifts to family and friends.

Dues and subscriptions/books and magazines

If you belong to a union or an organization where you pay monthly or annual dues, list them here. You can also use this category for magazine subscriptions. However, magazine subscriptions can also be included in either business-related expenses or entertainment expenses; it's up to you. Make sure once you determine which category to use that you are consistent. Remember, the budget is for your eyes only, so only you need to feel comfortable with your category choice.

Vacation expenses

As for vacations, don't be surprised when hotels, airfare, food, and entertainment costs total up to a bit more than you anticipated. Vacations are important, however. Determine your financial picture, and plan your vacation accordingly. Two weeks in Europe will be less enjoyable if you know you'll be coming back to great debt. Determine what you are looking for from a vacation. Then decide where you can go to achieve your vacation goals. You'd be surprised to learn that there are usually more options and cheaper ways to enjoy a marvelous vacation than most people anticipate. Work with travel agents and keep a few options open.

Miscellaneous

This category is for those incidental expenses that don't quite fit anywhere else. There will inevitably be a few unexpected expenses that will fall into this category.

Other expenses for families with children

Child care, baby-sitting, extracurricular activities, stereo and computer equipment, lessons, and, of course, education are all possibilities. You can either combine them into one category called "Children's Expenses" or divide them into various categories. It's all a matter of prioritizing plus adding appropriate categories as your family grows.

SAVINGS AND YOUR BUDGET

Although the money is still yours, money set aside for savings is an expense, if only in that you can't spend it, at least for the time being. Most often (sometimes with some penalties) you can retrieve your money from whatever type of plan you've put it in whenever it's necessary to do so.

If money from your paycheck is in a direct deposit account, then you need not list it at all, assuming you are listing your "income" after such money has been taken out.

Saving for a Special Event

1. Prioritize correctly. Set aside money after you've covered the necessities of life but before spending impulsively.
2. Set reasonable goals. You may not be able to spend two months in the finest hotels of Europe, but you may be able to enjoy ten marvelous days in lovely accommodations.
3. Plan together. If the goal involves one or more others (e.g., as would a fiftieth anniversary party), decide together what is best. If necessary, list separately what you each want, then compare and compromise wherever necessary.
4. Plan ahead.

THE MONEY $ GAZETTE

Money-Saving Tips

1. Don't leave lights on when you're going out and curb other means of wasting electricity.

2. Seek out a less expensive long distance carrier or make long distance calls at non-peak hours. Also, beyond call waiting, don't pay for a host of new phone related features offered by the phone companies that you don't need.

3. Look for discounts and sales on clothing and appliances.

4. Visit a price club on occasion and stock up on foods that will last. This is particularly helpful if you have a large family.

5. Avoid unnecessary impulse purchases.

6. Don't always spend money on goods or services that you can make or do for yourself. For example, you can occasionally cut your child's hair, or make a greeting card yourself.

7. Don't buy three when one will do. This goes for ordering three premium cable TV channels, three magazine subscriptions, three pairs of sneakers, and so on.

8. Consider buying a used car over buying a new one.

9. Take care of what you own. From car care to keeping the heads clean on your VCR, the better you maintain what you have the less often you will need to replace it.

10. Don't be suckered in by every new technological time saver. Universal remotes, automatic phone dialers, and other gimmicks have proven to be completely unnecessary. This also includes upgrading your computer software every time a highly promoted newer model comes out with a handful of added features.

INVESTMENTS

From the money you made on the cattle plantation in Alaska to the money you put into the stock market, investments will fall on both sides of your budget. Unfortunately, you cannot know in advance (other than dividends) which investments will land on the income side. Therefore, you should list investments as an expense, since it is not money you can utilize at present.

Regular monthly investments must be included, but other investments are often the result of a budget showing that you are in the black. Essentially, if your budget works as you would hope, you can have more capital to invest.

Essentially, much of the money you spend is an investment. For example, you hope that the home improvements, besides improving the quality of life, will raise the value of your home, or that the money you spend to send your children to school (or on your own night courses) will pay off in their success (or in helping you reach your own business or personal goals).

KEEP IT ALL ON PAPER

Whether you are using a notebook or a computer program, it is important for tax purposes, as well as for backup purposes, that you keep copies of all your receipts, canceled checks, pay stubs, and all other paperwork accompanying your income and expenses. Should you lose a page of your budget, have a computer glitch, or a tax audit, good record keeping and backup files are vital. Keep an occasional (monthly) hard copy of your budget on hand in case your computer crashes at any time.

BUDGETS FOR DIFFERENT TIMES IN LIFE

A budget for a twenty-four-year-old and for a sixty-four-year-old will include a lot of the same items; however, the priorities placed on those items and the money allotted will change significantly over those forty years. For example, at twenty-four, an automobile is really a mode of transportation, usually for one. It will not be a vehicle that needs to last many years and can often be a used car. At thirty-four,

Millionaires and Used Cars

The average American who is worth a million dollars or more typically got there by running their own business...and by being frugal. The average millionaire for example, drives a used car that is several years old.

Buying a new car every year costs a lot of money because cars depreciate (decrease in value every year). And a car depreciates most quickly when you first buy it.

This is in sharp contrast to the purchase of a home, which will almost always *appreciate* in value, at least in the long term. In fact, the moment you drive your new car off the dealer's lot, it's worth a lot less that when it was "brand new." Insurance and excise tax and sales tax are higher on a new car.

a car may need to accommodate the entire family and will therefore need to be larger and more durable. A second car might be necessary as well. At sixty-four, you may want a lot of room for grandchildren or have saved up enough to get that special top-of-the-line car that you've always wanted. Or, you might decide that since you're living in a golfing community and rarely ever go for long trips, you can lease a car and spend more time riding a golf cart on the links. The point is that the expenses will vary.

Another example might be the money a single person spends on weekly dances or trips to trendy clubs compared with the money a couple with children spends on paying a weekly baby-sitter so that they can go out—a different idea but the same line item (social events/baby-sitter costs). (Naturally the evening out is factored in.) The single person spends $100 for an evening out, including a new shirt; the married couple spends $25 on the sitter and $75 on the evening out.

Juggling a budget is not unlike the clown trying to spin ten plates at the top of ten poles. At first you get a couple of plates spinning, and then as life progresses, you keep adding on plates. The more people in your family, the more expenses you can expect and the more difficult it will become to create and manage your budget or savings plan. Naturally, as income increases, it should get easier to manage the spinning plates. But don't be fooled: you still need to remain in control. Many people believe that once their income goes up they no longer need to worry about a budget. Although you may gain flexibility, a budget will still keep you abreast of where you stand financially at any given time, which is always important to your financial picture.

BUDGETING FOR MILESTONES

Planning for weddings and other major events means you will need to adjust your budget for a specific period of time. Unlike saving to pay for college tuition or putting aside money for retirement (which are both covered later on), these are specific events that will cost a significant amount of money at one time. While a wedding need not cost as much as a year of college, it can cost more, depending on the size and scope of the occasion.

The idea in preparing for any potential major expense (be it buying a car or planning a trip to Europe) is to set up a savings plan with enough advance time to allow your money to work for you. Also allow for inflation, as costs will be higher for a wedding in five years than they are now. Often, saving for a special event, such as a vacation, is a strong incentive to put money aside regularly.

CALCULATIONS AND SAMPLE BUDGETS

Initially calculated from monthly amounts, your budget should show how much money is needed annually in each category. Then, on a monthly basis, you should keep running totals and divide by the number of months to see how you are doing.

For example, if you estimate, based on a daily sampling for a month, that you will spend $90 monthly on transportation, your total for that year would be $1,080. Some of us like to play it safe and budget to a higher number, usually increased by about 10 percent. Thus, you might list $1,200 as your annual transportation budget.

Suppose that at the end of March your three-month total is $480. You would divide the total by three months and find that your monthly total is actually $160. That would put you at $1,920, or $720 over your annual budget. Your options would be (1) to find a less expensive mode of transportation, or (2) to find another area on your budget that is running under and readjust your amounts.

Although the first option may not be practical, the second should work for you. By keeping track and looking for someplace to readjust your budget, you can solve the problem. Keep in mind that you shouldn't jump to conclusions based on one month. And don't be fooled by seasonal changes or other factors that can cause a category to shift. For example, if your electric bills are lower in January, February, and March, think twice before lowering the budgeted amount for electricity. Otherwise, you may be surprised when the summer comes and the air conditioner raises your electric bill significantly. In short,

Budget Tips from a Planner

Financial planner M. Eileen Dorsey, MBA, MS, CFP, of St. Louis, Missouri, is among many planners who point to the idea of "Buy now, pay later" as one of the premier stumbling blocks on the road to a successful budget. Ms. Dorsey emphasizes the need to be very careful with credit cards. Be sure you can pay your monthly balance in full, particularly if you are retired and/or living on a fixed income.

According to Ms. Dorsey, "You should set up your personal budget as you would a business budget. A lot of people work in financial areas at their jobs but don't bring the same rules to their budgets at home."

"It's also important to spend a few hours and analyze your budget," adds Ms. Dorsey. "Compare where you are at a certain point this year to the previous year, and see where you are spending more or less money. Many home finance computer programs will easily set this up for you."

keep a solid gauge on what is going on monthly and whether it will equal your annual budgeted amount.

SAMPLE BUDGET

FAMILY BUDGET		

Income

His annual income (net pay)		$45,000
Her annual income (net pay)		$30,000
Stocks/savings accounts (roughly) dividends and interest		$ 3,000
Investment, capital gains		$ 2,000
		$80,000

Expenses

	ANNUAL	MONTHLY
Mortgage (including insurance)	$15,000	$1,250
Insurance premiums	3,000	250
Medical	5,000	415
Travel/vacation	2,500	210
Food and daily items	15,000	1,250
Clothing	6,000	500
Entertainment	6,000	500
Utilities and telephone	4,000	335
Auto	5,500	460
Business/work related	2,000	170
Home related	3,000	250
Gifts	500	40
Charitable contributions	500	40
Miscellaneous	1,500	125
Child care	5,000	415
School	500	40
Savings	3,000	250
Total	$78,000	$6,500
Available cash	$2,000	

There are several ways you can set up your budget. This sample budget includes both incomes in a two-income family, plus the money earned from stocks, savings accounts, and one investment. This family is able to put away $3,000; part goes into a plan to send their son to college and part goes into a 401(k) plan. At the end of the year, if they stay on their budget, they will have $2,000 left over to put into their savings and/or to buy something special, or to take a vacation. With any luck the budget should balance or be in their favor!

Budgeting for Vacations

Factoring in at the start of the year how much you think you can set aside for your vacation will help you determine where you can afford to go. If you have a particular destination in mind, check out the airfare and cost per day with a travel agent or through guide books to that destination of choice. The best travel season for most people is the summer. However, if you can travel at a non-peak time of year, you can usually spend less. As for your budget, you should start setting aside money at the start of the year.

If you are planning to travel in August, you are looking at budgeting your trip through seven months. Therefore, if the vacation will cost $2,500 for two people, you need to put aside $357 a month for the seven months leading up to the trip. If you have a lump sum coming in, you could simply put it in a short-term low-risk account for six months and gain some interest on it.

Budgeting for the trip, however, may mean that you should move another major purchase to the fall, when the vacation line on your budget can be replaced with payments for another item.

Personal Finances and Your PC

Yes, you too can use your PC to manage your personal finances. From budgets, record keeping, and banking to investing and planning your financial future, your computer can be your own financial resource center.

Get Organized!

Electronic organizers are a good way to keep track of appointments, phone numbers, and important information, when you're on the go. However, you should also be organized at home, with a filing system that suits your needs. You can buy hanging files for your filing cabinet and label accordingly to satisfy all your financial needs. If you'd like, you can order the Financial Planning Organizer from Homefile, Inc. (1-800-695-3453). The organizer has laminated file dividers that provide a quick-find index so that you can locate your important papers quickly.

The two leading programs in the area of personal finance are Quicken from Intuit and Money from Microsoft. While each presents their new annual editions, you need to assess before upgrading which features, if any, you may need. There are various other programs devoted to personal budgets and finance, such as MECA Software's Managing Your Money. Long-time spreadsheet programs such as Excel or even Lotus can be used as well, should you already have them on your computer. Although not as comprehensive as some of the budgeting programs, they provide spreadsheets and do basic calculations.

Different variations of the Intuit Quicken, and Microsoft Money programs include budgeting, banking, investing, financial planning, mortgage information, and more. Most programs will help you by doing basic calculations quickly and allowing you to compare your current data with that of previous months or years—providing you've entered them.

Depending on the features, the costs of the latest PC home finance software generally runs from $25 to $125. The latest programs are designed to be user friendly even to those who are not computer savvy. They also tap into the power of the Internet. Look for a program that doesn't require that you change your approach to finance management.

The ability to pay bills online, as well as make other financial transactions and investments, is now at your fingertips. There are a wealth of online sites devoted to finance, including sites from Microsoft and Quicken. Be careful, however, because the objective of many Web sites, although they offer advice, is to sell you something—that's why they are there. There is a great deal of basic information if you browse carefully, but very little actual "unbiased" advice exists in cyberspace. So be very selective when taking investment tips from the Internet and always double check them. Also check the date when the information was posted. While a lot of sites are updated regularly, some are still providing you with information from 1996.

THE MONEY $ GAZETTE

Selecting a Personal Finance Program for Your PC

Besides the most common brands, Intuit Quicken and Microsoft Money, there are other programs available, and you should spend time scouting the latest computer magazines if you want to truly check out the financial software picture. These are the questions to ask yourself:

- What is applicable to my PC?
- What features do I need?
- How simple is it to set up and start using the program?
- Am I paying for a wealth of (impressive but unnecessary) features that don't suit my needs?

- Is the program too technical, or does it presume that I have a certain level of financial knowledge?
- How easily can I link up to the Web?
- How well does this program accept existing financial data and information?
- How much am I spending on a financial program?
- Will this program be my financial assistant or my enemy?

If you plan to do your banking online, you should make sure that your program has the power and capability to establish online accounts with relative ease.

How much you involve your computer in your financial matters is ultimately a question of comfort level. Computers can "run the whole show," provided you are at the controls. Many people, however, find that they are still most comfortable with a combination in which they utilize their computer for record keeping, budgeting, and even checkbook balancing, but still do their own banking and bill paying.

FAMILY BUDGET WORKSHEET

ASSETS	ACCOUNT	BALANCE	LIABILITIES	ACCOUNT	AMOUNT
LIQUID ASSETS			**MONTHLY PAYMENTS**		
Savings-1		$	Mortgage		$
Savings-2		$	Electric		$
Checking		$	Telephone		$
CASH FLOW			Water		$
His Annual Income		$	Insurance		$
Her Annual Income		$	Loan Payments		$
INVESTMENTS			Food and Daily Items		$
CD-1		$	Auto		$
CD-2		$	School		$
IRA-1		$	Savings		$
IRA-2		$	**MISCELLANEOUS**		
Money Market		$	Entertainment		$
Securities		$	Clothing		$
Bonds		$	Credit Card-1		$
T-Bills		$	Credit Card-2		$
Mutuals		$	Credit Card-3		$
INTEREST			Alimony		$
Yield on Bonds		$	Child Care		$
Yield on T-Bills		$	Public Transportation		$
Other Interest		$	Business/Work Related		$
MISCELLANEOUS			Home Related		$
Life Insurance		$	Gifts		$
Retirement Account		$	Charitable Contributions		$
Property		$	Medical		$
			Travel/Vacation		$
			Taxes		$
Total		$	Total		$

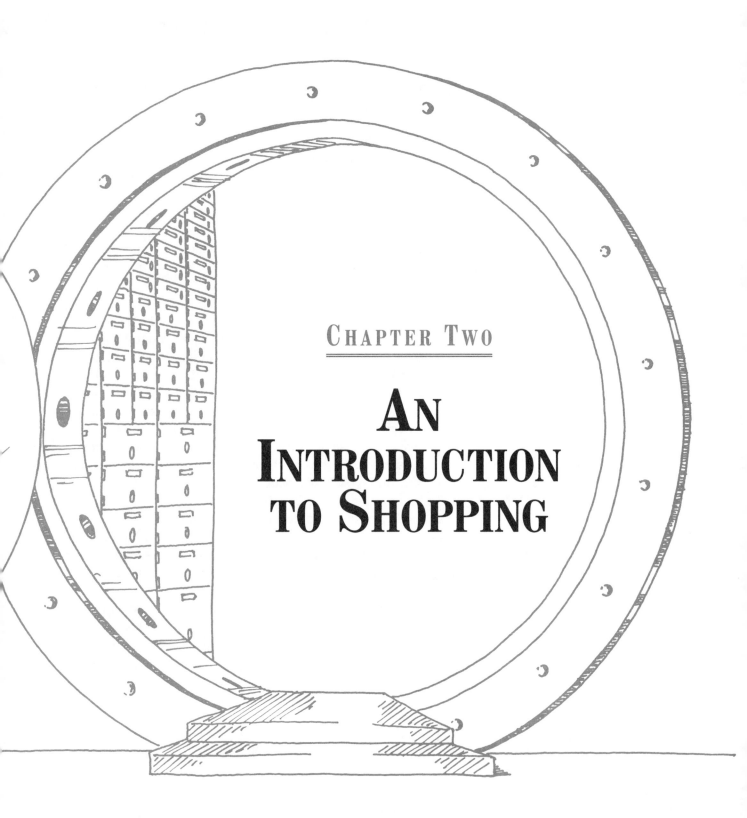

CHAPTER TWO

AN INTRODUCTION TO SHOPPING

Beyond the major purchases, such as a home and a car, there are numerous other items on which you can spend your hard-earned cash. Washers, dryers, stereos, televisions, furniture, recreational and fitness equipment, computers, clothing, hobbies, and numerous other goods make up our vast consumer spending index.

This area is where you can run into trouble, particularly with credit cards. The trick is to be selective and focus on the things you *really* feel are important to your lifestyle. We all need most of the above mentioned items; the question is, How many and at what price? This is where your budget should guide you, not restrict you. The careful, smart shopper can have a significant amount of *stuff*, as George Carlin calls it, without spending a fortune.

Buying guides such as *Consumer Reports* will tell you what the best rated products are, but then it's up to you to look around for the best prices. Browsing the Internet, reading local papers, and on occasion, simply waiting until the newest "fad" is no longer the hottest selling item are ways of saving money when you shop. When a brand new product hits the market, it's always priced higher. VCRs, for example, cost much more when they first hit the market. The same is true for movie videos. However, today the video stores carry thousands of film titles that can be had for $19 to $29. And most "used" videotapes sell for $8.

The idea is not to be "cheap" but to be savvy and to spend top dollar only on selected items or where time is of the essence (or you may miss out). Don't hold back, for instance, on a chance to see a Broadway show that you've been dying to see in the hopes of discounted prices; the show could close in the meantime.

On the other hand, a $200 pair of sneakers may be on sale next week for $129. Better yet, you might get a slightly lesser known brand that has a high rating in the fitness magazines for $99. Do your homework.

People who buy the latest advertised top-of-the-line computer, for example, when they rarely ever use one, are not shopping as wisely as they think they are. "It's the best on the market" means little if it'll hardly ever be used or if a less expensive model would serve the same functions.

Impulse buying is another route to debt and trouble. Tell yourself to wait three days and then, if you still feel you need the item, buy it. You'd be surprised how many "must have" impulse items are less appealing a few days later.

Catalog and Internet shopping is also a way of dishing out your money and running up your credit card bill. Buy through reputable retailers. Too often, lesser known mail order companies don't have the item you want and "allow" you to select something else. They also have different pricing in different parts of the country. And, too often these companies go out of business, sometimes holding your money. Those that do send you merchandise are not always sending the highest quality goods.

Also be very leery of the plethora of junk mail offers both in your mail box and online. Most of these are indeed JUNK. Don't get suckered in.

Here are some other shopping tips:

1. Brand names may be more costly, but (depending on the item) you usually get higher quality merchandise. In other words, don't drink a brand of soda you hate because it was ten cents cheaper than a Coke or a Pepsi. On the other hand, if two electric can openers serve the same exact purpose and meet your needs, why buy the better known brand name for $9 more?

2. It's usually not in your best interest to buy merchandiser extended warranties. This new concept has you betting that your merchandise will break. Warranties from the manufacturer usually cover the first year or two, possibly three. For years people bought items and, if they broke, would simply have them repaired. Today you pay for repairs in advance. And according to retailers surveyed, less than 20 percent of the warranties sold are ever put to use.

3. While it's important to shop at reputable companies, it's also important to deal with merchandisers that specialize in (or at least have an idea about) the merchandise you are buying. In other words, your local supermarket may be a well-known, reputable place to buy groceries and other household products; however, it may not be the place to purchase a home computer. Conversely, an electronic store may sell you a name PC at a good price, but they may not sell the best shelves for your work space. Shop in the right stores.

4. Sometimes smaller stores and their friendly personalized approach can be beneficial if you need more information.

They can also make you feel comfortable should you need to bring the item back.

5. It's also a good idea to get everything in writing, save receipts, and double check the return and exchange policy on whatever you buy.

THE "WATCH OUTS!"

No matter where you shop, there will always be something to "watch out" for. Here are some examples:

- Watch out for deals that sound too good to be true, particularly those that have you spending very little and getting a whole bunch of extras.
- Watch out for "free trial offers"; they'll usually get you in the end or start billing you because you didn't return the item by a certain date.
- Watch out for "buy now, pay later" specials. Deferred billing means you'll be hit with a big bill later.
- Watch out for bait and switch operations in which you're lured into the store to buy an item only to find out they don't have it. BUT (they will say), you can buy something else that is "just as good" and only a little more expensive. You can also leave the store!
- Watch out for new-fangled time-saving devises that will save you a few minutes while costing a lot more money while giving you more aggravation. Determine which time savers are right for you and which will end up on the shelf. Don't buy the latest *gadget* just because it is there.
- Watch out for items that may be difficult to assemble.

FRUGAL DOES NOT MEAN CHEAP

A frugal person enjoys comfort, attractive surroundings, good food, and the finer things in life. These people do, however, often find a less expensive way of achieving such happiness. Being cheap, on the other hand, means denying yourself the pleasures and the good things in life to avoid spending money. Essentially, a frugal person cuts corners at the right time and in the right places to avoid spending more money to achieve the same desired goals. A cheap person cuts out or alters his or her desired goals.

Individuals differ tremendously in their wants, needs, and lifestyles. Some people want the finest luxuries in their home but do not need all the extras in their car; others are comfortable with a more simple lifestyle around the house but need to splurge on one annual vacation. Pick and choose those areas that are most important to you and decide where you need to spend money and where you can gain satisfaction without having to spend a lot. You'd be surprised at how many good things in life don't really require you to spend.

Here are some (of many) other money saving ideas:

- Area rugs and throw rugs instead of wall-to-wall carpeting create the luxurious "less is more" feel of the nineties.
- Refinishing, re-covering, or painting old furnishings can often create a better look than *always* buying something new.
- Vacation off-season and always try to avoid tourist traps.
- Barter whenever possible. If you do tax returns and your neighbor is a contractor, for example, work out a sky light installed for a tax return done.
- Pass down children's clothing to family and friends. People do this at all income levels because kids simply outgrow things very quickly.
- Set up a fitness program on your own that doesn't necessitate membership in a high priced health club (and the need for lots of expensive fitness attire). Often a local Y or gym has the same facilities for less money and a less pressured, friendlier atmosphere as well.

GARAGE SALES

Garage sales are very popular across the country, with millions of dollars changing hands every weekend as Americans clean out their junk and make it someone else's. Garage sales provide opportunities to pick up items that you might not find elsewhere or commonplace items at lower prices. When approaching a yard or garage sale have some idea of the items you may be looking for. Otherwise, you can end up spending money on items you don't need. Plates, silverware, linens, tablecloths, pillows, desk chairs, computer mouse pads, coffeemakers, books, umbrellas, toys and games, videotapes, cookware, and furniture are all items you can find in good condition and at good prices at the right sale. In addition, garage sale shopping can be fun.

Electronic Organizers

Priced from $10 to over $200, electronic organizers come in a wide range of prices with a wide range of features. Sharp, Casio, Texas Instruments, and Royal are among the leading companies making these miniature versions of the personal secretary. Check out memory (256k or 512k are common) and PC connectivity capability. Other common features to look for include data communication, calendar, schedule, to-do list, anniversary, expense log, conversion, telephone list, calculator, games, and clock. Get the functions you need, plus an extra battery.

COMPARATIVE SHOPPING LIST WORKSHEET

ITEM #1:	DESIRED FEATURES:	
MODEL:		
Store:	Store:	Store:
Price:	Price:	Price:

ITEM #2:	DESIRED FEATURES:	
MODEL:		
Store:	Store:	Store:
Price:	Price:	Price:

ITEM #3:	DESIRED FEATURES:	
MODEL:		
Store:	Store:	Store:
Price:	Price:	Price:

ITEM #4:	DESIRED FEATURES:	
MODEL:		
Store:	Store:	Store:
Price:	Price:	Price:

ITEM #5:	DESIRED FEATURES:	
MODEL:		
Store:	Store:	Store:
Price:	Price:	Price:

ITEM #6:	DESIRED FEATURES:	
MODEL:		
Store:	Store:	Store:
Price:	Price:	Price:

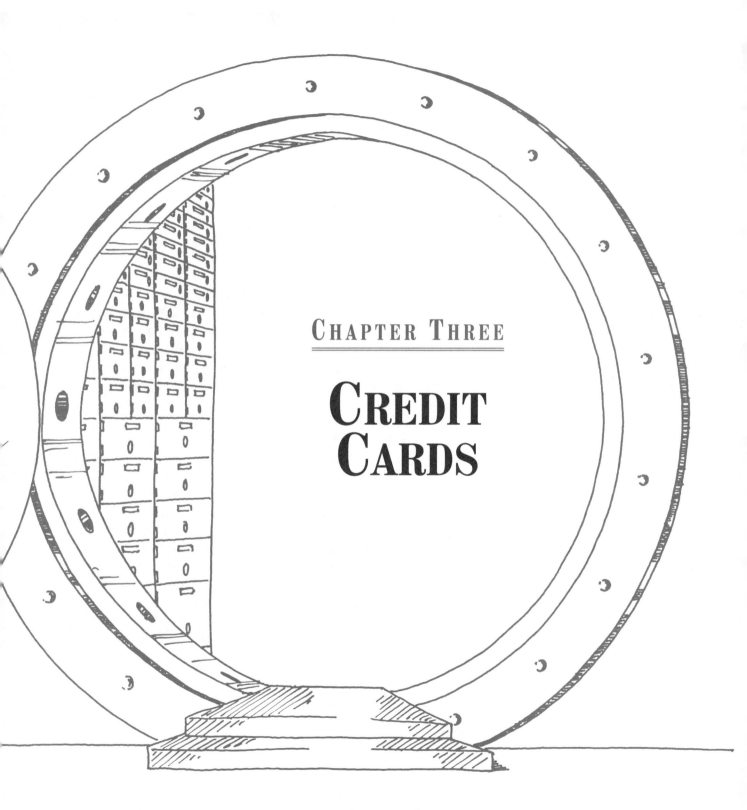

CHAPTER THREE

CREDIT CARDS

They come in gold, with holograms, offering special bonuses, no limits, and all sorts of wonderful ways in which you can drive yourself into debt. They are, as one major company puts it, *everywhere*. We're talking about credit cards.

From department stores to gas stations to the local food emporium, every retail outlet, catalog, home shopping network, and Internet site will offer you the chance to pay on your credit card. They make shopping from home via computer or television very easy. They are the technological IOUs that allow for tremendously increased purchasing power. You can use them wisely and get a number of freebies, including frequent flier mileage, discounts for hotels and rental cars, gift certificates, and other benefits. Credit cards can benefit you in many ways. They can also mean trouble.

Americans now charge over $600 billion on credit cards a year, and the amount is still growing. So how does one control the urge to whip out that plastic card and walk away with goods and services?

First, there are individuals for whom credit cards are a convenient way to avoid carrying around a lot of cash. These people pay their monthly bills in full and on time. They know how much they can charge in a given month and are always able to pay in full. And they enjoy the credit card benefits. Essentially, they manage their money well and use credit cards without a problem.

However, too many individuals end up spending money they don't have. Spend now, pay later is the basic premise of credit cards. The individual who, by his or her nature, seeks instant gratification is more likely to run into credit card debt than the person who plans ahead.

The credit card industry is hoping that their tantalizing sales approach, led by commercial television, which puts consumer goods in front of the average American, tempts you to just go out and buy. Apparently the temptation is great, as the credit card industry is booming. Purchasing power can be dangerous!

So how do you curb the credit card habit? If you are on the brink of falling behind on your credit card payments, you can easily turn it around by becoming stricter with yourself. You need to start making rules to guide you.

You could, for example, employ a rule that you use credit cards only for major expenses and in emergencies. You keep track each month of how much is in your checking account (or can be moved immediately into the account) to cover each large purchase ($300 or more). You then make a note of all credit card transactions and keep an eye on the checking account balance, since it will be from there that you pay the credit card bill.

It's suggested that you carry some cash at all times. Losing $100 by misplacing your wallet or purse, or even by being robbed, is a small "investment" compared with throwing thousands of dollars into interest charges and late payment fees.

Prior to the 1950s and the consumerism spearheaded by the television generation, people actually used cash (honest!). Today you will see many individuals paying for even their smaller items with a credit card: $25 for groceries, $15 at the gas station, $12 for lunch, and so on. These little items add up and can come back to haunt you later on.

Since impulse buying is the root of credit card trouble, Tracey McBride, author of the *Frugal Luxuries* books, suggests literally putting the freeze on your credit cards. "Keep them in the freezer," suggests Tracey. "That way every time you need to use it, it will take time to thaw out before it will run through the machine. You can't microwave it or you will destroy the plastic strip. This will give you that extra amount of time to think about your purchase."

Another idea is to prevent credit card phone orders by using a phone cord that will not reach the place where you keep the credit card. Thus, you have to put down the phone and then get the card. The bottom line is to make sure you have time to think before "whipping out" the card.

HOW DO CREDIT CARDS WORK

A 1998 survey showed that 75 percent of Americans did not really know how credit cards worked. Most of those people had at least one credit card.

Grace Periods

A *grace period* is the period of time you have to pay the full bill and not incur finance charges.

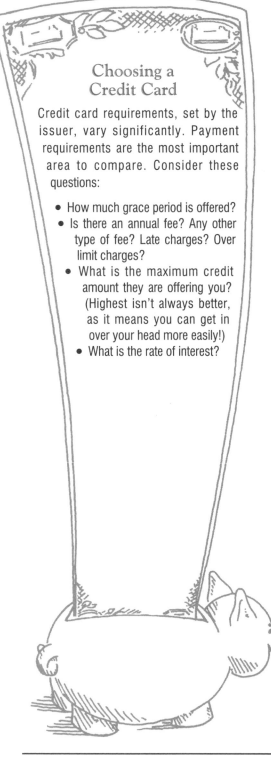

Choosing a Credit Card

Credit card requirements, set by the issuer, vary significantly. Payment requirements are the most important area to compare. Consider these questions:

- How much grace period is offered?
- Is there an annual fee? Any other type of fee? Late charges? Over limit charges?
- What is the maximum credit amount they are offering you? (Highest isn't always better, as it means you can get in over your head more easily!)
- What is the rate of interest?

It's in your best interest to understand how the credit card industry works. The more you know, the more you'll understand why it's important to be responsible with these cards.

Basically, the issuer, be it a bank, store, or other institution, extends you a loan to buy goods or services. They may set a limit, such as $2,000 to start with, meaning that that's the maximum you can borrow from them at any given time. You receive a monthly bill, and if you pay it in full and on time, you do not incur other charges, and, in fact, the card issuer generally then raises your credit limit. Some stores, in conjunction with credit card companies, offer a grace period when you purchase large items; after a certain amount of time, usually three or six months, you can make a full payment, with no finance charges. However, if you don't pay in full, the interest rate can be as high as 16 or 18 percent.

Although many credit card companies offer special services, usually to "preferred customers" with high-credit limits, it is worth your while (if you do not feel confident that you will pay in full every month) to seek out low-interest-rate cards, even if they do not offer frequent flier mileage and other such amenities. Some, but not many, credit card companies still charge annual fees. They may offer various services and their interest rates may be lower, but you still pay a fee for the convenience of being able to spend your own money without using cash.

CHOOSING A CREDIT CARD

The most popular credit cards offered today are Visa and MasterCard. Companies, banks, and corporations sponsor these cards. Both of these cards extend to you a line of credit. You can pay them back at your own pace, but you will incur interest on the amount owed and, possibly, late payment charges.

The American Express card is a charge card, but unlike a line of credit, American Express essentially pays the bill for you. They, therefore, do not allow you to pay in increments, expecting you to pay the balance in full for whatever you have charged at the end of the thirty-day cycle. They make money on the fees they charge to merchants and the yearly fees they charge to cardholders. American Express also offers the Optima card, which allows you to make monthly payments in the same manner as Visa and MasterCard.

You can also look at what privileges cards offers, such as frequent flier mileage, savings on long-distance calls, store discounts, and so on. Be careful that "extras" don't have fees or other requirements attached. Some companies offer to help you do practically anything, anyplace in the world. They fail, however, to remind you that you may have to sign up for this special service in advance or charge up to a certain amount on the card. Many of these "rewards" are only offered on certain cards (gold cards, platinum cards, kryptonite cards, etc.). This doesn't help you when your car breaks down and you are stranded with a "basic" card.

It's to your advantage to stick to a few credit cards that you know you will actually use and can pay in full at the end of the month. Don't be taken in by everyone who wants to send you a free credit card—this only leads to too many cards and can be your credit downfall (not to mention the paperwork of sending out payments and keeping track of them all). Also, be cautious that low rates are not just an introductory offer to suck you in. Rebates and other great offers, including rental car discounts, tickets to shows, and so on, can also be used as hooks to lure you in. Not that some of the most reputable cards won't offer added "rewards" that you can take advantage of; but when you are seeking out a low rate credit card to get out of debt, your first concern should be that *fixed low rate*.

The benefits and offers of competing cards is mind boggling. Here's a sample of some of the cards from various categories and their current offers. *Keep in mind that promotions change rapidly: By the time you read this, there may be new offers and other options available.*

GOLD CARDS

The *Chase Gold Card* is a *Visa* card that offers two programs to choose from: Flight Rewards, from which you can earn free airline tickets, or Retail Rental, which gives you a 5 percent discount at a selected retailer (there is a $25

Special Deals

Other cards you might check out include the following:

- AMEX Golf Card offers exclusive golf privileges and discounts.
- AT&T Universal Card offers a calling card and credit card in one.
- Blockbuster Visa offers Blockbuster rebates, discounts, and free rentals!
- Bravo Card lets you choose your billing date (you can't choose "never").
- Chase Visa Ultimate Rewards lets you accumulate points toward freebies.
- First USA Platinum Card offers a credit line of up to $100,000.
- Fleet Gold Card offers cash back on all purchases.
- Quicken Platinum Card lets you earn free or discounted air travel.
- Sheraton Club International lets you earn miles for every dollar, plus gift certificates.
- Six Flags Entertainment Visa offers discounts (where else?) at Six Flags Great Adventure!

Gone with the Old

Years ago the most popular credit cards were gas credit cards. Now general credit cards such as MasterCard, Visa, and American Express get the bulk of purchases. Today Debit cards—cards that immediately take money out of your account—are quickly increasing in popularity.

membership fee required for either plan). Both are accepted worldwide and offer auto rental insurance and merchandise protection as well.

The *American Express Gold Card* has no pre-set spending limit and allows you to earn free travel, car rental discounts, hotel discounts, and/or shopping sprees. Requiring an additional $25 membership fee, the AMEX Gold Card provides for a purchase protection plan/buyers assurance plan.

CASH BACK CARDS

The *Discover Card* offers up to 1 percent cash back based on the level of purchases, $500 flight insurance, a twenty-five-day grace period, and no annual fee.

US West MasterCard offers up to 2 percent cash back on all purchases and up to 2 percent cash back on all phone calls made with the card. There's a twenty-five-day grace period and no annual fee.

HOTEL CARDS

Caesars Gold/Custom MasterCard offers you discounts on entertainment, dining, and merchandise, particularly at Caesars Palace. In fact, you can earn cash bonus checks for Caesars properties.

Marriott First Card offers points toward special discounts, including five thousand points when you sign up and one additional point for every dollar charged. You'll also receive travel insurance.

FREQUENT FLIER CARDS

American Airlines Citibank Advantage Card offers one American Airlines mile for every dollar you charge. There is a twenty-five-day grace period and the classic card annual fee is $55 (the gold card is $85).

Delta SkyMiles American Express offers one SkyMile for every dollar charged and a twenty-five-day grace period. The annual fee for the classic card is $29 (the gold card is $49).

The list goes on and on. There are cards offering discounts for everything you could possibly want. Shop around. If you are a frequent flier, look for frequent flier mileage; if you are going on vacation, seek out hotel or car rental deals. You can pick and choose cards that have good interest rates, extend you a substantial credit limit, and have perks or extras that are tailored for your lifestyle. There's even an American Kennel Club Visa, with an introductory 5.9 percent APR and, more importantly, a picture of a dog on your card!

SECURED CREDIT CARDS

With secured credit cards, you put up a deposit in advance, usually somewhere between $500 and $3,000. This is your line of credit, so you are essentially borrowing against yourself. The reason for doing this, however, is to make sure you pay your charges every month (there's usually an annual fee). Secured credit cards are good for building up a credit rating (showing you can pay on time). If you want to acquire other credit cards, apply for a loan, or get a mortgage, a secured credit card is a good starting point.

Building a good line of credit, where the issuer increases the amount you can charge on the card, will occur as you use the card and pay your monthly bills on time. This will enable you to charge higher amounts. A good line of credit will also make you a "good credit risk" which is important if you ever apply for a mortgage or another type of loan in the future.

For college students, secured credit cards are good "starter cards." BUT make sure they pay their own deposit and fees, or they will not get the point of a credit card. Also, get secured cards only through reputable financial institutions directly. Don't hand over your deposit to a fly-by-night company.

DEBIT CARDS

The opposite of a credit card is a debit card. These cards will, through modern technology, deduct the amount of your purchase directly from your bank account. If you do not have the money in the account, the charge will not go through, thus

A Credit Card Tip

If you should find a lower rate credit card, you can transfer a balance to that card. This means that you still owe money on a credit card, but the interest rate is now lower. Some credit cards offer special rates for balance transfers. Be sure there are no other fees attached.

Switching to a lower rate card (without cash advance fees) means that if you owe $500 on your Visa Card at 14 percent and you transfer to MasterCard (at 12 percent), you will owe the same $500 but at 12 percent instead of 14 percent.

Debit Card Downfalls

Although debit cards take some of the worry away for credit card abusers, there is a downside. If lost or stolen, a thief can possibly clean out your account rather quickly.

eliminating the possibility for you to go over your limit and mount up interest charges. Visa, MasterCard, and other companies offer debit cards, but they are not nearly as widely hyped, simply because the companies can make more money off you by watching you run your credit card bills sky high.

Your ATM bank cards can also be used as debit cards. Usually such cards are offered as a bonus for opening an account at a certain bank or for signing up with an investment firm. It's worth inquiring when opening a bank account whether the bank can issue you a debit card or you can use your ATM card as such.

YOU AND YOUR CREDIT RATING

In school, if you did not adhere to the rules, your bad behavior would forever be written on your "permanent record." Your credit rating is just like that "permanent record." It follows you around throughout your life. It can help you make a major purchase if your credit is good and work against you if the rating is not good.

To qualify for credit and loans, you'll need to prove yourself worthy in the eyes of the lenders. Biased as it may seem, especially in this day and age of companies merging and new opportunities allowing (sometimes forcing) people to make several job changes, lenders like to see that you have stayed at one job for a period of time. They like to see that your bills are paid on time. They also want to know what your assets, earnings, and investments look like. They try to cover all bases when determining whether you are a good bet when it comes to borrowing money or extending a line of credit. Many credit card companies make it fairly easy to qualify for their card. In many cases, they are satisfied knowing you can come close to meeting your monthly balance. The reason is that they want more business.

Your credit report is tracked by a credit bureau. The credit bureau, however, acts like a library: They don't write the books or, in this case, credit reports; they simply take in and assimilate the information given to them by the companies with which you do business. Anyone making transactions in our modern society has some credit bureau keeping tabs on their payment history and habits. Through stores, banks, financial institutions, and other means, the credit bureau builds up a report on you that will be checked when you apply for a credit card or a loan.

If you want to build a good credit rating, start with a store credit card; they are usually easy to acquire. Another option is to start with a secured card, as mentioned earlier. Once you start with a low limit and pay off your bills on time, you will begin to build a good credit report, get higher credit limits, and qualify for more cards.

There are three major companies handling credit ratings in the United States: Trans Credit Union, Experian Information Solutions, and Equifax. These credit bureaus are not in the business of issuing or denying credit cards. They establish your credit reports from the reports given to them. You have a right, by law, to see your credit report.

You may very well be listed with two or all three of the credit bureaus, since different businesses work with the three companies. It's a good idea to check all three credit ratings, especially if you are about to buy a home or make some other significant purchase involving a loan or mortgage. Don't be surprised if they differ. Also, don't be surprised if there's an error. Due to the incredibly large number of people listed (nearly two hundred million in the United States), errors are made. Errors are more commonly made by a merchant incorrectly reporting your purchases or failing to report that you've paid off a delinquent bill. You must prove that an error is just that. Common mistakes include putting someone else's information on your form and neglecting to list follow-up information on a loan that you have paid. Getting errors corrected is a long and tedious process. Get something in writing and make sure to notify all the credit bureaus. Be polite but persistent, as it's important to have credit rating errors corrected while maintaining your "good name."

Too Many Cards?

If you apply for a card every time you receive an application in the mail, it will be marked down on your credit rating or credit report. Applying for many cards can make a lender nervous because they see that you *could* run up a large amount of debt. Essentially, this is the concern: A lender doesn't want to think that you already owe twenty-five other people.

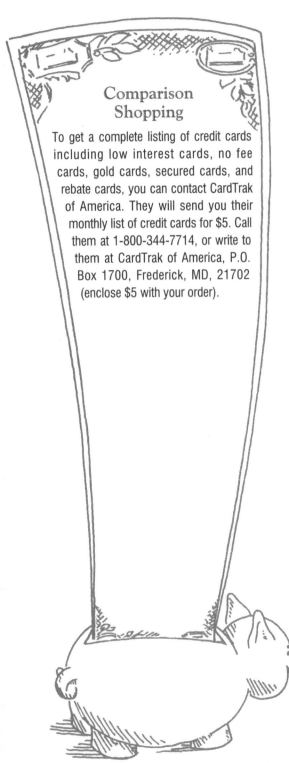

Comparison Shopping

To get a complete listing of credit cards including low interest cards, no fee cards, gold cards, secured cards, and rebate cards, you can contact CardTrak of America. They will send you their monthly list of credit cards for $5. Call them at 1-800-344-7714, or write to them at CardTrak of America, P.O. Box 1700, Frederick, MD, 21702 (enclose $5 with your order).

These are the "big three" credit bureaus:

Trans Credit Union
Trans Union National Consumer Disclosure Center
25249 Country Club Boulevard
P.O. Box 7000
North Olmstead, OH 44070
1-800-916-8800

Experian Information Solutions
Experian Consumer Assistance Center
P.O. Box 2350
Chatsworth, CA 91313
1-888-397-3742
www.experian.com

Equifax
Equifax Information Service Center
P.O. Box 740241
Atlanta, GA 30374
1-800-685-1111

You can check on your credit reports and get copies from all three credit bureaus through a company called Credit Com (1-800-777-9700). There is a charge of around $30.

If an error has not been corrected or you cannot get satisfactory results from a credit bureau, call either the office of the attorney general in your state or the Federal Trade Commission in Washington, D.C.

Essentially, a good credit rating, like a good report card, is a plus. Showing that you are responsible when it concerns money matters is the most significant step. For the most part, however, the idea that you can stay within your means is the key. There are minor delinquencies and major delinquencies when paying off credit. Someone who is late paying three bills and then recovers and is consistent about paying their bills from that point forward will show a minor delinquency. This can happen because of a life crisis and is not usually frowned upon. However, if a debt is turned over to a collection agency or the company has listed it as bad debt or a loss, you fall into the major delinquency category, also known as a major derogatory. Either way you are in big trouble creditwise.

Delinquencies stay on your report for seven years once paid off. Outstanding debts remain on your report until they are paid off.

To keep yourself on track, look at what creditors look for:

1. *Missed payments.* Creditors examine how often you miss a payment, how long ago you missed it, and whether you have outstanding payments. They also look to see whether you have a consistent level of debt and the amount of debt versus your credit limit. If you owe, say, $1,000 but your credit limit is $10,000, that's a low percentage of the amount of debt that you could have accrued. However, if you owe $9,000, or 90 percent, they will be more leery about offering you more credit.

2. *Time of credit.* If you've been a credit card holder for twenty years and have paid your bill late only five times, it's not significant.

3. *How much debt you COULD have.* The other aspect that comes into play in your credit report is how much debt you have and how much you could have tomorrow. If you keep opening accounts, there is a greater risk you could be in debt tomorrow. Your spending habits then become more consequential.

If your credit rating has essentially gone down the proverbial drain, you may need to correct it. For help, you might call:

The National Foundation for Consumer Credit
(they have regional offices)
1-800-388-2227

Keep One In Your Maiden Name

Women who share cards with their husbands often neglect to double check that they have their own individual credit rating. Credit card companies may not even list you jointly. Should you get divorced or should your husband die, you then have no credit rating. Request at least one credit card in your legal name (Mary Smith, not Mrs. Richard Smith), even on joint accounts.

Make sure that the person you work with is a proven professional. Amateurs can get you in even more credit trouble, and scam artists can simply rip you off, since you are vulnerable. Credit fixers have a number of offbeat approaches to correcting your low credit rating, such as creating a new line of credit for you under a "new" identity. This is illegal, as are most of these "bright ideas." AVOID CREDIT FIXERS!!

The second best way to start bailing yourself out of a bad credit rating is to repay your debts. Pay off the biggest ones first and then establish a consistency of payments on credit cards, utilities, rent, and other such items.

The best way to avoid a wealth of debt and a bad credit report is not to get into trouble in the first place. Fight the urge. DON'T OVERSPEND ON YOUR CARD(S)! (There's more on credit card debt in Chapter 4.)

LOST OR STOLEN CREDIT CARDS

Keep the toll-free number of the issuer of your card handy in the event your card is lost or stolen. Copy it down and keep it with your phone numbers at home. If the card is lost or stolen, report it immediately so that the issuer can cancel the card. You will not be billed for subsequent charges to your card. If the card has already been used, you may be liable for a small amount.

You should always review your credit card bill carefully, since it's important to note any charges that obviously do not belong to you. People have discovered that they lost their credit card(s) by noting such erroneous charges on their bills. Also, through phone sales as well as other means—such as copying the imprint of your card (many places have more updated systems to avoid this)—good scam artists can get your credit card number and charge items to your account. Most major credit card companies have no problem voiding such payments, if you've established a good credit rating. If erroneous charges show up with any frequency, cancel the card and get a new one. An alert credit card company will call you or even request identification at the point of purchase if the card is used for a series of transactions in a short period of time.

PROFESSIONAL CREDIT HELP

There are thousands of advertisers and merchandisers willing to tell you how to spend your money, since they don't get anything if you don't. So there's nothing wrong with seeking some help to avoid spending. As one frustrated car owner said, "The salesman gave me fifty reasons to buy the damn car. I wish someone had given me fifty good reasons not to!"

There are counselors and groups that work with people who are having a problem with spending and are in debt. The National Foundation for Consumer Credit (NFCC) (1-800-388-2227 or www.nfcc.org) is a good place to turn for credit education and counseling. Nearly fifty years old, the non-profit organization offers consumers confidential money management and homeowner counseling. With nearly fifteen hundred offices in the United States and Canada, the NFCC offers thousands of educational programs each year on budgeting and credit management to more than a million families.

A counselor will look over your credit card invoices, see where your balances are, and put you on a program. Like joining Weight Watchers and getting a menu to follow, they will work out a spending program. However, unlike Weight Watchers, who cannot contact all the local restaurants in your neighborhood, a counselor can call your lenders and ask them to waive the late charges or other additional fees and even reduce the interest rate. Often it is to the lenders' benefit to help you at this juncture, because if you end up filing for personal bankruptcy, the interest rates will be waived and they'll receive less than 100 percent on the dollar. (There's more on personal bankruptcy in Chapter 4.)

Also, you can be the one to notify your lenders that you are having trouble. Many lenders are receptive, especially if you've been paying them off on a steady basis and some circumstance, such as an emergency, has caused you to fall a month behind. It is best to approach the lending company early on, rather than wait until you are deep into debt. Keeping the lines of communication open is often to your advantage.

THE MONEY $ GAZETTE

Credit Card
Survival Top Ten List

1. Learn about your credit cards. Know the interest rate, billing due date/grace period, credit limit, and all other pertinent information. Also know exactly how the interest is compounded.

2. Avoid gimmicks.

3. Stick with known credit card companies, reputable merchants, and familiar banks.

4. Pay all cards off in full at the end of every month.

5. Pay your bills on time. (There's nothing worse than being able to pay your credit card bill in full and stupidly neglecting to send in the payment.) Paying bills by computer allows you to pay all the bills at one time. It also gives you proof that you paid the bill.

6. Don't charge small expenditures like food and gas.

7. Get rid of (or simply don't take) cards that you do not, or will not, use; keep a limit of three or four.

8. Make sure anyone else who is eligible to use your card has learned good spending habits.

9. Read your credit card bills carefully and report any errors.

10. Don't get suckered in by offers of deferred billing that promise no payment now but show up three months later with finance charges for the three months.

CREDIT CARDS OFFERED COMPARATIVE WORKSHEET

CARD NAME	ANNUAL FEE	GRACE PERIOD	APR	MAXIMUM CREDIT OFFERED	PERKS/BENEFITS

CREDIT CARDS HELD WORKSHEET

CARD NAME:	STATEMENT DATE
ACCOUNT #:	DATE PAID
CREDIT LIMIT:	AMOUNT PAID
INTEREST RATE:	REMAINING BALANCE

CARD NAME:	STATEMENT DATE
ACCOUNT #:	DATE PAID
CREDIT LIMIT:	AMOUNT PAID
INTEREST RATE:	REMAINING BALANCE

CARD NAME:	STATEMENT DATE
ACCOUNT #:	DATE PAID
CREDIT LIMIT:	AMOUNT PAID
INTEREST RATE:	REMAINING BALANCE

CARD NAME:	STATEMENT DATE
ACCOUNT #:	DATE PAID
CREDIT LIMIT:	AMOUNT PAID
INTEREST RATE:	REMAINING BALANCE

CARD NAME:	STATEMENT DATE
ACCOUNT #:	DATE PAID
CREDIT LIMIT:	AMOUNT PAID
INTEREST RATE:	REMAINING BALANCE

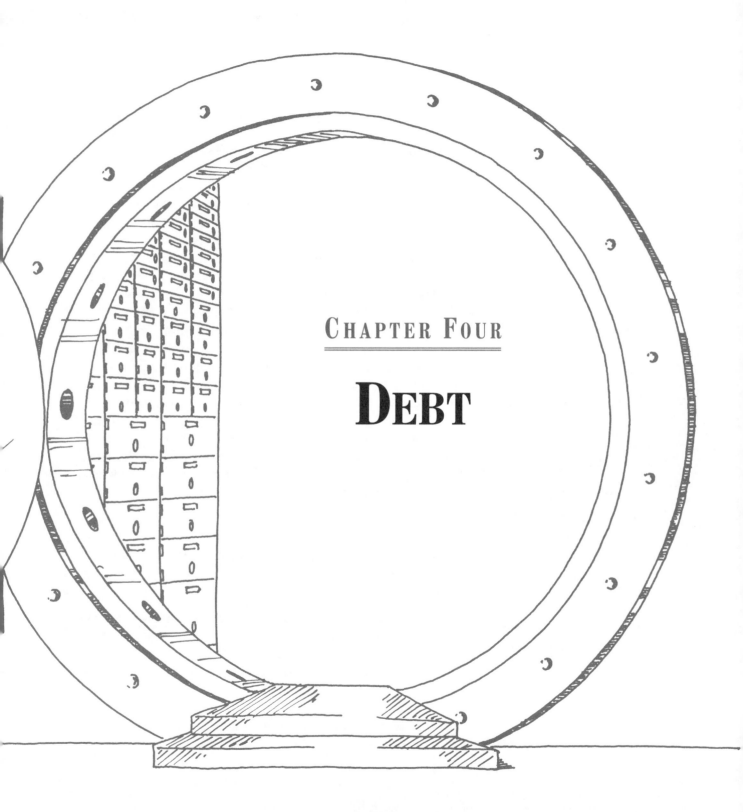

CHAPTER FOUR

DEBT

The number of people in debt in the United States is rising at a steady rate. It's a stressful, difficult lifestyle that traps many individuals, some through poor money management or bad spending habits and others through an unexpected turn of events, such as a job layoff, personal injury, or illness.

Although credit card debt is setting new records, debt is not new. In fact, being pursued by creditors today is far less traumatic than being sent to debtors prison, which was once the punishment for falling behind in your payments. And in ancient Rome, debtors and their families were actually sold into slavery.

Debt today is due in large part to consumerism and the amount of goods and services easily available. Let's face it: From the side of a bus to behind home plate at the ballpark, there are advertisements everywhere. Products and services are all around us, and credit cards make them more easily accessible than ever before. However, people need to take some responsibility for their spending habits. It's important to determine what you can and cannot afford, either at present or at the end of the month, when your credit card bill shows up in your mailbox. Essentially every time you use your credit card, you are taking out a loan. If you were to ask someone to lend you $20 for gas every time you needed to fill the tank, you would know that you owe this person money and that the amount is adding up. However, the plastic card makes it easy to forget because the lender is an anonymous source.

STAYING OUT OF DEBT

For those who are worried about heading into debt, you can evaluate your current situation and determine ways to avoid it. Here are some suggestions:

1. Keep a close watch on your monthly or weekly spending. Are you staying within the limits of your budget? Do you have a budget? (For information on budgets, see Chapter 1.)
2. Avoid using credit cards for small items. Small payments can add up into one large debt. (For more information on credit cards, see Chapter 3.)
3. Make sure you have money set aside to cover your credit card payments and pay in full at the end of each month.

4. The first month you fall behind on your payments, change your spending habits. Discipline yourself, have willpower, and give up one area of unnecessary expenditure.

5. Take out loans only for major purchases, such as car or home buying, and make the monthly payment with interest your top priority when you get paid.

6. Borrow only for emergencies.

7. Develop a plan of putting aside money so that you always have some reserve. You'll be surprised how much better you'll sleep at night knowing you have money tucked away.

8. Shop wisely and seek out good deals. Avoid impulse buying and think about what you really want and need.

9. If you're not good at disciplining yourself and handling money wisely, have it deposited directly into your account. Many people do this simply to avoid the hassles of having to deposit it themselves. It's a nineties way of having your money work for you and not having it slip through your fingers into someone else's cash register.

10. If you do go into debt, do not assume that if you ignore it, it will go away.

Amazingly enough, item 10 is one of the most frequent causes of personal bankruptcy and major debt-related headaches. It is very common for people to avoid their debt, change the subject, throw the pile of bills into the drawer, or even tear them up. But, this kind of action will not make the problem disappear. Bills need to be paid, and there's no way around it. In addition, interest fees continue to accumulate. If you see debt staring you in the face, stare back and fight; if you try to ignore it, you'll end up digging yourself into deeper trouble.

Often, if you approach lenders before the debt gets out of hand, they will help you work out payment schedules. As mentioned earlier, it doesn't help either side if you eventually reach bankruptcy. When a lender needs to call a collection agency, it is usually because the person in debt has not made any effort to develop a plan to get out of it.

Despite what you see in the movies (where the tough guy threatens to break your arm if you don't pay up), you are protected by the law from collection agencies. Collection agencies cannot

Budgeters are not Debtors!

One of the best ways to avoid getting into debt, is to carefully track your spending. People who know exactly what they are spending are much less likely to fall into debt than those that don't!

Also, try to use your credit cards as little as possible. One of the easiest ways to budget your small expenses is allow yourself a fixed amount of cash for those weekly expenses each week. The smaller the pile of cash—the less you have to spend! Not fancy, but it really works!

Beware the Credit Card Mushroom!

Try real hard to pay off your credit card debt each month. If you don't, you'll have to pay not just the credit card charges but interest to boot—often at the maximum amount allowed by law. And if you're payment is late, you'll get hit with a hefty late charge!

Worst of all, if you start to let your credit debt slide by without getting paid one month, the tendency is easy to let it slide the next month, and the next month.

Many people also have a tendency when they reach the spending limit of one credit card to start using their other cards—this is how the trouble can really mount! Many, many Americans go on to rack up $15,000 and $20,000 in credit card debts this way . . . often with relatively small individual purchases.

threaten you, injure you, harass you, or go by any other means than the courts to force your hand. The courts can garnish your wages, repossess property, and so on. BUT, do not assume that because you owe a lender money you are no longer protected by the law.

CREDIT CARD DEBT

One of the biggest drawbacks to the new "buy now, pay later" philosophy is that if you don't plan well and manage your money wisely you won't always be able to pay later. And the interest charged by most of these card companies is significant. Credit card companies are betting heavily that you won't be able to resist the rich seductive lure of consumerism.

Some sixty million American families are in debt, and the majority of that number are there thanks to those little plastic cards. The question is: How can you get out of debt once it starts mounting?

Often people who find themselves sinking further into credit card debt find themselves trying to use one card to pay off another. This works for a while, but eventually it catches up with you. Ultimately, you can lose all your credit, which will make home buying, renting a car, and many other expenditures extremely difficult. Once the debt begins to accumulate, you should immediately try to consolidate it onto one card with a low annual percentage. Look for a low rate card of around 12 percent and, before signing up, make sure you can transfer your existing debts onto the new card. Bank Rate Monitor will help you find lower rate cards.

For some spenders, the only way to avoid credit card catastrophe is to eliminate the card completely until you have acquired the self-discipline it takes to use it properly. There are support groups and counseling services offered that help people who cannot control their spending. Many credit card abusers join these groups to get help. (For more on credit card troubles, see Chapter 3.)

BAILING OUT

If you find that you are already in debt, there are ways to start bailing yourself out, short of an unexpected windfall of cash (like winning the lottery, which is not the method to bank on).

Borrowing from friends and family works for a short time. Initially, good friends may be happy to help you if they can afford to. Over time, however, this resource, and possibly your friendship, will dissolve. Pretty soon people won't be so quick to return your phone calls. If you do borrow from friends, pay them off as soon as you get your head above water. As for family, well, only you can determine how comfortable you feel about borrowing from relatives.

You can also borrow against your assets, the biggest of which is your home, if you have home equity. Home equity, the difference between the value of the house and the remaining loan balance, can be the basis for a loan at a low interest rate. You may also own a cash value life insurance policy that you can borrow against.

Another option is to sell off or cash in investments, starting with those that do not hit you with penalties. If the debt is just starting to accumulate, you might be able to nip it in the bud by selling off a few assets. Essentially, you can start slimming down assets much in the way the courts would do if you filed for bankruptcy, but your credit rating would not disappear and you'd have control over which assets you wanted to try to maintain.

You can, if possible, look for other ways to earn extra income that will be solely used to pay off the debt. From part-time tutoring to actual moonlighting, there are probably ways in which you can earn a few extra dollars to get out of debt, if you move while it's still a reasonable amount.

It's difficult living with bill collectors, banks, and credit card companies pursuing you for the money you owe. Unless you want to end up like Dr. Kimball in the TV show and the film *The Fugitive*, you should try to stop the chase before it begins.

If you need help to get out of debt, you might contact the Consumer Credit Counseling Service at 1-800-278-8811. They can be very helpful. Or call the National Foundation for Consumer Credit at 1-800-388-2227.

PERSONAL BANKRUPTCY

The last resort, should you find yourself in tremendous debt, is to file for personal bankruptcy. It is not an easy decision for people to make, but sometimes it is necessary.

Filing for bankruptcy is usually best advised when your debt has exceeded your annual income and is growing at a faster rate than your potential future income. It is also recommended when you are being sued by creditors. It is, however, a decision that must be well thought out and handled carefully by a good bankruptcy attorney, not someone advertising that they can solve all your problems. In fact, a good bankruptcy attorney will be the one who first looks to find other alternatives. One of the problems today is that too many people jump the gun and file at the recommendation of an overanxious attorney.

THREE FORMS OF BANKRUPTCY

Should you decide that your only alternative is to file for bankruptcy, there are three options: You can file under a Chapter 7, 11, or 13. Individuals generally file under a Chapter 7 or 13, while businesses primarily file under a Chapter 11.

Filing under a Chapter 7 involves liquidating your assets; you turn over the bulk of your assets (those that are not exempt by state or federal law) to the court, who sells them off to pay your creditors. All of your debt is discharged, and you do not use your future income to repay any remaining debt.

Each state has its own laws regarding exemptions or assets that cannot be sold off by the courts. Some states allow you to retain your house, but most include at least a portion of it as equity.

Personal bankruptcy is not pleasant. However, on a positive note, you are out of debt and can start again. All transactions are frozen in time when the papers are signed. Therefore, the creditors cannot come after you with a lawsuit. No more interest can be added, and nothing should be done by either party—the courts are in control at this point.

You should not try to hide assets by moving them into another area. It is not wise to try to fool the courts by hiding assets; fraud carries stiff penalties. Also, once you have entered into an agreement with a lender, of any kind, from that agreement on, almost any of the money you've moved is fair game for your creditors. In other words, if you buy a home and then start sending $500 a month to a friend, the banks, if you ever declare bankruptcy, can go after the $500 monthly amount you sent to your friend, from the date the lending agreement was signed.

A Chapter 13 or 11 filing both include the taking of future disposable income and giving it to a trustee of the bankruptcy system who distributes the money to your creditors. The trustee then pays off your bills based on a payment schedule set up with your creditors. Depending on state laws, you often pay off less than the full amount on the dollar. For example, based on your income, you might be expected to pay only $30,000, over five years, of a $50,000 debt. The rest would then be dismissed. Creditors have to agree to the plan, and you can have up to five years (the average time is three years) to pay off the agreed-upon portion of the debt. You need to look at the earning capability of any disposable income, then you need to look at the asset base. This is feasible for someone who has fallen into debt but now has enough steady income to pay it back.

A Chapter 11 filing, designed primarily as a form of business bankruptcy, also allows you to maintain possession of your assets and proceeds, much like filing under a Chapter 13. It's used for very high amounts—the jurisdictional limits are $350,000 unsecured and $750,000 secured.

Coming out of bankruptcy is almost like entering the witness protection program, only they don't set you up in a new home with a new identity or credit rating. You also have no chance of a credit rating for at least ten years. After that, your chance will improve; but it will be a slow recovery process.

Bankruptcy can be a mixed bag emotionally as well. Some who have gone through it feel a sense of relief that the nightmare of an increasing debt is no longer swallowing them alive. However, they also feel like they have been blacklisted from the consumer oriented society that we have all become accustomed to. Counseling during this time period is important, as it helps the individual feel a sense of self-worth.

Some of your debts, such as child support, taxes, and student loans, will remain after bankruptcy. However, you will be able to receive social security, disability, unemployment benefits, and in most cases, your pension.

Most likely you won't join the nearly ten million Americans who have filed for personal bankruptcy in the 1990s. However, if you do, you are not alone, and you can begin again and rebuild. Many people have, in time, successfully rebounded from bankruptcy and found themselves in lucrative careers and very comfortable lifestyles.

Questions to Ask a Bankruptcy Attorney

- Does the attorney practice bankruptcy law exclusively?
- How well known is the attorney to the local court?
- Does the attorney handle bankruptcy filings under Chapters 7, 11, and 13?
- Will the attorney sit down with you to determine other alternatives or go straight to bankruptcy as the answer?
- Has the attorney ever been a bankruptcy trustee? (If so, it shows that he or she has been intricately involved in the process.)

CREDITORS WORKSHEET

LENDER	AMOUNT DUE:
TYPE OF LOAN:	MONTHLY PAYMENT:
ACCOUNT NUMBER:	BALANCE:

LENDER	AMOUNT DUE:
TYPE OF LOAN:	MONTHLY PAYMENT:
ACCOUNT NUMBER:	BALANCE:

LENDER	AMOUNT DUE:
TYPE OF LOAN:	MONTHLY PAYMENT:
ACCOUNT NUMBER:	BALANCE:

LENDER	AMOUNT DUE:
TYPE OF LOAN:	MONTHLY PAYMENT:
ACCOUNT NUMBER:	BALANCE:

LENDER	AMOUNT DUE:
TYPE OF LOAN:	MONTHLY PAYMENT:
ACCOUNT NUMBER:	BALANCE:

LENDER	AMOUNT DUE:
TYPE OF LOAN:	MONTHLY PAYMENT:
ACCOUNT NUMBER:	BALANCE:

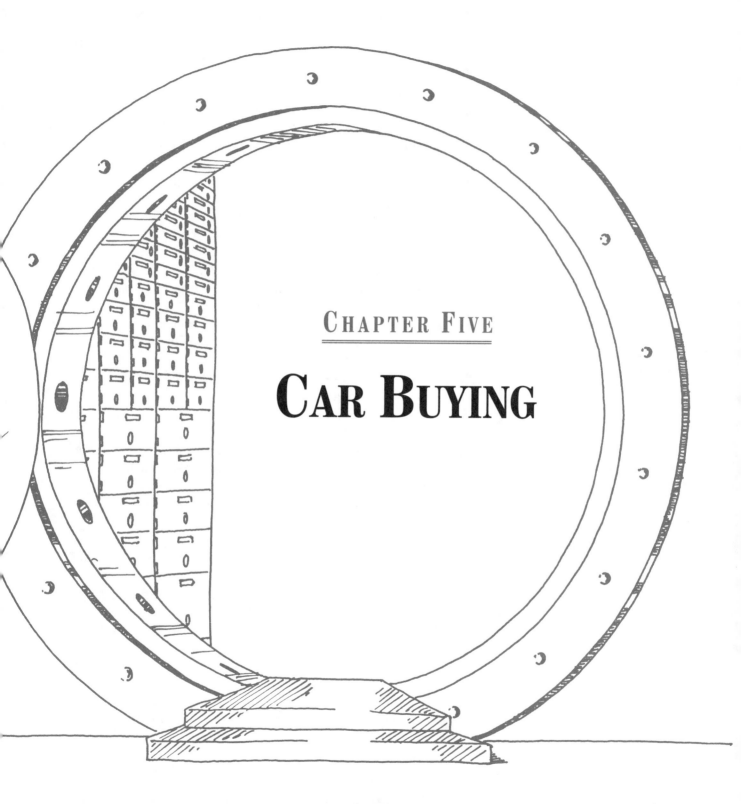

CHAPTER FIVE

CAR BUYING

Next to home buying, car buying seems relatively easy. Financially it certainly is. However, there are thousands of cars in the marketplace, and the selection process can be a tad overwhelming.

Therefore, before comparing what various cars have to offer, the first thing to do is assess your own needs. Next, zero in on your price range. Then, decide whether you are buying a car (new or used) or leasing a car.

Finally, peruse the automobile magazines. Car enthusiasts love writing about cars, and there is a wealth of information available for a small price. *Car and Driver, Motor Trend, Road and Track,* and *Autoweek* are just a few of the many magazines you'll come across. You should also look at *Consumer Reports*, a magazine that compares and rates the quality of the cars.

It's to your advantage to be "buyer savvy" when you enter the dealership. There is enough information available in magazines, in books, and on the Internet that you should know the dealer price of the car that interests you. You should also know if the dealer is offering any special deals or incentives.

Once you have a fairly good idea of what the car should really cost and the model you are most interested in, you can venture into the dealership. Dealers will immediately turn on the charm, become your best friend, ask if they can call you by your first name, and practically invite you over for Thanksgiving dinner. Despite their charm, the bottom line is that a number of things have to fall into place before you buy a new car:

1. Do you feel comfortable in the car? "Feel" is very important. If a car feels too big and overwhelming or too small and cramped, it may not be the car for you. You should have a sense of comfort and control.
2. Does the car meets your current needs? A larger car for a family or a smaller car for a single person might be in order.
3. Look at various features such as gas mileage, trunk space, leg room, acceleration, and handling. Make a checklist that includes features of significance to you.
4. Determine which "extras" you need and which ones you do not need. Be selective!

5. Be ready to haggle, negotiate, and haggle some more, and if necessary go elsewhere—there are plenty of dealerships around. Don't jump at the first sporty car you see. Shop around; get the best deal. Car dealers are very competitive, which explains why you see car ads on television every two minutes. A car is not an impulse buy and should never be the result of a high-pressure sales pitch.

6. Find out about the warranty. Usually the manufacturer gives a warranty for three to five years or for up to a certain number of miles. Look closely at what the warranty covers. The power train, including transmission and engine, are most important. Also, be careful in regard to extended warranties offered by the dealerships or anyone else, as they might be out of business before the warranty even goes into effect. You might also sell the car before this warranty kicks in.

7. Consider financing. Can you buy a new car outright or will you be paying it off? If you'll be financing the car, it's to your advantage to have a line of credit available to you through a bank or other lending institution. You can also finance with the dealer but this can be more costly.

8. Determine whether a new car or used car is a more valuable purchase than repairing your present car. A new car is an expense, not an investment. A car, unlike a house, will not become more valuable over time, unless you keep the car in good working condition until it is no longer made and becomes an "antique." For most of us, though, a car will depreciate over time. In fact, most cars will depreciate by 25 percent during the first year. Some folk will tell you that the value of a car goes down by 10 percent once you drive it out of the showroom.

9. Take a test drive. It's very important to test drive any vehicle you are thinking of buying. See that the car does not drift to one side, that the alignment is straight, that the steering is easy and smooth, that the

Child Seats

Will you require child seats? If so, determine how easy it is to install and remove them from the car. Sometimes installing a car seat properly into a car (with the seat-belt configuration) is an aggravating task.

Insurance

Don't forget about insurance! It's very important to get insurance that covers fire and theft. When renting a car, you might choose to bypass the insurance for the two or three days you have the car or the insurance may be covered on your credit card. When leasing, however, you'll rest much easier knowing you are insured, because if the car is stolen, guess who has to pay for it?

brakes work smoothly and quickly at a variety of speeds, that the sight lines are good (no major blind spots), that the car accelerates well (try a road with a hill), that the gears shift smoothly and easily, and that there are no unusual sounds. You might also check the ease at which you can operate lights, windows, wipers, and other dashboard features. When you are finished, check the engine and look under the car to see that there are no leaks. The bottom line is that you should make up a list of all the functions and check them out in a test drive.

10.   Seriously consider having a mechanic double check the car. Mechanics can find things you may have missed.

And when you're ready to buy, look over the paperwork very carefully, especially the fine print. Then make sure you obtain the title forms and proper registration. Also, make sure you have proper auto insurance, which is required in most states.

FINANCING A NEW CAR

Paying cash for a new car sounds absurd to some. After all, where are you going to come up with an extra twenty to fifty grand? However, if you consider that you save for the down payment on your home, college tuition, a wedding, or even your retirement, you can see exactly where the money can come from. Much in the way you will pay off a car, through monthly payments, with an interest rate, you can set aside the money (without the interest rate) and save up for a car. In fact, the money will grow, and you will be saving significantly if you can set aside money in a new-car account.

Don't despair if you have to play the auto finance game. BUT, do your homework. Keep in mind that additional costs, beyond financing (the loan and interest), can include fees for paperwork and credit reports.

As for financing, first apply for a line of credit; this is a way of determining that you can indeed qualify for a loan. Car loans can come from banks or finance companies. They can also come from credit unions or dealers, or you can borrow against your insurance or even your retirement fund. And there's always Mom, Dad, or your rich uncle.

Check with several lenders before choosing the financing that is best for you. Look for the best interest rates and the best loan terms. While a thirty-year loan is common for a house, long-term loans for a car aren't very common, since you won't have the car that long. Three or four years should be enough time to pay off a car. Do the math carefully. A longer term loan (four or five years) may sound better because you'll be paying less on the principal on a monthly basis. BUT, you'll be making more payments and paying more overall in the end.

Here is the "financing" bottom line:

1. Shop around for lenders.
2. Find out the annual percentage rates (APR), or interest rate for the loan and the terms.
3. Try to stay under four years with your loan.
4. Get a fair market value price on your old car as a trade in.
5. Watch the ads for the best deals and incentives for buying.
6. Be ready to put down about 15 to 20 percent up front.
7. Get the loan or at least the line of credit approved before going to the dealerships.

Other car costs, before you even hit the road, will include insurance and licensing fees. Then comes the cost of maintaining a car. Warranties will help with repair costs, but gas and regular maintenance are both line items for your budget. Regular maintenance includes checking the oil, antifreeze,

tires, belts and hoses, wipers, and so forth, and will help keep your car in good condition in the long run. And finally, don't forget to add the inspection fee to your car expense list.

LEASING

Leasing a car is one of the "in" things to do in the nineties. Leasing allows you the opportunity to drive a more expensive car for less money. However, you do not own the car in the end.

Leasing is essentially a way of "renting" a car at a lower rate. It's a good idea if you are not planning to stay in an area for more than a year or if you use your car primarily for business purposes. (You can deduct part of your leasing if you use the car for business.)

It's important that you very carefully read your lease agreement, as there can be hidden charges. Look for hidden charges for excess mileage or for features included on the car that you do not need.

Should you lease? Is it for you? The answer depends on your needs and your finances. The right leasing situation can be more affordable than buying a car. But remember: We said "THE RIGHT" situation. As when buying a car, you should shop around and negotiate the lease deal. You want the best deal up front because lease agreements can be hard or costly to get out of.

One nice features of leasing is that you can plan the lease for as long as you choose. Also, lease payments are usually lower than financing. If not, then why are you leasing? Another plus is that you can drive a car that is out of your buying range. At the end of the lease, if it's a typical "close-ended lease," you can walk away from the car, paying only for some extra mileage charges or perhaps for some expected wear and tear. And some agreements allow you to purchase the car after the lease terminates, at a lower cost (the residual value). GET ALL OF THIS SPELLED OUT IN THE LEASE AGREEMENT.

Many people shy away from leasing because they don't understand all the complexities (and those who lease cars certainly don't make it any easier). Also, people often feel that if they pay money for something, they want to own it.

LEASING SITUATIONS

Some people move to a new city and lease a car until they are comfortable in their new environment. Then, when they feel more secure, both emotionally and financially, they go out and buy a car. Others decide to lease a car at a low monthly rate, perhaps $300 a month, and invest an additional $300 a month during the two years of the lease. At the end of that time, they use the invested money to purchase the car they really want.

Here are some leasing tips:

1. Negotiate the lease VERY carefully.
2. Make sure the terms fit your needs. Don't lease a car for twenty-four months if you only need it for eighteen. Leases, as mentioned earlier, are costly to get out of.
3. Check other costs besides the monthly payment. There may be leasing company charges and other fees.
4. Perhaps most important, lease a car that you feel comfortable driving. Unlike renting a car for a long weekend, this is a car you will be driving for one to three years. Make sure you feel comfortable behind the wheel. Also, make sure to check carefully to see that you are leasing a quality vehicle (read *Consumer Reports*, the auto magazines, etc., as you would for buying a car). It's not uncommon for a person to get so absorbed in trying to figure out the complexities of leasing that he or she forgets completely about the car itself. Don't use the "well I'm just leasing it" theory to overlook things that might be frustrating or even hazardous to you as a driver.

BUYING A USED CAR

Used cars have also been very much in vogue in the nineties. If you are careful, shop wisely, and have the car checked out, you can often get a good deal with a car that has been owned before. No longer are used-car dealers the stereotypical wheeler dealer types who try to squeeze you into a lemon.

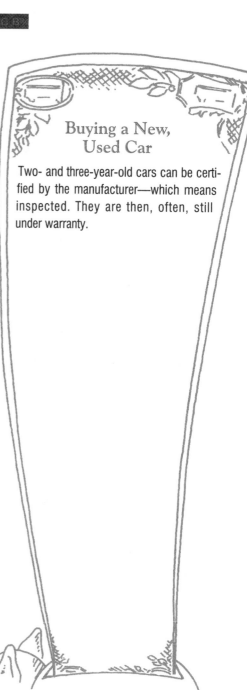

Buying a New, Used Car

Two- and three-year-old cars can be certified by the manufacturer—which means inspected. They are then, often, still under warranty.

Important Internet Sites

When in the market for a used car, it helps to do your homework. And where does anybody do homework these days? On the Internet, of course. Good car pricing Internet sites include www.edmunds.com, run by the people who publish the Edmunds car guides. Besides pricing, they provide reliability ratings and other information. Also look at www.autos.yahoo.com and www.carpoint.msn.com, brought to you by Microsoft. In addition, there are sites by America's Auto Mall, Auto Advantage, and The Car Lot.

The best thing the online sites can give you is a good feel for the pricing of the year and model car you are looking for. You can also find other suggested models in your price range. Information is a marvelous asset.

In fact, there are now giant used-car conglomerates, such as CarMax and AutoNation USA, that offer a wide selection of used cars in one huge outlet.

There are also numerous smaller dealers coast to coast who sell "late model" cars off their lots. If you buy a car off a lot, be sure to scout around and get some first-hand accounts from other satisfied customers. Get a feel for the reputation of the dealership. Also, find out about trade-ins. Trade-in allowances for your current car can often be in the area of 20 to 25 percent off the price of the car you buy.

The advantage of buying a used car is, obviously, that you save money. You do, however, have to pay sales tax on the car based on your state's sales tax rate.

The first step, naturally, is to find the car you want. The National Association of Automobile Dealers issues an *Official Guide to Used Cars*; this guide lists the going rate for the year and model of every car. Of course, you have to be the final judge. No matter what the book says or what the odometer reads, you have to feel comfortable with the condition of the car and the price.

So, Where Are the Cars?

Besides the car lots and newly founded super stores, there are many other sources for locating used cars, including newspaper ads, the Internet, auto auctions (where you can come away with some great deals), and fleet car sales (in which a car service sells off a number of their vehicles to make room for newer models). Don't be scared off by higher mileage on fleet cars. Often cars that are part of a car service or rental company receive far better maintenance (on a daily basis) than other cars because they are vital to the company's business. Since they need to sell off these cars before the newer models arrive, you can often buy them at a good price.

Autos are auctioned off by the Department of Defense, the U.S. Marshall's Office, the IRS, U.S. Customs Service, police departments, and as part of estates. Sometimes even movie companies and various other places that use cars for business reasons have cars available for sale. Then there are the many cars that have been leased out. Often businesses will lease those company cars that everybody wants. Once the leasing days of the cars are over, they too can be found at auctions or sold off the lot by the leasing companies. In fact, leasing has presented a whole new level of high-quality relatively new used cars.

A FEW THINGS TO LOOK FOR WHEN BUYING A USED CAR

How old is the car? Used cars are usually three to six years old.

How old or new are the parts in the car? What has been re-built or re-rebuilt? Be a good car detective and decipher clues regarding replacement parts or paint jobs. Look for the factory serial numbers on the fenders or inside the hood. If they're not there, then the parts have been replaced. See if the paint feels smooth or if dents or scratches have been painted over.

What about mileage? The average is 10,000 to 15,000 miles per year. Again, if the car has been well maintained, the mileage can be higher. Don't go by mileage alone. A car at 20,000 miles that is four years old is not a better deal if it was the lead car in a twelve-car pileup or a student driver car with gears that were shifted incorrectly for three years. Keep in mind that an incorrect odometer is illegal for resale purposes. However, it's not easy to determine if an odometer has been tampered with. Look for rust, loose sliding gear shifts, worn seats, and other signs that the car has traveled more than the odometer indicates.

Can you get a warranty if you want one? Don't overpay for this. If you get the car checked out by a good mechanic, you may save an extra $1,200 on a warranty that may not cover everything anyway.

Can you still get parts for that car? If you buy directly from someone (no dealer involved), make sure you are getting all the paperwork that goes with the car, including the transfer of title to prove ownership and possibly the owner's manual to provide you with information on operating the vehicle.

HOTTEST SELLING CARS

Among the top selling cars in the late 1990s are the Ford Explorer and Taurus, the Toyota Camry, and the Honda Civic. Vans are very popular, as are jeeps and pickup trucks. In fact, the top selling vehicles in 1997, according to *CRA Automotive News*, were the Ford Series F-pickup and the Chevrolet C/K pickup. Other highly rated cars in recent years include the Saturn SL Sedan, Ford Contour, Dodge Intrepid, Chevrolet Monte Carlo, Oldsmobile Aurora, and, for those of you who've read the other chapters of this book and invested wisely, the Mercedes Benz E320. Minivans and sports utility vehicles are also very popular. In fact, it's estimated that nearly two million sports utility vehicles will sell in the next year.

Among the best selling and highest rated used cars (three to seven years old) are the Ford Taurus LX, Honda Accord, Lexus LS400, and several models from Toyota.

MODEL:	MODEL:
MAKE:	MAKE:
YEAR:	YEAR:
BASE PRICE: $	BASE PRICE: $
EXTRAS:	EXTRAS:
TOTAL PRICE: $	TOTAL PRICE: $

MODEL:	MODEL:
MAKE:	MAKE:
YEAR:	YEAR:
BASE PRICE: $	BASE PRICE: $
EXTRAS:	EXTRAS:
TOTAL PRICE: $	TOTAL PRICE: $

LEASING VERSUS BUYING COST COMPARISON WORKSHEET

LEASING:		BUYING:	
Length of Lease		Term of Loan	
Down Payment	$	Down Payment	$
Monthly Payment (x number of months, including sales tax)	$	Monthly Payment (x number of months, including sales tax)	$
Title/Registration Fees	$	Title/Registration Fees	$
Insurance Premiums	$	Insurance Premiums	$
Company Provided Maintenance Charges	$	Estimated Maintenance Charges	$
Cost on Early Lease Termination	$		n/a
Total Leasing Cost this does not include charges for excess mileage	$	Total Purchasing Cost Minus fair market value at time of comparable lease termination	$ $
		Net Cost of Car	$

Part II

SAVING AND INVESTING

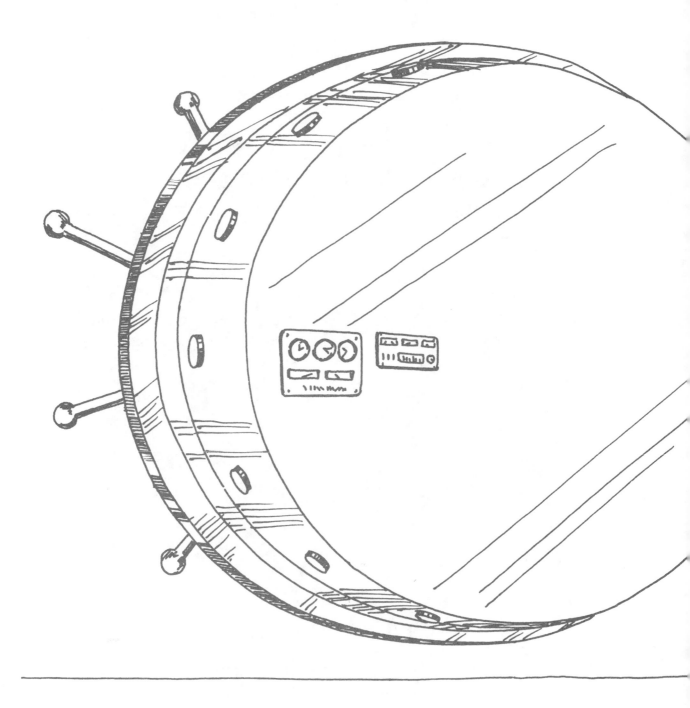

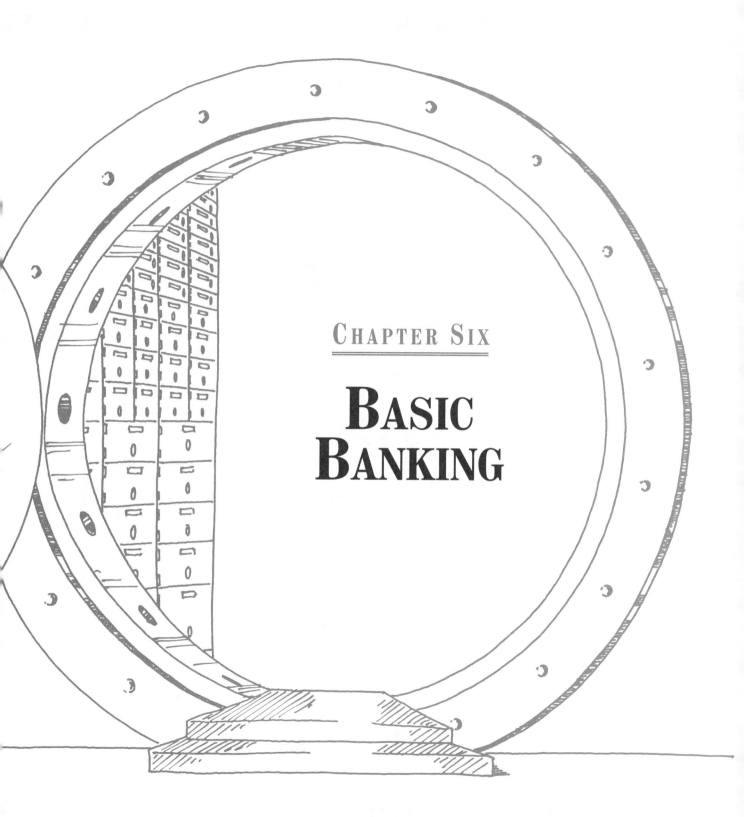

CHAPTER SIX

BASIC BANKING

It seems as though everyone, especially on television, has a new way for you to invest your money. People say, "It's only money," or "You can't take it with you," but that's easy to say when it's someone else's money.

The question is, Why not remain faithful to the banking industry? After all, it's a safe place to keep your money, at least since 1933 (when the FDIC was established). And it sure beats a hole in the mattress. From the most basic bank to the more established banking conglomerates, the concept of the bank is the same: It's a guaranteed safe place to keep your money. The FDIC insures each account for up to $100,000. So, if you're putting more than $100,000 in the bank, spread it around.

Opening various accounts can be advantageous. For example, a couple could each open an individual account, plus one jointly at their local Federal Mutual Ohio Boston New York Global Greenpoint Reserve, and another jointly at First Fidelity down the street. The couple's four accounts are then insured for a total of $400,000.

The money you place in banks, primarily in the form of "cash investments," goes into savings accounts, checking accounts, money market accounts, NOW accounts, CDs (certificates of deposit), or other types of accounts. These cash accounts are significant because they set the foundation for moving toward "riskier" investments.

In cash accounts you are protected and cannot lose the principal. Interest rates vary, and determining which account will pay the highest rate of interest and over how much time is a tedious chore worth doing. Investments, on the other hand, are more popular than bank accounts because they pay higher interest rates, and it's not advisable to keep huge sums of money in the bank when you can find safe investment options.

One significant feature of a cash instrument, such as a NOW account, is that you can have your money "now," via check, ATM, or withdrawal. CDs, T-bills, and other investments tie your money up for a period of time. Therefore, for money you need on hand, look to your friendly neighborhood bank. This is where you establish your "cash flow," or the cash coming and going from your account on a daily basis.

INTEREST

The concept of having your money grow in any short- or long-term investment is based largely on the concept of interest: For the right to hold and use your money, you will be paid based on the rate of the type of investment you have selected. The way in which money grows substantially over time is by compounding interest, that is, your interest keeps generating interest. The amount compounded quarterly will then grow and grow.

"COMPOUNDED DAILY"

The phrase *compounded daily* is one that we've all heard many times on bank commercials. It means that in a particular type of account your money grows every day. When putting money into an account, two important considerations are the interest rate and how often interest is compounded.

Interest rates vary from bank to bank, but not by much. In 1998 common numbers were in the 2 to 3 percent range for most savings accounts. Back in the early '80s interest rates were considerably higher on similar accounts, exceeding 6 percent. The interest rates dropped in the '90s as inflation slowed down.

VARIOUS TYPES OF ACCOUNTS

For many years, the most common bank account was the passbook savings account. It was the one account that offered interest (generally around 5 to 5.25 percent). You would take your passbook from your drawer or nightstand to the bank and have it stamped whenever you made a transaction. Typically, a trip to the bank meant presenting your passbook to the teller; all transactions were kept in that handy little book.

Today such accounts still exist; however, statement accounts have become more popular. Now banks send you a monthly or quarterly statement. Such accounts generally pay 2 to 4 percent, and there are often minimum amounts required to

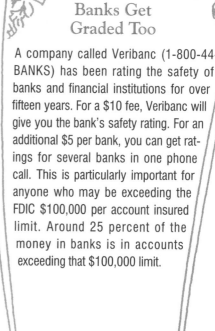

Banks Get Graded Too

A company called Veribanc (1-800-44-BANKS) has been rating the safety of banks and financial institutions for over fifteen years. For a $10 fee, Veribanc will give you the bank's safety rating. For an additional $5 per bank, you can get ratings for several banks in one phone call. This is particularly important for anyone who may be exceeding the FDIC $100,000 per account insured limit. Around 25 percent of the money in banks is in accounts exceeding that $100,000 limit.

Overdraft Accounts

Overdraft accounts are dangerous. If you spend more money than you have in your checking account, the bank will loan you the extra money to cover your expense. And they will do this every time. They will also charge you a very high rate of interest for this feature. You then have to pay off the overdraft or carry an ongoing balance with high interest. You're better off simply keeping track of approximately how much is in your checking account!

maintain an account without having to pay extra bank charges. As more banks appear on the horizon and there is more competition, banks must offer more attractive plans with higher interest rates.

Passbook or statement accounts are for those who don't meet the minimum for CDs or larger investments. They are for people who need liquidity as well as for anyone who just finds them convenient and easy to understand. Often seniors will continue to use passbook accounts simply because they have been doing so for many years. There is nothing wrong with this. Even individuals with large sums of money tied up in investments often maintain a standard statement or even passbook account to keep some available cash.

CHECKING ACCOUNTS

A recent survey found that major banks now have an average of seven different types of checking accounts. For most of us, that's five or even six choices too many.

Negotiable order of withdrawal (NOW) accounts are the most commonly used checking accounts. Until recent years, checking accounts did not offer interest, but because of various competitive accounts and the vast number of banks, most checking accounts offer a low interest rate. Most NOW accounts allow for unlimited check writing but require you to keep a minimum balance of at least $500, $1,000, or $2,000. Some will allow you to have a minimum balance between several "linking" accounts; thus, if you have x amount of money between three or four different accounts in the same bank, you won't be charged a fee for going under the NOW account minimum.

Some banks still charge you an amount per check. It's up to you to shop around and determine whether the interest will outweigh the bank charges when you open a NOW account. NOW accounts are mainly for people who write a steady number of checks but can maintain a minimum checking account balance to receive interest.

Deluxe accounts, which are loaded with extra features such as free travelers checks and other services, are also offered, as are *club accounts*, which may be tied in with other bank services such as various discounts. Many banks offer *self-service accounts* that tie to an ATM to encourage ATM use. Basic checking accounts still exist, and for three or four dollars a month, they allow you to write about ten checks. These *lifeline accounts* are good for people who have a limited need for a checking account. Students may benefit from such an account. It does not pay interest, but it does not require them to keep a significant balance in the account.

The ideal checking account is one that doesn't cost money to maintain, has a low minimum balance, allows you to write as many checks as necessary, pays interest, and provides you with up-to-date statements regularly.

MONEY MARKET BANK DEPOSIT ACCOUNTS

MMDAs came into existence in the mid 1980s because banks wanted to compete against mutual funds. Money market deposit accounts pay slightly higher interest rates (around 2.5 percent) than NOW or passbook savings accounts because they limit the number of checks, ATM withdrawals, or electronic transfers you are able to make to only three per month.

This is where banks can be very competitive, as they vary their rates depending on the overall state of interest rates. They may pay higher rates if you have more money invested in the account. On the other hand, they may charge bank fees if you drop below a certain minimum balance.

One wise move would be to use a money market account as a place to park cash that is not invested and may be needed to write checks. You can keep money in this account and use your three transfers to move enough money to your checking account to write checks and cover the minimum in that account. This way you are getting the better interest rate in the money market deposit account while using the checking account to send out checks. You can also wait until you've built up this account to later invest some of the money in higher yield (though more risky) investments.

Money market deposit accounts are for people who want a liquid account, may want to write some checks, and want less risk than mutual funds. They are insured by the FDIC, which makes some people feel more comfortable. They are also part of your

Shop Around for a Bank!

Not all banks charge the same rates, so shop around for the best deals! Then carefully consider which type of account is best for you. Maybe two types of accounts is the best solution. You may decide to keep a small amount of money in a checking or similar account with check-writing privileges and a larger amount of money in a savings account that doesn't allow check-writing, but pays a higher interest rate.

A Safe Investment Except For Inflation

CD's are one of the safest investments you can make, because they are FDIC insured—and they typically offer a much better interest rate than a savings account. But they do not offer a good hedge against inflation. To protect yourself against inflation, you'll need to invest in stocks or other assets that appreciate over time.

local bank, so you keep your money "close to home." It's a no-risk, "higher level of comfort" account with check writing capabilities plus interest.

CERTIFICATES OF DEPOSIT

CDs allow you to secure the same interest rate for a fixed amount of time, and the principal will not fluctuate. Through your bank, or a credit union, you can purchase CDs for three months, six months, one year, or longer. Naturally, the longer you commit to with your CD, the higher your yield will be. On the other side of the equation is the early withdrawal penalty, should you need to cash in the CD before it is due. CDs are good short-term no-risk places to invest money while you investigate your longer term plans. They are a way of "playing it safe," particularly because they are insured by the FDIC.

Once you are sure that you can tie up a certain amount of money, be it $100 or $5,000, you can purchase a CD. Banks usually set a low minimum and do not charge for purchasing such a certificate. Interest rates will vary depending on the bank, the amount of money, and time frame you specify. Some banks even allow for designer CDs, which let you set the guidelines while the bank calculates the rate. Interest rate parameters are determined by the banks in conjunction with the demand and expected future demand for loans.

The annual percentage yield on your CD is what the CD will earn on an annual basis, combining the stated rate of interest and the compounded frequency. As we near the end of the 1990s, the annual yields generally run between 4 and 6 percent, depending on whether you purchase a six-month, one-year, or five-year CD. This is similar to short- and intermediate-term bonds. Not to rain on your CD parade, but the interest from your CD is taxable.

Among the places to scout CDs are the major money and investing newspapers and magazines including the *Wall Street Journal*, *USA Today*, *Money Magazine*, *Barron's*, and *Kiplingers Personal Finance Magazine*.

There is also a newsletter called *The 100 Highest Yields*, which is available by subscription (call 1-800-327-7717 for more information).

U.S. TREASURY BILLS

Backed by the United States government, T-bills, as they are widely known, are safe purchases because there is no threat of losing the principal. More popular before the mutual fund wave of the '90s (T-bill interest rates reached double digits in the '80s), they are sold at government auctions (every Monday except bank holidays) and offered for 13, 26, or 52 weeks. Essentially, the government determines the rate of yield at the treasury auctions. This determines what yield you will receive when you buy the T-bill. Current T-bill rates are typically in the 5 to 5.5 percent range. When you buy one, you immediately get a payment of interest (called the "discount"), and when the T-bill becomes due, you can reinvest and receive a discount payment again.

For example, let's say you buy a 26-week T-bill for $10,000. You then immediately receive a check for $300 (at an interest rate of around 6 percent) as your discount. It's the government's way of saying thank you. Then, after the six months are up, you will receive another check for the original $10,000 you invested. Or you can renew it indefinitely.

Treasury bills are investments made with the federal government. Therefore, you can bypass your local bank and purchase them from any federal reserve bank or from the Bureau of Public Debt at the Treasury Department. The interest can then be routed directly into your bank account or money market account by providing the routing number for your bank, plus the number of your account. Although the interest rate of the T-bill is set when you purchase it, you can earn additional interest from the money that goes into your bank or money market account. For more information, contact the Bureau of Public Debt, Treasury Department, Washington, DC, 20239 or talk with a banker.

As of 1998, anyone can buy Treasury bills in thousand dollar denominations starting as low as $1,000. Previously, the minimum T-bill investment was $10,000, so this is a real boon to consumers.

While T-bill interest payments are taxable at the federal level, they are not taxable at the state or local level, so if you reside in a state with high taxes, this might be an attractive

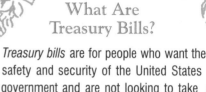

What Are Treasury Bills?

Treasury bills are for people who want the safety and security of the United States government and are not looking to take risks. Treasury Direct electronic services will let you reinvest by phone at 1-800-943-6864. You can also get account information.

investment. Also, the T-bill tax is paid when the bill becomes due. Thus, if you bought a six-month bill in August of 1999, the taxable income will not show up until 2000, and it will be reported on the return you submit in 2001.

THE FDIC

The Federal Deposit Insurance Corporation was created in 1933 (after the stock-market crashed in 1929, ushering in the Great Depression). It was established by Congress to insure deposits and serve as a safeguard in the case of failure in the banking system. In 1989, deposits in savings associations were also insured by the FDIC, which is backed by the credit of the United States and uses the Bank Insurance and Savings Association Insurance funds.

While the vast majority of banks in the United States are FDIC affiliated, not all banks are covered. It's worth checking to make sure your bank has the FDIC official logo.

Most types of deposits are covered by the FDIC, including deposits in savings accounts, checking accounts, NOW accounts, Christmas accounts, CDs, cashiers checks, money orders, certified checks, and traveler's checks, issued in exchange for money.

Treasury bills and Treasury bonds and notes can be purchased through a bank but are not purchased via book entries at the bank. In other words, the accounting entry is not maintained by the bank but by the Treasury Department. Treasury securities are essentially transactions between the customer and the Treasury Department, with the bank acting as a custodian. Therefore, if the bank fails and you are holding a Treasury security, you can request a document from the acquiring bank or from the FDIC that shows proof of ownership and can be redeemed at the nearest Federal Reserve Bank.

Although Treasury securities are not covered by the federal deposit insurance, interest and principal on those securities that are deposited into an investor's deposit account are covered by FDIC insurance up to the $100,000 limit. Treasury securities are backed by the full faith and credit of the United States government.

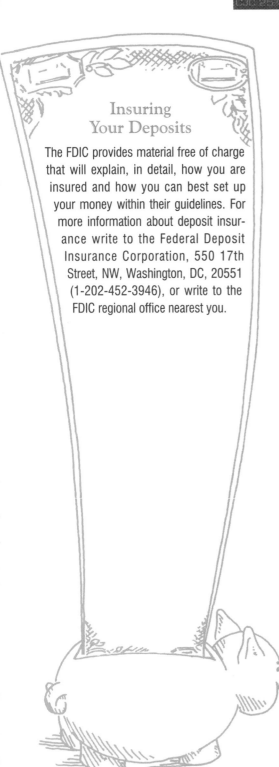

Insuring Your Deposits

The FDIC provides material free of charge that will explain, in detail, how you are insured and how you can best set up your money within their guidelines. For more information about deposit insurance write to the Federal Deposit Insurance Corporation, 550 17th Street, NW, Washington, DC, 20551 (1-202-452-3946), or write to the FDIC regional office nearest you.

Investments in mutual funds, stocks, bonds, and money market mutual funds are not generally insured by the FDIC. Safety deposit boxes are also not protected by FDIC insurance.

As previously noted, you are covered for $100,000 per account. Ownership is determined, according to the FDIC, by what is shown on the "deposit of account records" of the insured depository institution. The "deposit of account records" are signature cards, account ledgers, certificates of deposits, passbooks, and certain computer records.

If you want to exceed the $100,000 limit, you need to put your funds in different ownership categories. You can also get separate insurance coverage for money in retirement accounts such as Keogh plans, pensions, and profit sharing. Using various accounts, such as a CD, a NOW account, and a savings account at the same bank, under your own name or ownership, won't do it.

How to Choose a Bank

Despite mergers and acquisitions, there are still over nine thousand banks operating in the United States—down from some fifteen thousand in the '80s. Indeed, you still have a great many banks to choose from.

THE MONEY $ GAZETTE

When Choosing a Bank . . .

Here's what to look for when choosing a bank:

- Check the interest rates, and if you need a loan or mortgage, check those rates as well.

- What does the bank offer? Some banks offer broker services. Others have free home money management software such as Intuit Quicken or Microsoft Money. Free checking is always nice, too. There are numerous services banks can now include, beyond the "old" free toaster.

- Determine the convenience of ATMs. Does the bank have accessibility to ATMs in other locations? Is there a surcharge?

- Look at bank fees. For example, compare unlimited checks versus paying per check. Don't forget "account minimums." What are they?

- Does the bank offer online services? Do they have their own service, or are you going through a commercial server? What do they charge for home banking?

- Look to see whether they have linking accounts, which are common today. This basically means that your minimum in one account may be lower than the allotted minimum, but because your balance is higher in another account and they are linked together, you will not be charged a minimum fee.

- Location and hours are always important. Are they open on Saturdays?

- Visit the local branch and get to know the characteristics of that bank. What level of personal service do you want?

- And finally, how safe is your bank? Is it FDIC protected? Is it solvent? About to merge with a hardware store? In the "everything gets graded" '90s, you can actually check out the rating of a bank.

BALANCING YOUR CHECKBOOK

These are the three primary reasons for balancing your checkbook:

1. To make sure you do not write bad checks.
2. To be able to better utilize money sitting in your checking account earning a low interest rate.
3. To find any errors that the bank may have made on your account.

It is very simple to keep your checkbook balanced. Here are the basic steps you must follow in order to do so:

1. Enter each check you write, including the date, check number, payee, and amount paid.
2. Deduct the amount paid from the account balance.
3. Enter each deposit including the date and amount.
4. Add the amount deposited to the account balance.
5. Be sure to deduct all ATM withdrawals (this is commonly forgotten).
6. Be sure to add in any direct deposits (paychecks, interest, etc.).
7. Be sure to deduct any bank charges or fees charged to your account.

When you receive your monthly statement, follow these steps:

1. Compare the canceled checks to the checks written since the previous statement.
2. Do the same for any deposits made.
3. Since it takes checks a few days to clear and you may have written some after your statement was sent to you, you should list all outstanding checks (including those written in prior months) so that your checkbook will balance with the statement. Therefore, if you have $1,000 according to the statement's balance but you know you have two outstanding checks worth a total of $500, you should enter these and deduct them on the statement. Now you'll have a statement balance of $500. Keep track of these items so that you can see if they clear on your next statement.

Top Online Banking Websites

Online bank web sites include the following:

www.bankone.com (Bank One)
www.bofa.com (Bank of America)
www.chase.com (Chase)
www.citibank.com (Citibank)
www.firstunion.com (First Union)
www.fleet.com (Fleet Bank)
www.nationsbank.com (NationsBank)
www.norwest.com (Norwest Bank)
www.wellsfargo.com (Wells Fargo)

Magazines like *Money*, *Kiplingers*, and various PC magazines will occasionally rate and review the various online banking services. Look for these particular issues of the magazines or go online (or to a library) to look at back issues.

Some people want to balance their checkbook to the penny. Others have neither the time nor the patience and are satisfied knowing that they have enough money to cover their check writing needs. The choice is yours.

Many personal organizers and check balancing computer programs can also be used as well. It depends on the volume of checks you write as to whether or not software is really necessary. Make sure you double check your entries. Hard copies are always nice, just in case of a technological "glitch."

ONLINE BANKING

"I helped hold a bank up online," said one crook. "What did you do?" asked the other. "I drove the getaway mouse," responded the cyberthief.

"Online banking has exceeded the banking industry's expectations and is growing at an extremely rapid pace. By early 1998 over 700 banks offered online banking with the number expected to quadruple within the next couple of years," says Fritz Elmendorff of the Consumer Bankers Association.

Nearly five million American households are doing their banking online. Why the sudden popularity of banking by computer?

The most appealing aspect of online banking is accessibility. You are no longer at the mercy of the bank statement arriving on time in the mail or of "banking hours," and you can view your account whenever you choose. You'll be able to download statements, see that your checkbook is balanced, and pay bills whenever they come in—or program them to be paid on a particular date, from the comfort of your own home. And if paying bills online isn't enough technology for you, the next wave, e-billing, has already begun.

All you need to do is select a bank that has online banking accessibility and a platform or way of making the connection. Typically, Intuit Quicken, Microsoft Money, Managing Your

Money, or, in some cases, America Online will provide you the access you need. You can also receive proprietary software from the bank. You need at least a 486 microprocessor with 8 megabytes of memory (16 megabytes for some programs), and a minimum modem speed of 28.8. Most bank systems support Windows 3.1 and Mac, but you need to check. Some banks will only be found on the Internet, but most won't require you to be Internet users.

As is the case with all banking these days, when selecting an online bank, you need to look at the cost factor. While CitiBank offers both free online banking and bill paying, others offer free online banking but charge for bill paying at anywhere from $.50 per bill to $9.95 a month for twenty bills. The trick is to go online and "shop around." Learn what your bank offers, what you can download, and what the costs will be. Find a bank that meets your needs at a cost that is right for you.

There is still some concern over the safety of online banking. However, there have been fewer instances of hackers getting into banking systems than there have been of photocopied papers in a bank finding their way into the wrong hands. Both are very rare and prove that nothing is completely safe. People have been robbed leaving ATMs as well. Online banking is so safe, however, that most banks will not hold the customer responsible if a hacker gets in, which isn't to say there will not be an inconvenience.

While leaders in the banking industry will state emphatically that online banking is safe, there are still doubters. For that reason, there are companies like Traveler's Bond, a division of Traveler's Property Casualty Corporation, offering Safe Web Remote Banking (or Web banking) insurance. Other companies will probably soon follow suit.

Banks maintain a high level of confidence and stand behind online banking. It is most often a choice of preference based on the habits and computer comfort level of the individual.

Take My Money, Please

The saying "Out of sight, out of mind" can now be amended to "Out of sight and into the plan." A study conducted by the Employee Benefit Research Institute found that nearly 80 percent of those surveyed found that the best way to save for retirement is to have money automatically deducted from their paychecks. The same holds true for investing for college. Direct deposit is the wave of the new technical generation, which apparently supports the theory that if we don't see our money, we have a better chance of not missing it—and saving it!

BANK RECONCILIATION WORKSHEET

NUMBER	DATE	DESCRIPTION OF TRANSACTION	PAYMENT/DEBIT (-)		CODE*	FEE (-)	DEPOSIT/CREDIT (+)		$ BALANCE
			$			$	$		

*USE THESE CODES WHEN RECORDING YOUR NON-CHECK TRANSACTIONS

D-DEPOSIT   DC-DEBIT CARD   ATM-TELLER MACHINE   AP-AUTOMATIC PAYMENT   TT-TELEPHONE TRANSFER   T-TAX DEDUCTIBLE   O-OTHER

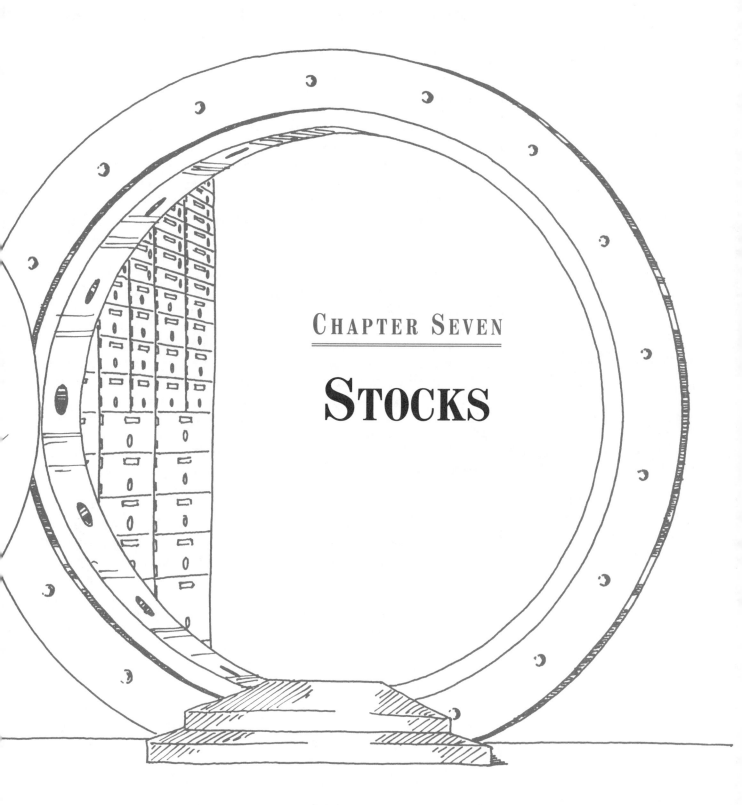

CHAPTER SEVEN

STOCKS

Not even the financial planners, market analysts, or *Wall Street Journal* mavens have totally figured out the stock market. Nonetheless, and despite its volatile nature over the past few years, it is still the place where many people are now sprucing up their portfolios. Intimidating to some, the market is accessible to people at all levels of income. However, because of the risk, it is not the place to invest if you do not have a cushion in a risk-free area. It is also not the place to invest if you do not feel comfortable taking some level of risk.

Although buying low and selling high is the basic premise, there are variations on that theme. Numerous financial studies show that holding onto a stock for a longer period of time, such as five to ten years, will reduce the risk of losing your money considerably. Over the long haul, stocks are a solid way of building your assets. The stocks in the Standard & Poor's 500 index have averaged a return of 9.8 percent annually since 1900.

The market, however, has had some major down periods along the way. The test of endurance for most investors is how tolerant they are during the setbacks. Not unlike a board game, which will eventually get you around the board space by space, occasionally you will have to take a step back. A stock that goes from 25 to 55 over ten years will have a week, month, and even a year of stepping back from 30 to 27. Setbacks, or "down periods," are not uncommon, as the market research will indicate.

The biggest risk, and the downfall of many investors, has been trying to play a volatile stock market on a short-term basis. The other big downfall comes from people who invest with long-term growth in mind but panic when the market has a setback and sell too soon. The October 1987 crash was an exception to the rule: people had a right to panic. However, those who held tight to their stocks saw them rebound. In many cases, it took a year or even eighteen months to undo the damage of that one fateful day. But in the end, stocks withstood and appreciated over time.

To increase your likelihood of holding onto winners, you might consider a stock mutual fund (see Chapter 8). A mutual fund diversifies your investment by purchasing several stocks. Good fund managers balance more volatile stocks with those that have shown greater consistency. They compensate for one bad choice with several good ones. Although they can be wrong, and mutual funds have lost money, the majority of them in recent years have performed well, some showing over 30 to 40 percent in annual returns.

STOCK BASICS

A company sells shares of stock to help raise equity to operate and grow. They anticipate growth and profits. Those profits will be reflected in the activity of the stock and those who have invested (own shares) will be along for the ride. The first time a company issues stock it is called an *initial public offering*. Companies that have issued stock previously offer what is called a *primary offering* when they offer new stock.

The detailed process of issuing stock is usually done through an investment bank, with whom the company works to determine how much capital is needed, what price they will sell the stock at, how much it will cost them to issue such equities, and so on. A company must file a registration statement with the Securities Exchange Commission, which then carefully investigates whether the company has made full disclosure in compliance with the Securities Act of 1933. The SEC then determines whether the company has met all the criteria to issue common stock, or "go public."

Prior to the stock going public, and while the SEC is determining that everything is in order (and this can take some time), the company generally issues a *red herring*, that is, a prospectus, letting the public know about the company and the impending stock offering.

When the stock is ready to be sold to the public, a price is issued in accordance with the current market. The best way for you to find out about an initial public offering is to have a broker who has a pulse on all breaking financial news. Companies will often call the leading brokerage houses and brokers with whom they are familiar so that they can inform their clients about such an offering. They look for investors who will hold onto the stock for some time. As is the case with anything new, these stocks are likely to be volatile at first and, thus, can be very risky. Sometimes it is best to wait to see where the stock settles.

The vast majority of stocks have been on the market for some time. They fall into several categories including blue chip stocks, growth stocks, income stocks, and cyclical stocks.

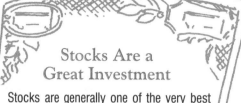

Stocks Are a Great Investment

Stocks are generally one of the very best investments you can make, especially if you can invest for a period of years. Because over a period of years the value of the stock market has always gone up. And it has outpaced the rate of inflation.

However, you need to understand that some years the value of all US stock markets have gone down. So no matter what stocks you invest in, there will be some months, even a year or two when the value of your investment actually decreases.

Also if you only own a few stocks—or stocks that are similar, such as all oil company stocks—the value of your stocks will fluctuate much more rapidly than if you own a wide variety of stocks. One of the easiest ways to own a very wide variety of stocks is to buy shares in a mutual fund—which itself owns shares in many different stocks.

How Much Risk Do You Want?

Some stocks are much riskier than others. Some stocks, such as a hot new public offering may jump as much as 100 percent on it's first day of trading. Other stocks may move less than 5 percent in value over an entire year.

But one of the great things about stocks is that you can pretty much decide how much risk you are willing to accept. Of course the more risk, the more chance the stock will go up quickly. The less risk, the less chance the stock will dramatically increase in value overnight.

Always keep in mind however, that all stocks are equity investments—they represent ownership shares in a company. And equity investments always have *some* element of risk. Occasionally a once solid company gets into trouble and the value of it's stock falls sharply. This is why you should always diversify your stock market investments (own a variety of different stocks).

Blue chip stock is issued by companies such as IBM, Procter & Gamble, and Disney. Such prestigious, established major companies have solid reputations in the market. Most have been around more than twenty-five years and show no signs of "slowing down." Not that you can't lose money on a major company, but it's highly unlikely over time. In fact, you will generally receive consistent dividend payments from these companies, which is essentially a bonus for owning stock.

Cyclical stocks are those of companies whose earnings are most closely tied to the business cycle. As the economy fluctuates these stocks will move up or down along with it. Stocks in automobiles, such as General Motors, for example, will be cyclical because when the economy is bad, fewer people will buy new cars, and when the economy is good, car buying will be up. Companies that make products such as food, are not cyclical since food is a constant in any economy. Stocks for which there is a consistent demand, regardless of the economic climate, are non-cyclical.

Growth stocks, as the name suggests, are issued by companies that are looking to grow. You may be on a roller-coaster ride with such a company at first, but if their prognosis is correct, they will grow successfully over time. The type of business a company transacts is an important consideration. When PCs and the Internet were just starting to catch on, companies offering new software and search engines were the hot ticket. As we head to the twenty-first century, the field may be oversaturated, so you have to pick more carefully. Nonetheless, a company providing the next wave of business technology or consumerism (whatever that may be) could be the growth stock to purchase.

There are different types of *income stocks*. Many are considered "safer" stocks, or "less of a risk." They pay steady dividends because frequently they are issued by long-time established companies, rather than by groundbreaking newcomers. Utility companies, for example, are often in this category. Prices do vary, but income stocks often compete with the bond market, where such steady income is similar. Stocks, however, can pay a higher rate—plus the stock can go up—whereas the bond principal remains the same. Many older stocks also pay dividends, which may make them more attractive to buyers. These, too, are often considered less risky stocks.

The bottom line is that there are numerous types of common stocks, but they all perform in the same manner. You buy them low and hope they go up! Evaluate the company you are looking to buy shares of and try to determine the outlook for their future, based on their past track record, their current stability, and their future goals.

Preferred stocks also need to increase in value for you to make money. They are somewhat like bonds in that they have a fixed dividend rate, paid every month or quarter. Most often these are offered by long-time stable companies. Preferred stocks are usually less volatile than common stocks. Also, companies pay preferred stock dividends before they pay common stock dividends. Some are *convertible stocks*, meaning they can be converted into shares of common stocks.

Stocks and You

When you buy shares of stock, you essentially become one of many investors in that company. A "public" company allows the public to become owners, or have equity, in the company. Stocks are, therefore, also known as *equities*. The price of the stock depends on how many shares have been sold. If the future of the company looks promising, then the stock becomes sought after and the price rises. Conversely, if the company experiences a downswing, shareholders sell and the price drops. Thus, your shares increase and decrease in value based on the buying and selling, or trading, of the shares of stock in the company.

Stocks are purchased at the current price per share listed for that stock. For example, one hundred shares of XYZ, listed at 20 on the exchange, would cost $2,000. Selling those same shares at 27 would bring you $2,700, or a $700 profit. Those are the bare basics.

As a shareholder of stock, you receive quarterly and annual reports. Such reports feature a wealth of details including the history of the business, the major players, and the earnings (gains or losses) of the company. Also, ownership of a common stock gives you voting rights, usually at one vote per share owned. Although you may enjoy having a say in company matters, the reality is that the major shareholders determine the direction the company will take. However, you are entitled to go to stockholders' meetings, if you so choose, to learn more about the direction the company is taking.

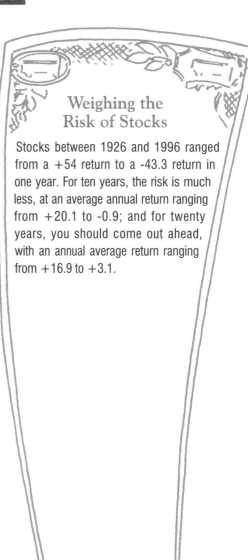

Weighing the Risk of Stocks

Stocks between 1926 and 1996 ranged from a +54 return to a -43.3 return in one year. For ten years, the risk is much less, at an average annual return ranging from +20.1 to -0.9; and for twenty years, you should come out ahead, with an annual average return ranging from +16.9 to +3.1.

There are also various types of stock and different classes. The most common type of stock is, oddly enough, "common stock." Anyone can buy common stock; thus the name. Classes of stock have been around for just over ten years and basically allow a company to sell different A, B, or C grades of stock with greater voting rights per share, to specific customers.

Unlike other investments, where there may be a binding time agreement (e.g., a retirement plan, from which you cannot withdraw money until you reach a certain age), you can hold onto stocks for as long as you choose, from several days to many years (unless, of course, the company goes out of business). Shares of stock can be willed, given through a trust, or gifted to another person. Shares of stock received by an heir to an estate are not taxable to the heir upon receipt, but a capital gains tax may have to be paid when the shares are sold.

SPLITTING

Stocks are also known to split. Splits usually occur when the price of a stock is heading toward $100 per share. Essentially it means that if you own 50 shares of a $100 stock and it splits, two for one, you will own 100 shares of a $50 stock. The value is still the same except the shares have doubled at the lower price. The positive aspect is that this usually means the company is optimistic that they can bring the stock up again, and you'll have twice as many shares the next time it reaches the century mark. Often a split is a signal for investors to buy in at the lower price, thus driving the price up.

Following a stock split, however, shareholders may initially sell, lowering the price of the stock, because they have more shares and may want to diversify. In other words, if you had 100 shares of IBM at $110 and now have 200 at $55, even though the value after the split is the same, you might want to buy another stock at or around $55 to diversify the second 100 shares. This practice isn't necessarily recommended, but it is one reason stocks sometimes drop after a stock splits. Once again, remember that holding onto a stock over time is the key to success in the market. Many stocks split, and then, at a later date, they rise to a point and then split again.

Don't Get Excited about Stock Splits

Technically stock splits do not affect the underlying value of your investment. The company that the shares represent ownership in is still the same business. And you still own the same percentage of that business.

Stocks can also split into thirds or more. One share of a stock at $105 can become three shares of the same company at $35.

Stock splits do not result in a gain or loss, or realization of taxable income to holders of the stock. If a stock splits in half, the tax basis for each share will be worth one half of the tax basis before the split.

WHERE TO LOOK

To keep up with day-to-day stock market activities, most people check their stocks in the local newspapers, *USA Today*, or the *Wall Street Journal*, if they want more detailed information. You can also tune in to CNN, FNN, or other financial radio or television networks, or go online. Your home computer is a marvelous place to do some searching. Nearly every company now has its own Web site, as do financial newspapers, magazines, and various information services. Most Internet services have financial information at your fingertips, allowing you to punch in the stock symbols and get the latest individual quotes or even set up your entire portfolio online and get the whole picture.

CHOOSING STOCKS

If you're going to buy shares of stock, it's to your benefit to do some homework. First, you should know something about the company you are investing in. Look at their annual report, look them up online, and find articles that talk about their future plans. Ultimately, although a strong past track record is very important, the stock price will only matter to you in the future, or once you've bought shares. Therefore, a stock that you or your dad made money on in 1977 is not necessarily the stock that will perform in 2001.

For many people, the best company to invest in is one that they are familiar with in their daily lives. If you are a pharmacist, for example, and you know a new drug is flying off the shelf, you might invest in that pharmaceutical company, after reading up on it of course. Likewise, if there is a product you are reading about for your own needs or items you find yourself becoming more familiar with for your children, these may be the companies to look up, since you are already familiar with their product.

You also need not dive in with a huge investment. Start slowly, get the feel for following the market, and then buy more. It's a good idea to diversify (which is why mutual funds are so incredibly popular). People like choices and diversification in everything.

This has been said before but is always worth repeating: The market can work best when played over a longer period of time, such as three, five, ten, or more years. The following stock prices indicate how over a couple of years you have a better chance of making money than trying to guess the highs and lows on a month-to-month basis.

GENERAL ELECTRIC Closing Price			
6/30/95	$28^3/_{16}$	2/28/97	$51^1/_2$
8/31/95	$29^7/_{16}$	4/30/97	$55^1/_2$
10/31/95	$31^5/_8$	6/30/97	$65^1/_{16}$
12/29/95	36	8/29/97	$62^9/_{16}$
2/29/96	$37^3/_4$	10/31/97	$64^9/_{16}$
4/30/96	$38^5/_8$	12/30/97	$73^3/_8$
6/28/96	$43^3/_8$	2/27/98	$77^3/_4$
8/30/96	$41^9/_{16}$	4/30/98	$85^1/_8$
10/31/96	$48^3/_8$	6/30/98	91
12/31/96	$49^9/_{16}$		

Thus, if you had bought 200 shares of General Electric at the end of June 1995 for $5,640, by July of 1998 it would have been worth just over $18,000. However, if you had bought on June 28 of 1996 at $43^3/_8$, two months later it would have declined to $41^9/_{16}$, and you would have taken a loss. General Electric is a fairly steady stock; others, particularly smaller, less established companies, can fluctuate much more in the short term.

Here are six more stocks that show the benefits of holding on over time while also illustrating how strong the market has become in the latter part of the 1990s:

THREE-YEAR REVIEW OF SIX STOCKS

	AMERICAN EXPRESS	COCA-COLA	EASTMAN KODAK	GM	INTEL	YAHOO
6/30/95	$35^1/_4$	31	$60^5/_8$	$46^7/_8$	$31^{11}/_{16}$	—
9/29/95	$44^3/_8$	$35^1/_4$	$59^1/_4$	$46^7/_8$	$30^1/_{16}$	—
12/29/95	$41^3/_8$	35	67	$52^7/_8$	$23^3/_8$	—
3/29/96	$49^3/_8$	$33^3/_4$	71	$53^1/_4$	$28^7/_{16}$	—
6/28/96	$44^5/_8$	$35^1/_4$	$77^3/_4$	$52^3/_8$	$36^3/_4$	13.86
9/30/96	$46^1/_4$	38	$78^1/_4$	48	$47^3/_4$	14
12/31/96	$56^1/_2$	$48^3/_4$	$80^1/_4$	$55^7/_8$	$65^1/_2$	11.22
3/31/97	$59^7/_8$	$43^1/_2$	$75^7/_8$	$55^3/_8$	$69^9/_{16}$	$18^9/_{16}$
6/30/97	$74^{15}/_{16}$	$48^1/_2$	$76^{15}/_{16}$	$55^{11}/_{16}$	$70^{15}/_{16}$	$23^1/_4$
9/30/97	$81^7/_8$	$57^1/_2$	$64^{15}/_{16}$	$66^{15}/_{16}$	$92^5/_{16}$	$50^1/_8$
12/31/97	$89^1/_4$	69	$60^9/_{16}$	$60^5/_8$	$70^1/_4$	$69^1/_4$
3/31/98	$91^3/_4$	$57^3/_4$	$64^7/_8$	$67^3/_4$	$78^1/_{16}$	$92^7/_{16}$
6/30/98	114	$66^1/_8$	$73^1/_{16}$	$66^{13}/_{16}$	$74^1/_8$	$157^1/_2$

STOCKS AND THE NEWS OF THE DAY

Worldwide news has an influence on the market because the world's economies intermingle. Most news stories have an effect (or could potentially have some effect) on finance in some part of the world. Thus, news has a "ripple" effect on international finance.

Here is a simple scenario: If a region of Japan were to be hit by an earthquake, shutting down its operations so that companies there could not send computer parts to major companies in the United States, the U.S. companies would then have to look to other resources to stay afloat until the Japanese company could reopen. If the American companies were forced to slow down production, their stocks would subsequently drop, as would the stocks of the retail stores carrying the product. Investors could sell or, knowing that this was a temporary situation that would soon right itself, buy the lower stock at a faster rate. Subsequently, trading would be affected.

Some History

The oldest and most prominent stock market is the New York Stock Exchange (NYSE), which was established in 1792. The American Stock Exchange joined the ranks later on, comprising the Boston, San Francisco, and Chicago exchanges. There are several other exchanges including the over-the-counter market, commonly known today as the NASDAQ (including NASDAQ SmallCap), plus numerous foreign markets around the globe.

Since the inauspicious start of the NYSE, when twenty-four prominent brokers and merchants gathered on Wall Street to forge a securities trading agreement, the market has grown into the driving force behind the United States economy and has had an impact on the world market (and vice versa). Having set up shop at 40 Wall Street, with its own constitution (in 1817), the stock market has been affected by major events and has subsequently left its mark in the annals of history.

The market shuts down only on rare occasion. It did so for a week following the assassination of President Lincoln, and it shut down early when President Kennedy was shot.

Often the situation is not as cut and dried as the previous example. Political events, such as a change in government, often lead to expectations of changes in laws and policies, which may affect the market. Sometimes the sheer emotional aspect of a news story prompts buying and selling. As long as people are part of the equation, emotions are involved as well, and the stock market can be affected.

STOCK MARKET INDICATORS

The diversity of household name companies is part of what makes the Dow such a significant indicator. While forecasters continually try to predict what the new high will be for the Dow and when it will top 10,000, it might be worth noting how the Dow is compiled. The thirty stocks are all represented equally, each being added to reach a total number that is then divided by a specified number, which varies due to stock splits and various factors in the market. While your biggest concern is not the Dow as a whole but the individual stocks within it that you own, the Dow does act as a good barometer of the overall market.

The S&P (Standard & Poor's) 500 index is the other leading player in the business of evaluating, analyzing, and disseminating market information. The index includes 500 stocks, but unlike the Dow, they are weighed differently—the higher the value of the company, the more heavily it is weighed. Widely respected because of their in-depth coverage of the market, the S&P 500 has become the standard by which experts judge their success at selecting stocks and mutual funds. Few actually beat the S&P index (although many claim to).

Standard & Poor's Equity Investor Services include numerous products, such as the Compustat data base, which provides information on nearly nine thousand active U.S. companies, including twenty-eight years of monthly market data and a lot more. Other S&P Equity Service Products include ComStock, Stock Guide, Corporate Records, Stock Reports, and directories of the S&P 500, the S&P MidCap 400, the new S&P Small Cap Index, securities dealers, pension funds, and just about any other type of investment opportunity. A catalog can provide you with a listing of software and books. Many are used by brokerage houses, financial planners, and financial institutions. Standard & Poor's address is 25 Broadway, New York, NY, 10004-1010 (1-212-208-8786).

Who is Dow Jones?

The leading indicator of the stock market for over one hundred years has been the Dow Jones, which is considered the most significant pillar of American capitalism. The Dow represents thirty blue chip industrials, plus transportation and utility components. Occasionally these companies change, such as Woolworth's recent departure or the addition of Disney in 1991. However, many of these companies are staples in American business, which explains why when the Dow drops, investors are concerned.

Allied-Signal

Aluminum Co. of America

American Express

AT&T

Boeing

Caterpillar

Chevron

Citigroup

Coca-Cola

DuPont

Eastman Kodak

Exxon

General Electric

General Motors

Goodyear Tire & Rubber

Hewlett-Packard

IBM

International Paper

Johnson & Johnson

J.P. Morgan

McDonald's

Merck

Minnesota Mining & Manufacturing

Phillip Morris

Procter & Gamble

Sears, Roebuck

Union Carbide

United Technologies

Wal-Mart Stores

Walt Disney

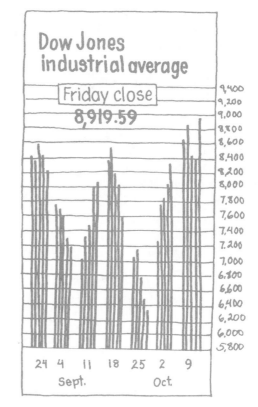

How Now Dow Jones?

Who were Dow and Jones? Charles Dow and Edward D. Jones were newspaper reporters with the Kiernan News Agency in New York at the start of the 1880s. In 1882 they formed Dow Jones and Company, which delivered news information to financial institutions. By 1883 they began printing a small paper containing the news of the day. This was the precursor to the *Wall Street Journal*, which began in 1889 with Dow as editor. Here he published his updates and ideas regarding finance. And it was here that his first theories appeared and became the standard by which theorizing and analyzing the stock market and the financial world was judged.

ACTUALLY BUYING STOCKS

If you are comfortable with picking stocks, have done your homework, and feel confident that you know what you are doing, you can call a discount broker or buy stocks directly from the company, which is far less common. If you are looking for more guidance, want more detailed reports, and seek advice, you can go to a full-service broker. Full service, as the term implies, will provide you with more information. Recommendations will also be made by full-service brokers. In some cases a full-service broker can buy and sell for you on his or her own (at your discretion, of course). Naturally, a full-service broker takes a higher commission.

When signing up with a brokerage firm, you will receive a new account agreement. Look over the agreement carefully before signing. There are a few decisions you will be asked to make regarding an account with a brokerage firm.

First you must determine who will have the decision-making capacity regarding the account. Does the representative have *discretionary authority* to make decisions for you? This is up to you and usually not advised until you are very comfortable with the broker. Advice and discretionary authority are not the same thing. Also, can anyone else contact the broker on your account? Your spouse? Your son or daughter? Another decision involves how you will pay for your investments. It is common to maintain a cash account in which you can pay for each transaction as it is made. A margin account allows you to borrow money from the brokerage house to buy securities. You then pay interest on the account. Margin accounts can be dangerous, because if the loan becomes greater than the value of the stock, you are liable for the balance. Essentially, you are playing with borrowed money.

In a margin account, you can, for example, buy 1,000 shares of a $40 stock (worth $40,000) at what is known as a margin call. If the margin call is 50 percent, it means you are buying the 1,000 shares of ($40) stock at $20,000. This leaves a debit balance of $20,000, while the buyer has an equity balance of $20,000. Each is at 50 percent. The debit and equity balance will always equal 100 percent. If the stock goes up, so will the equity amount; if it goes down, the debit amount will rise, and you will be responsible for whatever percentage it goes up to.

Should your broker have the authority to buy equities on your behalf? You must make clear the level of risk you are willing to take, or will allow him or her to take with your money. Do you want to play the market aggressively or be a little more conservative with income stocks? Once you sign the agreement and specify your intentions, the account agreement and/or a subsequent contract can be legally binding.

Keep in mind that because the stock market, during its operating hours, is like a living organism; it keeps on moving. Therefore, if you call to buy a stock at 23, it could be $22^7/_8$ or $23^1/_4$ when the broker is actually able to purchase it or sell it for you. When purchasing, you can set a limit and say to the broker, for example, "If it's over $23^1/_2$, don't purchase it." Besides a *limit order* to buy or sell at a specific price or better, you can also place a *stop limit order*, which becomes an order to buy as soon as a trade occurs at the target price. Conversely, a *sell stop limit* means that as soon as a stock reaches a certain target price, or drops to a certain price, it is to be sold. There are various other orders you can place, such as a *day order* to be placed that day only.

CARE TO DRIP OR DIP?

Dividend Reinvestment Plans (or DRPs, sometimes called Drips) and *Dividend Investment Plans* (DIPs) are plans in which you can purchase stock directly from a company. The plan essentially has you starting with a small amount of money and reinvesting it as you receive dividends. It is a way of starting small and letting your money buy more shares as it grows through dividends. It is almost like a stock bank account, except the results should be much better over time.

Another nice feature about a DRP, besides that it allows you to start off small, is that you can buy stock consistently without having to do anything. In most cases you can add to the amount by purchasing more shares if you choose. Otherwise, you can let the dividend reinvestment grow into substantial capital on its own.

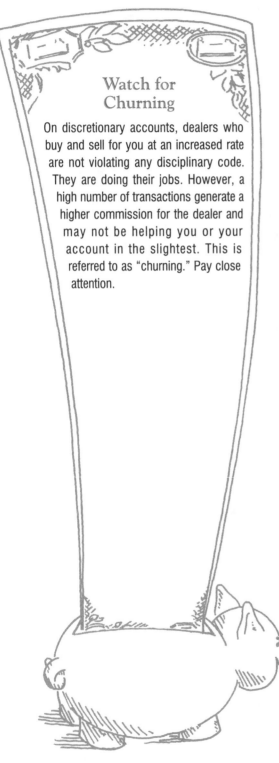

Watch for Churning

On discretionary accounts, dealers who buy and sell for you at an increased rate are not violating any disciplinary code. They are doing their jobs. However, a high number of transactions generate a higher commission for the dealer and may not be helping you or your account in the slightest. This is referred to as "churning." Pay close attention.

Naturally, where there is an opportunity to buy, there is always a middleperson. So what else is new? Although you can often purchase a DRP or DIP directly from the company, you can also go to a transfer agent such as Chase Mellon or Boston Equiserve. They can provide you with more options while making it easier in terms of paperwork and administration for the company. Since they are hired by the company, you are not charged a fee.

OTHER CONSIDERATIONS WHEN BUYING STOCKS

There are other considerations when buying stocks:

1. Don't believe everything you read. Many hot tips have gone askew over the years. Take all "can't miss" candidates with a grain of salt and do your own research.
2. Avoid "peer pressure." You can get suckered into buying or selling because everyone else says you should. Again, listen to what others say but make your own determination.
3. Determine whether you need a full-service stock broker or a discount broker.
4. Save the business section. From the *Wall Street Journal* to FNN to *USA Today*, there are numerous ways to follow the stock market. Make a habit of checking up on your stocks on a daily basis. Most online services provide easy access to the day's stock prices, with many providing information about the company as well. You can always read material from the S&P or from Value-line.
5. Do some bargain hunting. Unlike the Titanic, sometimes a sinking ship will rise again. Keep an eye on stocks that don't appear to be doing well at present but may be heading for a rebound. These can be good purchases. You need to find a valid reason why a stock may go back up, such as some new technology, forthcoming product, merger, or acquisition.

6. Get a second opinion. You should double check a "recommended stock" with someone whose financial knowledge and opinion you respect.

7. Keep the word *risk* in mind. Don't let it scare you, but remember that stocks promising greater short-term rates of return are also riskier, meaning your chance of losing money is also greater.

8. Pay attention to any announcements, such as information about a stock split, made by the company you own stock in. Mergers, buyouts, reorganizations, third-party actions, and other factors can affect your investments. Read any such notices or announcements carefully.

9. Insider trading does exist. Be wary of any recommendation from an "inside source" regarding any confidential information, a prospective merger, a new product, and so on.

10. Stay within your limit. If you have set aside $10,000 for the stock market and your stock has risen by 5 points, it's not uncommon to invest the profits, if you choose. On the other hand, if you've lost money, don't beg, borrow, or steal another $10,000 to reinvest.

All in all, the market is the place to be (at present), if you have money to invest and can handle some level of risk. IT IS NOT THE ONLY PLACE TO BE! Don't put all your money in the market, no matter how good it looks.

CHOOSING A BROKER OR BROKERAGE HOUSE

There are a number of factors you need to consider when determining which broker or brokerage house will handle your transactions. It's worth your time to evaluate any dealer of securities before putting your confidence in one to handle your account. First and foremost, as noted previously, you need to determine whether to go with a full-service broker or a discount brokerage house. They both have access to the same stocks; the difference is in how much advice, input, and "service" you want.

Prior to consulting a broker, determine your financial goals and objectives. It's important to know what you are looking for and to determine your level of risk. It is also important to have a solid idea of your current financial situation.

When evaluating brokers, get answers to these questions:

- What is the sales background and experience of the broker?
- What is the history of the firm or brokerage house?
- How much are the commissions? (Commissions vary widely, depending on whether you are using a discount or full-service broker. Also factored heavily into the equation are the number of shares you are buying and the price per share.)
- What fees will you have to pay when opening, maintaining, or closing an account?
- Is the brokerage firm a member of the Securities Investor Protection Corporation? (SIPC can help consumers to some degree if the firm goes bankrupt.) Ask if the firm has other insurance.
- Are the account representatives accessible? Who covers for them?
- If you're dealing with a full-service brokerage house, what services do they provide and what is their market strategy and philosophy?

The National Association of Securities Dealers can answer your questions and alleviate your concerns about the practices of a particular dealer or look up his or her past record regarding any disciplinary actions taken or complaints registered. They can also let you know if the broker is licensed to do business in your state. (Call NASD at 1-800-289-9999.)

Companies file annual reports, quarterly reports, special reports, proxy statements, and other information with the Securities and Exchange Commission (SEC). You can look up reports at the SEC's public reference rooms in Washington, DC, New York City, and Chicago. The SEC has a Web site at www.sec.gov. The address of the SEC is U.S. Securities and Exchange Commission, 450 5th Street, NW, Washington, DC, 20549. You can also inquire or register a complaint about a broker or brokerage house by contacting the SEC Office of Consumer Affairs at 1-202-942-7040.

To obtain further information on stocks and investing (besides from newspapers, magazines, and online Web sites), ask for brochures and other literature directly from the stock exchanges:

American Stock Exchange	212-306-1452
New York Stock Exchange	212-656-3000
Pacific Stock Exchange	415-393-4000

ONLINE TRADING

A lot of people are using online trading as a way of expediting their transactions. On the other hand, a lot of people prefer to talk to a real person when dealing with their money. The choice is yours. Online trading allows you to make transactions day and night. However, before you jump at this new techno-trading possibility, there are a few things to consider:

1. The idea of quick trading and easy access lends itself to short-term wheeling and dealing. After all, if you are going to hold the bulk of your stocks for five to ten years, occasionally buying or selling a few shares, why not just have a discount broker you can call? Therefore, it is important that you assess your reason for online trading. Are you playing the market on a short-term basis? And, if so, will you abuse the new trading technology? The problem (as with credit cards, off-track betting, and other means of "easy spending") is that people tend to overdo it. Online trading opens up a can of worms for people who are impulsive. It can make trading TOO easy.

2. Ask a few computer-related questions. If your system is down and you are unable to get online or the site itself is down, what do you do as your stock plummets or your hot up-and-comer becomes everyone's hot up-and-comer? Make sure there is an alternative way of reaching the online broker and getting whatever information you need.

3. Paperwork is important. You need records of all transactions. Make sure you can and do obtain them.

Trading On the Internet

Be careful when jumping on the bandwagon of the latest trend. Internet-related companies are popping up at a staggering pace, meaning that they can't all survive. Once upon a time, at the start of the automobile boom, nearly five hundred car companies opened their doors. Nearly half of them disappeared at an "accelerated" pace. In any trendy, flourishing industry, players rise to the top, but many others disappear.

SOME INDEPENDENT BROKERS

The following list of independent brokers is reprinted by permission of Mercer, Inc., 379 West Broadway, New York, NY, 10012 (1-212-334-6212). Mercer also sells an annual detailed discount-broker survey including bank-broker and commission comparisons.

Accutrade
4211 South 102nd Street
Omaha, NE 68127
1-800-882-4887; 1-402-330-7605
E-mail info@accutrade.com
www.accutrade.com

Advisors Group Corp.
51 Louisiana Avenue, NW
Washington, DC 20001
1-800-777-1500

AMERITRADE
140 Broadway
New York, NY 10005
1-800-669-3800
E-mail www.ameritrade.com

Andrew Peck Associates
111 Pavonia Avenue
Jersey City, NJ 07310
1-800-221-5873; 1-201-217-9500
E-mail apainc@aol.com
www.thehost.com//peck/

Arnold Securities
830 Second Avenue South
Minneapolis, MN 55402
1-800-328-4076;
   In-state 1-800-292-4135;
   1-612-339-7040

Baker & Company
1940 East 6th Street
Cleveland, OH 44114
1-800-321-1640;
   In-state 1-800-362-2008
E-mail thenahan@bakernyse.com
www.bakernyse.com

Barry Murphy & Company, Inc.
77 Summer Street
Boston, MA 02110
1-800-221-2111; 1-617-426-1770

Berlind Securities
One North Broadway
White Plains, NY 10601
1-914-761-6665

Bidwell & Company
209 SW Oak Street
Portland, OR 97204
1-800-547-6337
E-mail info@bidwell.com
www.bidwell.com

Brown & Company
20 Winthrop Square
Boston, MA 02110
1-800-225-6707
www.brownco.com

Bruno, Stolze & Company
Manchester/270 Office Center
12444 Powerscourt Drive, Suite 230
St. Louis, MO 63131
1-800-899-6878; 1-314-821-1990

Bull, Bear Securities, Inc.
11 Hanover Square
New York, NY 10005
1-800-262-5800; 1-212-742-1300
E-mail BulBear@aol.com
www.bullbear.com

Burke, Christensen & Lewis
303 West Madison Street
Chicago, IL 60606
1-800-621-0392
E-mail BCLI@ix.netcom.com
www.bclnet.com

Ceres Securities Inc.
P.O. Box 2209
Omaha, NE 68103-2209
1-800-628-6100
E-mail info@ceres.com
www.ceres.com

Charles Schwab
101 Montgomery Street
San Francisco, CA 94104
1-800-435-4000
www.schwab.com

Computel Securities
A division of
 Thomas F. White & Co.
1 Second Street, 5th Floor
San Francisco, CA 94105
1-800-432-0327
E-mail support@rapidtrade.com
www.computel.com

Consolidated Financial
 Investments
287 North Lindbergh,
 Suite 201
St. Louis, MO 63141
1-800-292-6637; 1-314-991-4030

Downstate Discount Brokers
259 Indian Rock Road, North
Belleair Bluffs, FL 34640
1-800-780-3543

Empire Financial
220 Crown Oak Centre
Longwood, FL 32779
1-800-900-8101
E-mail biztool.com
www.lowfees.com

E*Trade Securities
4 Embarcadero Place
2400 Geng Road
Palo Alto, CA 94303
1-800-539-2651
E-mail service@etrade.com
www.etrade.com

Everen Securities
2 North LaSalle Street
Chicago, IL 60602-3702
1-800-621-4480
www.ptdiscount.com

Fidelity Investments
161 Devonshire Street
Boston, MA 02110
1-800-544-8666
www.fidelity.com

First Union Brokerage Services
301 South College Street,
   5th Floor
Charlotte, NC 28288
1-800-326-4434; In-state
   1-800-358-9292
www.firstunion.com

Freedom Investments
555 Madison Avenue
New York, NY 10022
1-800-221-1660
www.tradeflash.com

Freeman Welwood & Company
1501 Fourth Avenue, Suite 1700
Seattle, WA 98101
1-800-729-7585
E-mail fwseattle@fwlink.com

Investors National Corporation
1300 North State Street
Bellingham, WA 98225
1-800-728-1266
E-mail inc@saturna.com
www.saturna.com

Jack White & Company
9191 Towne Centre Drive, Suite 220
San Diego, CA 92122
1-800-233-3411
E-mail jwx@pawws.com
www.pawws.com

JB Oxford & Company
665 Wilshire Boulevard,
   3rd Floor
Beverly Hills, CA 90212
1-800-500-5007
E-mail sales@jboc.com
www.jboxford.com

J.D. Seibert & Company
20 West 9th Street
Cincinnati, OH 45202-2024
1-800-247-3396

John Finn & Company, Inc.
205 Dixie Terminal Building
Cincinnati, OH 45202
1-800-743-7059

Kashner Davidson
   Securities Corp.
77 South Palm Avenue
Sarasota, FL 34236
1-800-678-2626

Levitt & Levitt
135 South Lasalle Street,
   Suite 1945
Chicago, IL 60603-4303
1-800-671-8505
E-mail info@levitt-levitt.com
www.levitt-levitt.com

Maloney Securities
130 East Jefferson,
   2nd Floor
Kirkwood, MO 63122
1-800-218-4625
E-mail bobhock@pobox.com
www.stocktrader.com

Marquette, DeBary Company, Inc.
477 Madison Avenue
New York, NY 10022
1-800-221-3305
E-mail debary@spacelab.com
www.debary.com

Max Ule
26 Broadway, Suite 200
New York, NY 10004
1-800-223-6642
E-mail maxule@maxule.com
www.maxule.com

Montgerson & Company
135 South LaSalle Street,
   Suite 1000
Chicago, IL 60603-4109
1-800-621-2627; 1-312-263-3100

Muriel Siebert & Company
885 Third Avenue,
   17th Floor
New York, NY 10022-4802
1-800-872-0711; 1-212-644-2400
www.siebert.com

National Discount Brokers
7 Hanover Street,
   4th Floor
New York, NY 10004
1-800-888-3999
E-mail help@ndb.com
www.ndb.com

Olde Discount Stockbrokers
751 Griswold Street
Detroit, MI 48226
1-800-823-5400; 1-313-961-6666
www.olde.com

Peremel & Company, Inc.
Woodhome Business Center
1829 Reistertown Road,
   Suite 120
Baltimore, MD 21208
1-800-666-1440

Prestige Status, Inc.
271-603 Grand Central Parkway
Floral Park, NY 11005
1-800-782-8871
E-mail pstat1@aol.com

Quick & Reilly
26 Broadway
New York, NY 10004-1899 or
67 Wall Street
New York, NY 10005
1-800-672-7220; 1-212-747-1200
www.quick-reilly.com

Recom Securities, Inc.
619 Marquette Avenue, South,
  Suite 142
Minneapolis, MN 55402
1-800-328-8600; 1-612-339-5566

Regal Discount Securities
209 West Jackson Boulevard,
  4th Floor
Chicago, IL 60606
1-800-786-9000; 1-312-554-2240
E-mail
  webmaster@regaldiscout.com
www.regaldiscount.com

R.F. Lafferty & Company
50 Broad Street
New York, NY 10004
1-800-221-8514
E-mail inforfl@aol.com

R.J. Forbes Group
1150 Broad Hollow Road
Melville, NY 11747
1-800-488-0090
E-mail webmaster@rjforbes.com
www.rjforbes.com

Rodecker & Company
4000 Town Center
Southfield, MI 48075
1-800-676-1848; 1-810-358-2282

Russo Securities
128 Sand Lane
Staten Island, NY 10305
1-800-451-7877; 1-718-448-2900

Savoy Discount Brokerage
823 3rd Avenue, Suite 206
Seattle, WA 98104-1617
1-800-961-1500
E-mail info@savoystocks.com
www.savoystocks.com

S.C. Costa Company, Inc.
320 South Boston Avenue,
  West Lobby
Tulsa, OK 74103
1-918-481-7090

Scottsdale Securities
12855 Flushing Meadow Drive
St. Louis, MO 63131
1-800-619-7283; 1-314-965-1555
E-mail info@scottrade.com
www.discountbroker.com

Seaport Securities Corporation
19 Rector Street
New York, NY 10006
1-800-SEAPORT

Shearman Ralston, Inc.
17 Battery Place, Suite 604
New York, NY 10004-1102
1-800-221-4242

Shochet Securities, Inc.
2351 East Hallandale Beach
  Boulevard
Hallandale, FL 33009
1-800-327-1536; In-state
  1-800-940-4567

State Discount Brokers
27600 Chagrin Boulevard
Cleveland, OH 44122
1-800-222-5520
E-mail
    sbruce@state-discount.com
www.state-discount.com

Sterling Investment Securities
135 South LaSalle Street,
    Suite 2100
Chicago, IL 60603-4402
1-800-782-1522

St. Louis Discount
    Securities, Inc.
200 South Hanley, Lobby
    Suite 103
Clayton, MO 63105
1-800-726-7401; In-state
    1-800-421-6563

Stockcross
One Washington Mall
Boston, MA 02108
1-800-225-6196;
    In-state 1-800-392-6104

Summit Financial Securities
    Group
305 Route 17 South
Paramus, NJ 07652
1-800-631-1635

Sunlogic Securities, Inc.
5333 Thornton Avenue
Newark, CA 94560
1-800-556-4600
E-mail stock@sunlogic.com
www.sunlogic.com

Tradewell Discount Investing
25 Broadway, 7th Floor
New York, NY 10004
1-888-907-9797
E-mail info@tradewell.com
www.tradewell.com

Tradex Brokerage Service
20 Vesey Street, Suite 800
New York, NY 10007
1-800-522-3000

T. Rowe Price Discount
    Brokerage
100 East Pratt Street
Baltimore, MD 21202
1-800-225-7720
E-mail info@troweprice.com
www.troweprice.com

Tuttle Securities
307 South Townsend Street
Syracuse, NY 13202
1-800-962-5489

USAA Brokerage Services
9800 Fredericksburg Road
San Antonio, TX 78288
1-800-531-8343

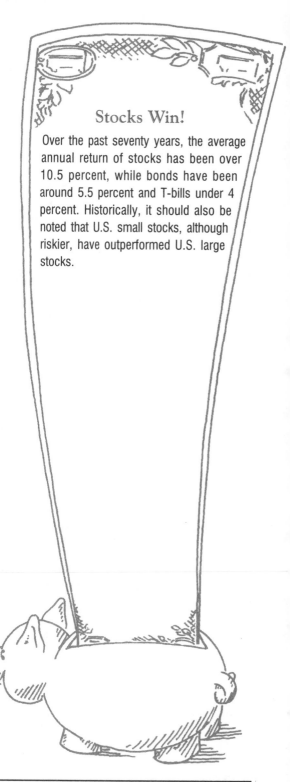

Stocks Win!

Over the past seventy years, the average annual return of stocks has been over 10.5 percent, while bonds have been around 5.5 percent and T-bills under 4 percent. Historically, it should also be noted that U.S. small stocks, although riskier, have outperformed U.S. large stocks.

The Vanguard Group
Vanguard Financial Center
Valley Forge, PA 19482
1-800-992-8327
www.vanguard.com

Voss & Company
6225 Brandon Avenue, Suite 120
Springfield, VA 22150
1-800-426-8106

W.J. Gallagher & Company
2920 Garfield, Suite 303
Missoula, MT 59801
1-800-935-6633

Wall Street Access
17 Battery Place
New York, NY 10004
1-800-925-5781
E-mail webmaster@wsaccess.com
www.wsaccess.com

The Wall Street Discount
    Corporation
100 Wall Street
New York, NY 10005
1-800-221-7990
E-mail info@wsdc.com
www.wsdc.com

Wall Street Equities
40 Exchange Place
New York, NY 10005
1-800-447-8625

Washington Discount Brokerage
100 Wall Street
New York, NY 10005
1-800-843-9601

Waterhouse Securities, Inc.
100 Wall Street
New York, NY 10005
1-800-934-4430
www.waterhouse.com

Wilshire Capital Management
120 Broadway, Suite 960
New York, NY 10271
1-800-926-9991
E-mail info@wilshirecm.com
www.wilshirecm.com

Wisconsin Discount Securities
7161 North Port Washington Road
Milwaukee, WI 53217
1-800-537-0239

York Securities
160 Broadway, East Building,
    7th Floor
New York, NY 10038
1-800-221-3154

Young, Stovall & Company
9627 South Dixie Highway,
    Suite 101
Miami, FL 33156
1-800-433-5132

Your Discount Broker
855 South Federal Highway
Boca Raton, FL 33432
1-800-800-3215; 1-407-367-9836

Ziegler Thrift Trading, Inc.
7333 Marquette Avenue, Suite 106
Minneapolis, MN 55402-2340
1-800-328-4854
E-mail info@ziegler-thrift.com
www.ziegler-thrift.com

SYSTEMS AND STRATEGIES

There are numerous systems and strategies to playing the market, but the only one that works is the one in which you come out ahead. Dollar cost averaging is very popular. Essentially you invest x amount of dollars into a stock on a regular weekly, monthly, or bimonthly basis. This allows you to buy more shares when the stock goes down and less when the stock is high, which is where the averaging comes from.

For this system to work well, it is important for you to invest consistently. It is also recommended that you do so with a few stocks (around four or five) at one time, which means your winners will balance out your losers. You'll be able to hang onto what appear to be losers for a longer time because you will have other stocks balancing them out. Essentially, buying several stocks and creating your own portfolio is akin to creating your own personal mutual fund. However, you are the portfolio manager. Can you handle the pressure?

Not unlike mutual funds, it is advantageous to invest in several industry groups. The market is broken into a number of groups. Some of the more timely industries include the following:

- Health care information
- Home building
- Manufacturing, housing
- Manufacturing, recreational vehicles
- Air transport
- Computer software and services
- Financial services
- Home furnishings

- Retail building supplies
- Office equipment and supplies
- Textiles
- Cement and aggregates
- Advertising
- Auto parts
- Environmental
- Industrial
- Restaurant
- Retail stores
- Cable television
- Telecommunications equipment

Some of the less timely industries include the following:

- Copper
- Metals and mining
- Paper and forest products
- Petroleum
- Steel
- Shoe manufacturing
- Natural gas
- Publishing
- Electrical equipment
- Coal/alternate energy
- Machinery

If you read that an industry may be on the rebound, you might take a risk while holding onto stocks in more timely industries in your portfolio. Watch for changing trends. You may also diversify between high-cap and low-cap stocks, that is, larger and smaller companies. You might have a few Dow Jones blue-chippers paying dividends and a couple of more volatile new high-growth, high-risk stocks in emerging young companies. Balance is important in a portfolio.

Another way to maximize your investments is to look up the fifty-two week high and low for a stock (easily located online or in any number of stock market programs or in the financial section of a paper). The high and low give you a good indication of the parameters of this stock. Assuming you have read about and feel comfortable with the company, look to purchase this stock when it is as close to its fifty-two-week low as possible. One way to do that is to use "open orders" to have the stock bought at the price you want it. Therefore, if the stock does not drop to that price, you don't purchase it. This plan is more effective if you choose several stocks and place open orders on them. This way, if you've selected fifteen at very low prices, it's likely that two or three will reach the price at which you are looking to buy them. This takes patience; but you'll have several stocks selected at very low prices over the course of six, twelve, or eighteen months.

Some advisors suggest that you start with the bigger, large-cap stocks; then once they've gone up, sell some of the shares and "play with found money" (your profit) by putting it into small- or mid-cap stocks, which traditionally perform well, but can be more risky. You also need to select more carefully. While your money grows over time in the large-cap stocks, you can follow the smaller and medium-sized companies to determine what you will buy once you sell off some of your shares.

There are many other systems. Some have you reinvesting the profits into other areas, such as bonds; others have you planning to sell off each stock once it reaches a certain level or percentage gained. The bottom line is to pick a strategy that works for you and stick with it.

FUTURES

If you recall the movie *Trading Places*, you may remember that the climactic scene centered around the buying and selling of a commodity, orange juice, and that in the end Eddie Murphy and Dan Aykroyd walked away with a great deal of money. Whether it's orange juice, soybeans, wheat, or a precious metal such as silver or gold, you can invest in your favorite commodity in the futures market.

A lot of money has been made and lost in this risky (though exciting) venture. If you choose to play, you need to be on top of the game at all times. This is not a situation in which you can sit back and watch your money grow. Dealing with futures is akin to having your money riding on the roulette wheel. You have to pay constant attention to the daily commodity prices. Unless you have a good understanding of futures, it is probably best to steer clear entirely.

Not unlike the stock and bond markets, futures are based on the concept of buying low and selling high. With futures, you purchase a contract to buy or sell a specific quantity of a commodity at a set price in the future, hence the name *futures*. Essentially, you pick a price at which to buy, and that price is set in your contract. Then, you put a down payment, or margin, on the total price of the contract. In other words, you lock in the right to buy a specified amount of a physical commodity for a period of time at a certain price. At the end of that period of time, you own that commodity.

Perhaps an example will help. Let's say that you control 100 ounces of gold and that gold—the day you open the contract—is at $300 per ounce. You put down $500 as a down payment to control $30,000 worth of gold. Theoretically, you are liable for the other $29,500 upon the expiration of the contract. As the price of gold varies, you will either be credited the difference or be forced to come up with additional margin capital on a margin call. The reason futures is so much more of a gamble is that you could lose the whole $30,000, not just the $500 you put down. (With a stock, $500 invested is all you could lose.) On the other side, your $30,000 can make you a lot of money upon the slightest upswing in the price of gold. Buying and selling is brisk on the commodities exchange!

Futures is a method of controlling larger quantities of a product without paying a lot of money. Because you play with bigger stakes, futures are often in the hands of the "high rollers." Your investment may be only 15 percent of the cost of what that contract is worth; thus, you have a great deal of power.

MORE ON FUTURES CONTRACTS

Your futures contract locks you into the right to buy a commodity for a period of time. Contracts run in periodic months, with every exchange and contract having its own cycle. As the contract nears its completion, your margin requirements will increase, meaning you'll owe more and more money on that overall contract price.

Ultimately, at the end of the contract time period, you take delivery of that commodity. Since you don't want truckloads of orange juice or thousands of bushels of wheat to show up at your front door, or to be responsible for storage costs, you will sell the contract well before delivery. (Over 99 percent of contracts are sold prior to their conclusion.) As delivery day nears, brokers will encourage you to get out of the contract, which becomes increasingly hard to do once you've gone beyond what's known as a "notice."

In the end, provisions are made so that you don't end up with the commodity; however, you could end up with storage fees. In nearly all cases, the contracts end up in the hands of those who need the commodity, such as the product manufacturers.

Both futures selling and futures buying are ways to make money. After all, with futures contracts, there is a buyer for every seller. Subsequently, someone makes money and someone loses money, which makes this form of trading exciting and very risky.

There are commodity exchanges throughout the world, including electronic exchanges, all putting buyers and sellers together much like stocks, although you are dealing with a hard commodity. Originally, futures exchanges were created to give producers a way to hedge their corn crops with speculators guessing which way the price would go. Today the concept is still the same, except instead of just corn, there are a wealth of commodities you can buy on the various exchanges

Futures Aren't for Everyone

Don't invest in futures unless you have enough money saved that will allow you to pay off your margin calls should your speculation not go as planned. Futures can be a tough game to figure out, so don't depend on it as a means for retirement or college planning.

worldwide, including gold, silver, copper, platinum, soybeans, soybean oil, coffee, sugar, cocoa, cotton, cattle, hogs, gasoline, crude oil, propane, heating oil, and many others. You can also buy contracts on international currency such as the Japanese yen, Eurodollar, Canadian dollar, Australian dollar, Swiss franc, and so on.

There are other costs that are factored into the pricing mechanism. They are the insurance fees, exchange fees, broker fees, and storage fees.

Determining the right commodity to purchase can be a challenge unto itself. You need to learn about the commodity and the pricing. In the stock market, you look at the growth potential of a company; in the futures market, you look at supply and demand, production cycles, international monetary rates, and other factors that can cause prices to fluctuate. Even crop reports come into play, as they did in the movie *Trading Places*.

EXCHANGES AND RESOURCES

Futures are traded by futures brokers and have their own exchanges including the granddaddy of the futures market, the Chicago Board of Trade. Other leading exchanges include the Chicago Mercantile Exchange, London International Futures Exchange (LIFE), Minneapolis Grain Exchange, New York Cotton Exchange, New York Mercantile Exchange, and electronic trading on Globex, Globex2, Access, and other round-the-clock interactive trading systems.

There is a great deal of information you should study before investing in the futures game. For details, read *Futures Magazine*; it has articles about buying and selling futures. A site for online information is www.worldlinkfutures.com

The futures market is regulated, and all key players including exchanges and brokers are licensed by the Commodity Futures Trading Commission (CFTC), a federal agency that oversees the United States commodities market. Their address is 2033 K Street Northwest, Washington, DC, 20581 (1-202-418-5000). There is also the National Futures Association which oversees and maintains the conduct and standards of those in the field. Their address is 200 West Madison Street, Chicago, IL, 60606 (1-800-621-3570).

COMPARISON STOCK LISTING BEFORE PURCHASING WORKSHEET

	STOCK	STOCK	STOCK	STOCK	STOCK	STOCK
	PER SHARE PRICE	PER SHARE PRICE	PER SHARE PRICE	PER SHARE PRICE	PER SHARE PRICE	PER SHARE PRICE
Dates						
/ /						
/ /						
/ /						
/ /						
/ /						
/ /						
/ /						
/ /						
/ /						
/ /						
/ /						
/ /						
/ /						
/ /						
/ /						
/ /						
/ /						
/ /						
/ /						
/ /						
/ /						
/ /						
/ /						
/ /						

MONTHLY COMPARISON OF STOCKS OWNED (DATES/PER SHARE PRICES)

STOCK	DATE BOUGHT	NO. OF SHARES	PER SHARE COST	DATE PRICE	DATE PRICE	DATE PRICE	DATE PRICE	DATE PRICE	DATE PRICE	DATE PRICE	DATE PRICE	DATE PRICE	DATE PRICE	DATE PRICE	DATE PRICE

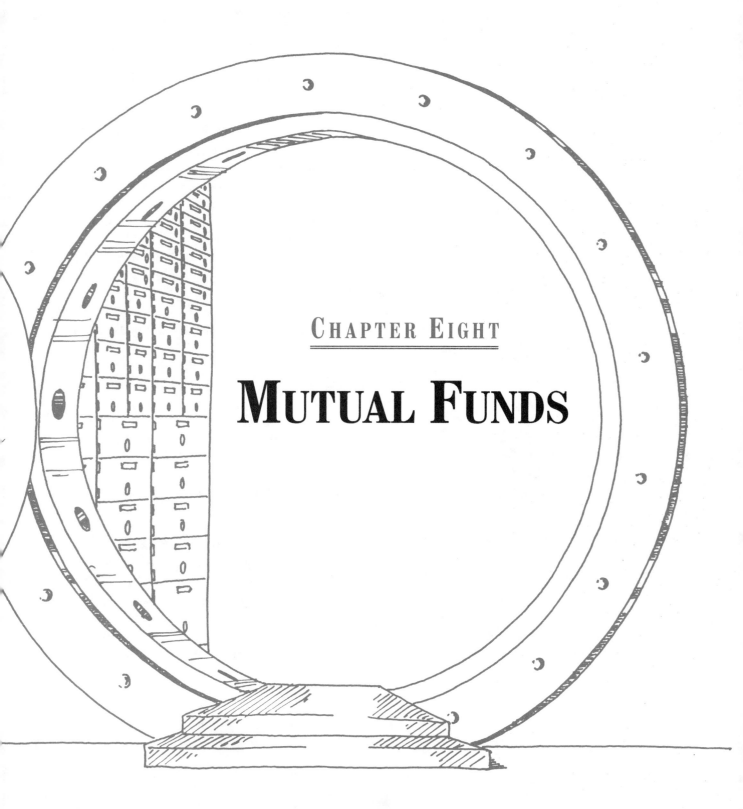

CHAPTER EIGHT

MUTUAL FUNDS

From cocktail parties to the hot topics on Internet sites, mutual funds are the "thing to do" in the '90s. Of course trends change, so be forewarned.

There is a lot of money being made in the right mutual funds. The key is finding *the right* mutual fund, when every financial magazine, financial expert, financial Web site, financial "anything" has THE mutual fund for you! So, buyer be careful. Remember, it's your money, your needs, and your goals that are of primary concern.

Mutual funds came into being over seventy years ago. They offer a way to play the stock market without having to pick individual stocks. They have also evolved into a way to invest in bonds or in cash vehicles without having to carefully select those either. In fact, one of the advantages of a mutual fund company is that experts make selections for you. The other advantage is diversification. It's the "don't put all your eggs in one basket" theory that makes mutual funds so attractive and so successful.

There are thousands of mutual funds to choose from to suit all investment needs. Magazines and newspapers such as *Money*, *Kiplingers*, *Forbes*, and the *Wall Street Journal* keep you apprised of the hottest ones. Online services at a wide variety of sites can also update you on the latest mutuals, with fund companies offering their own Web services.

Choose a fund according to your own situation and preferences as well as the historical performance of the fund and the outlook for the future. As a shrewd fund shopper you should evaluate the level of risk and assess the background of the fund manager. Naturally, the more you invest and the more "risky" the investment (such as a short-term aggressive-growth equity fund), the more carefully you need to select. Once you determine the type of fund for you, the next step is to shop for the best returns.

Mutual funds diversify your money for you. The manager must try to meet the goal of the fund, be it income in steady yields or growth. The risk factor depends on the type of fund. Low-risk funds provide a steady interest level but do not offer the growth potential of higher risk funds, which obviously take a bigger "gamble" with your money. All securities purchased by the fund are pooled and owned mutually by the fund's investors, who comprise the portfolio of that fund. Shareholders are paid based on the number of shares they own and the performance of the overall portfolio.

One item to consider when reviewing several competitive funds is operating expenses. Operating expenses, or expense ratios, generally run in the .70 to 1.50 percent range. This is one reason why mutual fund companies held over $4 trillion in assets in 1998. It is also part of the calculating that you need to do to determine which fund is really better for you. Better yields are not really better if you are paying too much in expenses for fund management.

Companies such as Dreyfus, Fidelity, Schwab, and others deal in billions of dollars and are sound companies. Although mutual fund companies are not protected by the FDIC, there is no need to worry about a company of this magnitude going out of business. It simply hasn't happened.

RISK VERSUS REWARD AND RISK VERSUS TOLERANCE

Base your determination of risk on how much you can afford to invest and what your goals are. Money market and fixed income mutuals are in the low-risk category; growth and aggressive growth stock funds are in the higher risk category. If you are just starting to save money for college tuition or retirement, with years ahead of you, you might decide on aggressive growth to build up your assets. If you are nearing retirement or college is a year or two away, you might decide to play it much safer and choose low-risk funds. The strategy is up to you; time affords you greater flexibility regarding risk.

Unlike the idea of risk/reward, which means that you take a risk in order to achieve a potential reward, risk/tolerance refers to how much risk you feel comfortable taking. It is a part of your personality that plays a major role in your investing strategies. In fact, it generally is the first question, or series of questions (often on a questionnaire), asked by a financial planner.

Here are some of the questions you might be asked to consider when determining your own level of risk/tolerance:

Mutual Funds Are a Terrific First Investment

If you haven't bought stocks before, you should first consider investing in a mutual fund. When you first buy stocks, you're probably not going to buy a lot of different ones. And if you only buy a few stocks, the value of your stocks is likely to jump around. But if instead you buy shares of a mutual fund—the mutual fund will be invested in many, many stocks and hence the value of your investment will move more gradually and be safer.

1. Your stock drops 3 points in two weeks after you buy it. What do you do?
   A. Buy more.
   B. Sit tight.
   C. Get more information about the company and hold it.
   D. Sell it

2. Your stock gains 5 points in the first month you own it. What do you do?
   A. Buy more.
   B. Sit tight.
   C. Get more information and sit tight.
   D. Sell it.

3. Through a broker your mutual fund has gained 21 percent over the past six months you've owned it. You read about another fund that has gained 31 percent. What do you do?
   A. Have your broker shift to the other fund.
   B. Ask him to track the other fund.
   C. Nothing.

4. Which makes more sense to you?
   A. $50,000 in the stock market
   B. $50,000 divided between stocks, bonds, and a money market
   C. $50,000 in a money market account

5. How often to you track your investments, or would you track investments?
   A. Daily
   B. Weekly
   C. Monthly
   D. Quarterly
   E. Less often

6. How often do you read about interest rates or the stock market?
   A. Daily
   B. Weekly

C. Monthly
D. Infrequently
E. Never

7. You just won $360 on the roulette table in Atlantic City. What do you do?
   A. Collect it and walk away.
   B. Put 75 percent away and play with the other 25%.
   C. Put 50 percent away and play with the other 50%.
   D. Put 25 percent away and play with the other 75%.
   E. Continue to play, using all of it.

8. Consider the same scenario as in question 7. You've been betting the minimum of $10. What do you do on your next couple of bets? (If you chose A in the previous question, skip to question 9.)
   A. Continue to bet $10.
   B. Bet $10 to $25.
   C. Bet $25 to $50.
   D. Bet $50 to $100.
   E. Bet the whole $360.

9. If someone told you that you could have $500 tomorrow or had a 50-50 chance of having $2,000 in three months, which option would you choose?

10. If you find a stereo (or similarly priced item that you are shopping for) at a good price, do you buy it or look for a better price elsewhere?

Basically the purpose of this type of questionnaire is to establish how you feel about spending money. Are you liberal or conservative? Are you somewhere in between? People selling you something will always try to sway you. The truth is, however, you cannot be "right or wrong" in answering any of these questions.

There are individuals who will jump at the chance to make money now and others who are content letting money accrue over time. There are many people that fall somewhere in between. Just as volatility measures mutual funds, tolerance measures your own personal "volatility" level.

Determine your Risk Level

Although investing in mutual funds is generally less risky than investing in stocks (because each mutual fund owns many stocks or bonds), there is a significant difference in the level of risk from one mutual fund to the next.

Only you can determine how much risk you are comfortable with. Be sure to understand the type of stocks or bonds that a mutual fund invests in. Also understand how much the stock or bond fund has fluctuated during the last few years. Is this a fluctuation level that you are comfortable with?

Some people are comfortable earning a safe 6 percent on an investment they know about and trust, and do not have to monitor carefully; others are willing to take a risk for a possible 15 percent return on their investment. It's up to you.

Mutual fund minimum investments range dramatically, with most being between $250 and $10,000. There are some at $100 and others at $25,000. Stay in your comfort zone.

The other part of doing your "fund" homework in the world of investments is determining the risk versus reward factor. One of the reasons the country has embraced mutuals so strongly in recent years is because they offer both ends of the spectrum and everything in between. And after all, don't millions of Americans flock to Vegas, Atlantic City, and the racetrack every year? There is something exciting, for many people, about taking some level of risk in hopes of financial reward. Others stay away from the gaming tables and play it safe. Your level of risk versus reward, or how liberal or conservative you are, should be the determining factor.

Funds always have some level of risk attached. But the risk is lower in short-term bond funds and much higher in junk bonds and stock funds, especially for the short term.

STOCK FUNDS

Stock funds are the most common types of mutual funds available. They are also probably the most exciting type and certainly the most active. Based on the volatility of the market, stock funds buy and sell stocks with your money. It is important, therefore, that you "play the market" through the hands of a skilled portfolio manager and that you have several stocks earning you money.

Like all mutual fund groups, stock funds have a variety of options. Aggressive growth funds are the most volatile. While the annual three-year return for the category was averaging over 22 percent as of early 1998, during the down market of 1990, funds averaged a -27 percent. The idea of short-term growth in the market is the most risky category and, therefore, where you need to be the most careful when making a selection of a fund and fund manager.

Long-term growth stock funds are slightly safer; you still deal with the market, but you play in a longer time frame. Over time, it has been proven, the stock market is a less risky investment. According to market experts, the annual performance of the best and worst stocks over a greater period of time is far less volatile. In fact, the longer you stay in the market, the less risk you are taking. The one-year best and worst performances since 1926 range from a +54 percent to a -43 percent; the five-year difference is +24 percent to -13 percent; and the fifteen-year span is +20 percent to +1 percent. (There's more on the long-term positive effects of the market in Chapter 7.)

Therefore, if you want to play more conservatively and think long term, you might be better with a long-term fund. These funds are often advisable for retirement planning. Stocks in these funds are proven to be—like the tortoise— slow but steady.

There are also growth and income funds that offer a little of each. They are less volatile because the portfolio is balanced between stocks that will perform best over a long term and provide dividends and stocks that will fluctuate and be bought and sold by the fund manager on a short-term basis.

International stock funds are risky. In recent years, the international market has not been strong, so be cautious.

BOND FUNDS

Bond funds provide steady interest because they invest in fixed income securities. The yields are usually a little higher than money market mutual funds but also a little more risky. If interest rates increase, the value of the bond fund can decrease, thus creating a greater risk to you. However, that depends on the type of bonds.

There are a host of bond funds to choose from that buy either short- or long-term bonds. Bond high-yield funds, for example, buy current high-yield bonds, also known as junk bonds. Municipal bond funds buy tax-free municipal bonds of varying maturities offered by states and local municipalities. International bond funds buy bonds issued by governments and corporations around the world. Other funds buy short-, intermediate-, and long-term bonds.

One of the advantages of bond funds over buying bonds individually is that when bond interest is paid, you may not be able to buy another bond, should you choose to, but instead have to funnel the interest into a money market account until you have enough to buy a bond. With a bond fund, you can have your dividends reinvested automatically. Also, bond fund managers are experts, or should be.

Last, but certainly not least, is the opportunity to buy tax-free funds if you are in a high-tax bracket. These will pay a lower yield, but if you are in a high-tax bracket or are living in a state or city with high taxes, you might benefit from the lesser yield. It may be to your advantage to make some dividend comparisons between taxable and tax-free funds. Tax-free bond funds are offered by most major fund companies.

MONEY MARKET MUTUAL FUNDS

Money market mutual funds (not to be confused with money market deposit accounts offered by banks) are popular investment vehicles offering steady yields. They are offered by fund management companies who invest in high-quality short-term investments, such as CDs and bankers' acceptances, and return a yield after deducting their operating expenses. They are share based, which means they offer a rate of $1 per one share, and, therefore, a "low-risk" option. Generally, they offer check writing privileges and let you sell off shares when you choose (the money is wired into your bank account or sent by check to your home).

Money market mutual funds are fashionable because they offer a lot of the positives that most people are seeking in their investments. Due to the competition brought on by the influx of so many fund companies, the yields are higher than bank interest, usually in the 4 to 6 percent range. They are for anyone who wants to maintain a low risk, earn primarily interest income, and have easy access to their money. In higher tax brackets, you can get a tax-free money market account, at a lower yield. Because they retain a constant $1 per share price, the seven-day yield is the best way to follow money market fund performance.

BALANCED FUNDS

Balanced funds invest in both stocks and bonds. This allows them the best of both worlds, paying high dividends and reaping the long-term growth benefits of stocks. Variety is the spice of life!

A good fund manager will be able to keep the appropriate balance by moving the majority of the fund revenues into bonds or cash instruments when necessary. Conversely, if the market is on the rise, the manager can invest more heavily in it.

LOAD VERSUS NO-LOAD FUNDS

Hand holding versus going solo is another way of phrasing it. Essentially, the difference between load and no-load funds has to do with the method by which they are purchased. Load funds are purchased through a salesperson, to whom you pay a commission. No-load funds are purchased by you directly, often through a toll-free number. How you purchase a fund depends primarily on how much time you have to do your mutual fund homework and how comfortable you are in your knowledge of funds. Between books, magazines, financial programs on radio and television, the financial network, and the Internet, there is a wealth of information out there from which you can make your own determinations. However, there are salespeople trained in the area of mutuals who have expertise that is not easily acquired. They can save you time and give you pointers.

Naturally, in the more complex, more complicated 1990s—where nothing is black and white and you no longer have a simple choice of Coke or Pepsi (but a dozen variations of each)—load and no-load funds compete heavily. They now offer middle-of-the-road funds. These "loaded no-loads" have catches to them, however, in that somewhere along the line you pay extra. For example, you may pay extra for selecting a "no-load" fund from a catalog or pay a $500 fee for a "personal finance report." You need to consider whether you are defeating the purpose of a no-load fund when paying any extra costs for a loaded no-load or a no-load loaded, or whatever new name they choose to confuse you with. Why not take a load off

How to Rank Funds

Periodicals such as *Value Line* tell you everything you could possibly want to know about mutual funds, including the "risk rank," 1-, 5-, and 10-year returns, holdings of the fund (in shares), tax status, estimated taxes on a $10,000 investment in the fund, how the fund rates against the S&P 500 index, and more.

Be forewarned: It can get overwhelming.

your mind and simply go with either the loaded funds OR the no-loads? (By the way, there are also back-end loads, which charge you a fee if you sell the fund within the first several years of owning it. The longer you own it, the smaller the fee.)

Since many mutual fund purchases are made through toll-free numbers, you can shop around for funds all over the country. The *Wall Street Journal, Kiplingers,* and other financial publications routinely list the best funds at any given time. The Money Fund Report from IBC in Ashland, Massachusetts (1-800-343-5413), keeps track of some 850 money market mutual funds, noting their seven-day yield, the companies' assets, and more. Companies with larger assets, such as Fidelity, generally pass lower expenses on to you.

READ THE PROSPECTUS

It's not always "easy reading," but you should read the prospectus before buying the fund, not to mention the leading up-to-date reports in the top financial magazines and in the many top-selling investment books.

The prospectus accompanies your fund application form, as mandated by the Securities and Exchange Commission. It explains the fund's goal—for example, to achieve steady income, income/growth, aggressive growth, and so forth—and how successful it has been over the last several years. It also apprises you of what types of stocks (or bonds) the fund purchases and gives you a breakdown. The prospectus tells you about the type of risk the fund takes, the background track-record information on the fund, the fees, whether the fund is taxed, the minimum investment allowed, whether you can reinvest dividends, and so on.

A typical prospectus tells you the number of years the company has been around. It also defines the type of fund and the goals. Here is an example:

Type of fund: Short-Term Bond Fund
Goal: High current income with preservation of capital
Fund strategy: Invests in investment grade debt securities while
    maintaining an average maturity of three years or less
Fund size: As of April 30, 1998, assets totaled over $742 million

The fund performance evaluates the returns over the past 1, 3, 5, and/or 10 years. The yield generated lets you know the income generated by the fund over a given period of time. Consider, however, that the past performance is only a guide and cannot assure you of future performance. Yields change daily, based on rising and falling interest rates, market conditions, and the response to other factors such as political and economical events.

The prospectus should answer all your questions about a fund. The magazines and books will tell you how that fund rates in regard to other funds, and the "experts" will tell you what they foresee that fund doing in the future. Once you've covered these bases, you've done your homework.

SO MANY TO CHOOSE FROM

Choosing the right fund can be a gargantuan task, with nearly ten thousand mutual funds of varying types in an oversaturated marketplace. So, what do you do?

First, determine your personal goals, based on your assets, income/expenses, and needs. Are you saving for retirement? Are you putting away money for college tuition? Did you just collect $25,000 above and beyond your budget from an inheritance and want to get some rapid growth on this new-found money? It is important to assess and evaluate your own situation to eliminate the funds that don't fall into the category in which you are looking to invest.

Most major fund companies offer a wide range of funds to meet the needs of any type of investor, from conservative newcomers to seasoned aggressive investors who already know their way through the jungle of funds available. Talk with other people you know who have invested in a particular fund and find out why. Talk to several professionals who analyze funds and read the top magazines. *Money Magazine*, for example, lists their top one hundred funds for each year. It's a good starting point.

Here are the names of just some of the many popular fund companies or families:

Getting Started

If you're considering your first investment in a mutual fund and are feeling hesitant, then start with a small investment and watch it perform for six months or a year, until you feel more comfortable with the process.

Also if the first time you invest, you are unsure of how risky a fund in which to invest—then invest conservatively. First-time investors can get a little nervous if their fund should slip in value even temporarily.

But most of all, the key to building wealth is to get started. Get started saving. And get started investing—even if you are first investing only a small amount.

Advantus	1-800-665-6506	Neuberger &	
Aim	1-800-347-4246	Berman	1-800-877-9700
Alliance	1-800-227-4618	Nicholas	1-800-227-5987
American	1-800-421-9900	North American	1-800-334-0575
American Century	1-800-321-3219	North Investors	1-800-225-6704
American Express	1-800-437-4332	Oakmark	1-800-625-6275
American Funds	1-800-421-4120	Oppenheimer	1-800-525-7048
Babson	1-800-422-2766	PaineWebber	1-800-647-1568
Bear Sterns	1-800-766-4111	Phoenix	1-800-243-4361
Clipper	1-800-776-5033	PIMCO	1-800-927-4648
Colonial	1-800-248-2828	Prudential	1-800-225-1852
Dodge & Cox	1-800-621-3979	Putnam	1-800-225-1581
Dreyfus	1-800-373-9387	Rainier	1-800-248-6314
Eaton Vance	1-800-334-6899	Rydex	1-800-820-0888
Excelsior	1-800-446-1012	Safeco	1-800-426-6730
Federated	1-800-245-4770	Saloman Brothers	1-800-725-6666
Fidelity	1-800-544-8888	Schwab	1-800-435-4000
Flag Investors	1-800-767-3524	Scudder	1-800-225-2470
Founders	1-800-525-2440	Security	1-800-888-2461
Franklin	1-800-342-5236	Seligman	1-800-221-2450
Gabelli	1-800-422-3554	Smith, Barney	1-800-451-2010
Goldman Sachs	1-800-621-2550	Stagecoast	1-800-222-8222
Harbor	1-800-422-1050	Strong	1-800-368-1030
Invesco	1-800-525-8085	SunAmerica	1-800-858-8850
Janus	1-800-525-8983	Templeton	1-800-292-9293
J. Hancock	1-800-225-5291	T. Rowe Price	1-800-638-5660
Kemper	1-800-621-1048	UAM	1-877-UAMLINK
Legg Mason	1-800-822-5544	USAA	1-800-531-8181
Lexington	1-800-526-0056	US Global Investors	1-800-873-8637
Loomis Sayles	1-800-633-3330	Vanguard	1-800-851-4999
MAS	1-800-354-8185	Van Kampen	1-800-421-5666
Merrill Lynch	1-800-Merrill	Vista	1-800-348-4782
MFS	1-800-637-2929	Waddell & Reed	1-800-366-5465
Morgan Stanley	1-800-282-4404	Westcor	1-800-392-2673
Nationwide	1-800-848-0920	WM Group	1-800-222-5852

These are among the categories of funds listed:

Aggressive growth
Long-term growth
Growth and income
Balanced funds
Investment grade corporate
High-yield corporate
Global bonds
Mortgage securities
U.S. government securities
Investment grade munis
High-yield munis
International general
International regional
Global stock

A REVIEW

So what have we learned so far? When looking at mutual funds, these are your concerns:

- What is the goal of the fund? Does it match your goal? (Short-term growth? Long-term savings? College tuition? Retirement?)
- What is the level of risk?
- Where is the fund investing your money? (Stocks? Bonds? Both?)
- What are the operating expenses or fees?
- Who is the fund manager?
- Is it a load or no-load fund?
- Where is the fund investing? (Stocks? Bonds? Both? REITS? Domestic? Foreign?)
- How has the fund ranked against other funds in the same category?
- What is the track record of the fund manager? (This is very important, since he or she calls the shots.) Has he or she been there long?
- How volatile is the fund?

Exclusive Funds to Watch For

Aggressive growth funds dealing with small companies often stop selling to *new* investors; therefore, you run the risk of being shut out. Close-ended funds, with a limited or set number of shares, can also close their doors before you have a chance to buy. If you learn about such funds early on, play it safe and invest minimally at first. This will get your "foot in the door," and you will no longer be a *new* investor. As for closed funds, if they are doing well and are converted to open funds, you will be able to purchase more.

- What is the minimum investment?
- What is the expense ratio of the fund?

The bottom line is that you are looking for a fund that has a well-planned, clearly defined strategy that meets your needs, has low expenses, has performed well, and is run by a manager you feel has a solid track record.

KEEPING TRACK

National and local newspapers, along with financial networks and online services, can keep you abreast of your fund's current value. The net asset value (NAV) is the current price per share of the fund. To obtain the current value of your fund, multiply the number of shares by the price. Then compare this to the price at which you bought the fund. For example, if you purchase a fund from Schwab at $10 per share for 1,000 shares, you will have invested $10,000 in the fund. If the fund grows to $11 per share (times your 1,000 shares), it will be worth $11,000.

	MUTUAL FUND TABLES				
	OBJ	NAV	WK	YTD	Retn./rank 4-yr.
Fidelity Invest: AMgr n	MP	19.24	-.12	+5.6	+13.7/D

What does it all mean? It's actually fairly simple. First, you have the name of the fund family and the specific fund. The OBJ, or objective, is the type of fund; in this case MP means mixed portfolio (a key accompanies the listings; it defines the various funds, such as CA for capital appreciation, SB for short-term bond fund, etc.). As mentioned above, the NAV, net asset value, is the current price at which you buy or sell shares of the fund. Then you have the movement of the fund by week (WK), year to date (YTD), and over four years; the final letter shows the fund's "ranking" versus other funds in the same objective category (some show 3- or 5-year returns).

You will often see what's called a "Down Market" category. This is not meant to discourage you but to reassure you that the better funds suffer less when the market goes bad. The number in that category gives you an idea of how the fund performed during tough times. Keep in mind that the income yield (how well the fund did to that point) is also factored in, so the decline is actually a little greater in most cases.

A volatility ranking tells you how much of a roller-coaster ride you can expect. Usually, it's a one-to-ten ranking with ten being the cyclone at Coney Island and one being a walk in the park (for those of you who have a nervous stomach *before* investing).

For mutual-fund-related software, browse www.Steelesystems.com on the Internet. You can even download a demo version of the program. You can order the personal version of *Mutual Fund Expert* for $45 (plus $5 shipping) from Steelesystems at 1-800-237-8400, ext. 729.

Every major money magazine and almost all fund families can be found online; try *www* and the name of the fund family or magazine or do a search. There is a lot of information on mutuals all around the Internet, as well as in books and periodicals. Remember to double check information to make sure it is current.

FUND MANAGERS

They're not as popular as baseball players—yet. But they are becoming the financial world equivalent minus the bubble gum cards. The top managers are renowned in the financial world. They write books and are frequent guests on financial talk shows. When their funds are yielding great returns, they are the toast of the financial world.

If someone is handling your money for you, it's important that you know something about this individual. Computers do not pick the funds; they only assist in generating the information and calculating the numbers. A good fund manager needs to have a proven track record over a period of several years. You should know the strategy of the fund manager and what type of stocks or bonds he or she specializes in buying.

Some managers take a more conservative approach, some try to keep expense costs lower, some do the bulk of stock selection themselves, and others work through numerous analysts. The bottom line is that you need to have confidence in the fund manager, so

Keeping an Eye On Your Fund

Here are some "watch outs" for mutual funds:

1. Watch out for a shift in investment strategies.
2. Watch out for a change of fund managers.
3. Watch out for a higher expense ratio.
4. Watch out for a fund that has a portfolio *du jour* (i.e., one that changes constantly).
5. Watch out for a fund that starts getting too risky for its own good.

These are not signals that you should abandon ship; they are simply indications that you should take a closer look at your mutual fund.

review his or her background carefully. Don't be dazzled by a young "hot" rookie fund manager who had one great year; it may have been a fluke. Look for managers with successful backgrounds. See how they fared in the down markets of 1997 and even 1990 (if they were out of school back then). See how their fund companies rebounded. See where their funds rate in the various money magazine listings, such as in *Kiplingers, Forbes,* and *Money.*

If a fund has changed managers often, that's not usually a good sign. Likewise, if a fund manager is at the helm of a different fund every year, that may not be reassuring either. Seek out consistency when dealing with investments. After all it's your money that's being played with!

BANKS AND MUTUAL FUNDS

To stay afloat in the competitive world of investments, banks are now in the mutual fund business. Not unlike going through a broker, you can buy mutuals through most banks. It's a matter of choice, with banks having their own managed mutual funds that perform well. Advantages include familiarity and comfort level. Plus many banks will give you a solid monthly statement that includes the fund balances along with your checking and savings account balances. It may also make it easier to make direct transfers from mutuals to and from your bank accounts. The disadvantage is that unlike a mutual fund family, the bank is in the banking business; so this is not where they specialize.

MUTUAL FUND COMPARISON WORKSHEET

NAME OF FUND	FUND OBJECTIVE	NAV	WEEK	YTD	4-YR.

MUTUAL FUNDS OWNED WORKSHEET (NOTE: REINVESTED DIVIDENDS ARE TREATED AS ADDITIONAL PURCHASES)

NAME OF FUND	FUND OBJECTIVE	PURCHASE DATE	NO. OF SHARES	NAV	1 MONTH NAV	2 MONTH NAV	3 MONTH NAV	4 MONTH NAV	5 MONTH NAV	6 MONTH NAV	1 YEAR NAV

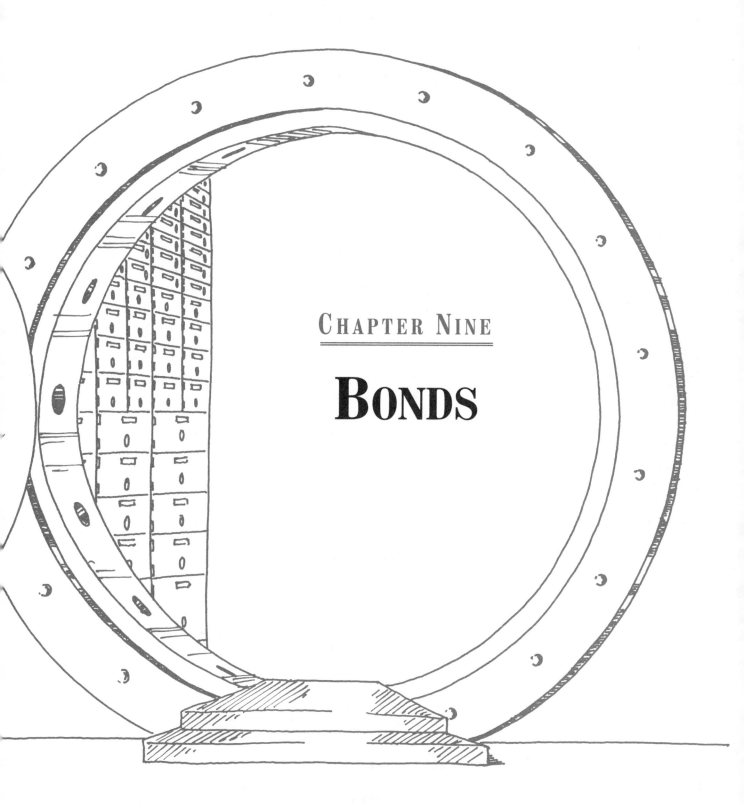

Chapter Nine

Bonds

The bond market is not glamorous, but it is a relatively conservative way to watch your money grow. Although you
rarely hear of bonds paying returns of 30 percent (okay,
you never hear that), high-rated bonds and government bonds are
a very safe investment.

But, what are bonds? A bond is, essentially, a loan from you
to a company or to the government. They are sold in specific
increments and pay interest. When buying a bond, you can purchase it at face value, at a discount, or at a premium, depending
on the interest rate of the bond and the interest rates of the
market. The maturity date of the bond determines when you get
your principal back. Bonds can be "called" earlier, which means
the lender pays you back at an earlier date (as stated in the
terms of the bond). You usually receive a premium, which is a
little something extra for your troubles. A bond is usually
"called" because the interest rate has dropped and the company
wants to issue bonds at the lower rate.

If the company does very well, unlike with a stock, you will
not benefit. Basically, with a bond, it's as though you lent $100 to
someone who promised to pay back $125 over the next year. If, in
the meantime, the person wins the lottery and has an additional
$2 million, he or she still pays you $125 over the next year. If, on
the other hand, the person's financial state is slightly worse, you
still get your $125.

The original bonds were of the U.S. savings variety. Today,
bonds can be bought from the government (federal, state, or
local) or from companies or corporations. For example, rock star
David Bowie has issued $55 million worth of "Bowie Bonds,"
backed by the future stream of royalties from his records and
income from tour earnings.

The wide variety of bonds has grown over the past twenty-
five years and includes everything from munis (municipal bonds)
to asset backed securities, zero coupon, and "junk" bonds.
There are also bond mutual funds (see Chapter 8) and combined equity/bond funds.

Before looking at the various types of bonds, it may be
worth learning a little more about bonds themselves. First, bond
prices vary in contrast to the interest rate. If interest rates rise

above the price at which you bought your bond, then your bond decreases in value. If interest rates drop, your bond is worth more. For example, if you buy a bond at 8 percent and the interest rate drops, the bond's value would increase—the 8 percent bond would be more valuable than bonds currently paying the lower rate—and vice versa. If you buy a bond at 8 percent and the interest rate rises to 10 percent, your 8 percent bond would not be as valuable as those bonds currently paying the higher interest rate.

As for interest rates, short-term bonds over the past fifty years have brought in average returns of over 4.5 percent; long-term bonds have brought in returns of around 6 percent. While these statistics may not be as dramatic as those equity funds, it is a steady rate of return over a long period of time.

Calculate bond interest in terms of $1,000. If the yield is 7.5 percent, then you will receive $75 per each $1,000 you invest. In other words, a bond that pays $75 has a 7.5 percent yield. Most bonds have a set or fixed interest rate, but some have a "floating" rate, which means that the interest can change over time.

TYPES OF BONDS

Bonds fall into several categories. Like all other investments, these categories vary in degree of risk. With any category of bonds, particularly long-term bonds, you have some degree of interest rate risk (rate fluctuations make the bond more or less valuable).

The different bond categories center primarily around credit risk and yield. Naturally, the riskier bonds also provide the higher yield, but that's always the case when you invest—or when you gamble, for that matter. (Think of it this way: Red or black on a roulette table are less risky bets, but they don't pay as high as one of the numbers.)

Categories of bonds run the gamut from Treasury bonds, which are essentially risk free, to bonds with government affiliated agencies like Fannie Mae and Ginnie Mae to municipals to investment grade corporate and, finally, to the riskier junk bonds. Before choosing a category, evaluate your goals. Next decide how much of your portfolio you plan to invest in bonds. Then, look at how much of a risk you are willing to take.

GOVERNMENT BONDS

U.S. government bonds are safe and solid investments. You do not pay state taxes, the bonds are backed by the United States government, and you can buy them directly from the Treasury Department, without paying broker fees. (For more information, contact the Bureau of Public Debt, Division of Customer Services, Washington, DC 20239, 1-202-874-4000). By laddering, or staggering, several bonds with different maturities, you'll have money coming in consistently over a period of time.

Treasury bonds have maturity dates in excess of ten years, with a minimum denomination of $1,000. Interest is paid semiannually at a rate that varies with each issue. Treasury notes can have shorter maturity dates of two to ten years. Depending on the issue, the minimum investment ranges from $1,000 to $5,000.

Zero coupon bonds (also known as CATS, TIGERS, LIONS, and just about any other member of the cat family) do not pay interest until the bond reaches maturity. The rate is higher, but you need to be patient. These bonds are good for a major future expenditure such as for a home or college tuition. Staggering four zeros to mature in each of the four years of college is a good "laddered" approach to help fund higher education.

In the area of savings bonds, EE savings bonds are issued at half their face value (or par value). Therefore, a $1,000 bond (face value) is purchased at $500. Interest accrues on the bond over a period of time. Series HH bonds, meanwhile, are interest paying bonds that mature in ten years. Savings bonds can be had in denominations ranging from $25 to $10,000.

Mortgage backed bonds often come from the Government National Mortgage Association (GNMA, or Ginnie Mae) or the two housing corporations that are not officially part of the government but play a large role in home mortgage secondary lending, Fannie Mae and Freddie Mac. These organization sell bonds that result from the purchase of numerous mortgages from either government agencies or lenders throughout the country. Essentially, your bond is in the home mortgage field. Government agency bonds are also issued (in nonmortgage areas) by Sallie Mae (Student Loan Marketing Association) and other federal agencies, including the

United States Postal Service (they offer a bond that will mature, come rain or shine, hail, sleet, or snow).

MUNICIPAL BONDS

Also known as munis, municipal bonds are always popular as part of a diverse portfolio. Municipal bonds are issued by states, cities, counties, and local governments. Although not glamorous, they are usually sources of steady income and low risk. They're not always graded, but when they are, they are almost always investment grade, particularly when secured. Yields are not generally high, but they are usually free of federal taxes. They are also usually free of state and local taxes—if issued by the state in which you reside. Therefore, you can accept a slightly lower yield if necessary.

CORPORATE BONDS

Corporations issue bonds to raise capital. They offer a host of different types of bonds, all of which are graded (or rated) on the ability of the company to repay the bond holders. Among the various types of corporate bonds are convertible bonds, which can be converted into shares of stock in the issuing company (either on request or after a fixed time frame), and the risky, well-documented, high-yield junk bonds.

Yields on corporate bonds are paid semiannually. Like stocks, corporate bonds are traded frequently. Trading is based on the price of the bond, which, like stocks, can fluctuate as a result of the company's financial outlook.

It's important to carefully study the company issuing the bond. Fortunately for most of us, bonds are rated. These ratings provide a significant indication of whether the company will default on the bonds (i.e., of whether the bonds will become your new wallpaper).

THOSE "INFAMOUS" JUNK BONDS

Small companies, or those in shaky financial straits, may sell what are known as "high-yield" bonds, or "junk bonds." They are often new companies trying to raise money to establish themselves or companies in trouble looking to re-establish themselves. Junk bonds offer a high yield but are a major risk because of their

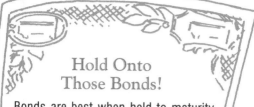

Hold Onto Those Bonds!

Bonds are best when held to maturity. Selling bonds can often be difficult, and you can lose money after transaction fees and commissions. Keep in mind also that because bond rates vary, you may not receive the same face value of the bond when you sell it.

greater chance of default (they do not receive investment grade ratings). Among several other downfalls of junk bonds is that they can be called when the company's financial picture improves, and the company can issue bonds at a lower interest rates. There is also the chance that the bond can be downgraded from a low rating to an even lower rating, causing the bond's price to drop. Be very careful with junk bonds—unless you are skilled in the bond trading market or have a diversified portfolio that can handle a junk bond or two.

BOND RATINGS

No, bonds are not uniformly rated. Like everything else, there are numerous types of ratings of bonds. Depending on the rating system used, the higher the rating, the better the bond, in terms of investment security. The more secure the bond, the easier it is to sell and the safer it is to own. Ratings are important with corporate bonds and sometimes with municipals; U.S. government bonds are secure.

Investment grade bonds are the highest rated bonds. Bonds issued by long-time stable corporations are usually rated higher because they are more secure, though not always.

Bond ratings are complex and require more scrutiny than simply reviewing the stability of the company. Another important factor is the company's financial picture (how solvent it is and its level of debt), plus past history and future financial outlook.

A bond may be graded poorly because of an unstable financial picture or because it is an offering from a new company that might not have previously issued bonds. Chris Phelps of Rowling, Dold and Associate, a financial planning and CPA firm in San Diego, California, compares these bonds with someone coming out of college: "When you're first out of college you have no prior payment history and are therefore considered a greater risk. It's the same with companies, when they are new, they are riskier."

Two of the most widely regarded rating systems are Standard & Poor's and Moody's. Standard & Poor's system runs as follows: AAA (highest rating), AA, A, BBB, BB, B, CCC, CC, C, and D. BB and BBB are the mid range—the lowest grade considered a reasonable investment. Anything in the C and D ratings have a high rate of default.

Moody's has a similar rating system: Aaa (highest), Aa, A, Baa, Ba, B, Caa, Ca, and C. Despite a penchant for the letter *a*, the system is similar to Poor's, with Baa and Ba ratings being the medium range, investment-grade bonds.

BOND COMPARISON WORKSHEET

TYPE OF BOND	ISSUER	INTEREST RATE	YIELD TO MATURITY	COST	CALL PROVISIONS

BONDS OWNED WORKSHEET

TYPE OF BOND:	TYPE OF BOND:
INTEREST RATE:	INTEREST RATE:
ISSUER:	ISSUER:
DATE PURCHASED:	DATE PURCHASED:
PURCHASE PRICE:	PURCHASE PRICE:
DATE OF MATURITY:	DATE OF MATURITY:
CALL PROVISIONS:	CALL PROVISIONS:
INTEREST PAYMENT DATES: / /	INTEREST PAYMENT DATES: / /

TYPE OF BOND:	TYPE OF BOND:
INTEREST RATE:	INTEREST RATE:
ISSUER:	ISSUER:
DATE PURCHASED:	DATE PURCHASED:
PURCHASE PRICE:	PURCHASE PRICE:
DATE OF MATURITY:	DATE OF MATURITY:
CALL PROVISIONS:	CALL PROVISIONS:
INTEREST PAYMENT DATES: / /	INTEREST PAYMENT DATES: / /

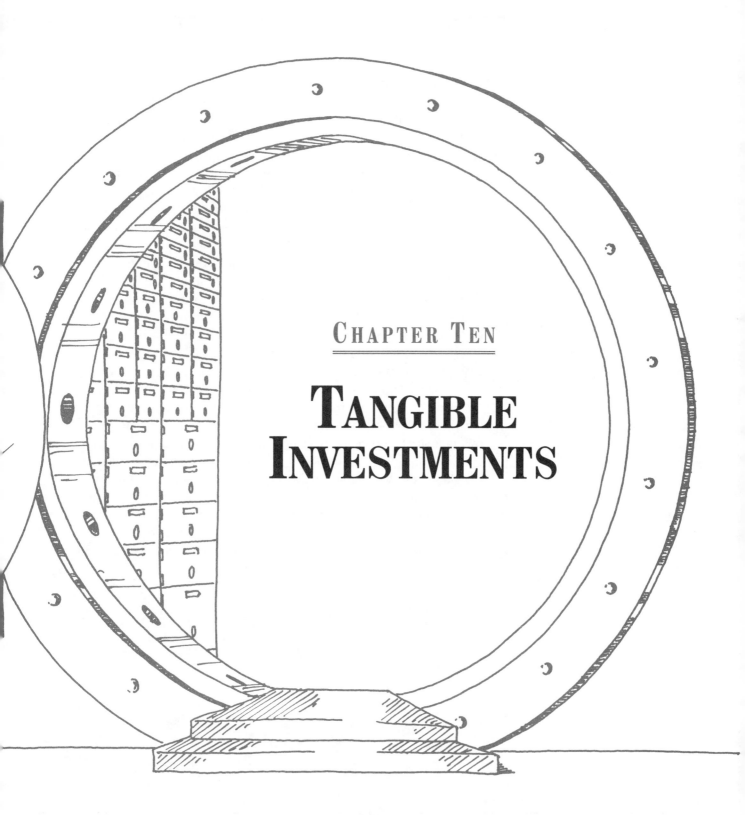

CHAPTER TEN

TANGIBLE
INVESTMENTS

REAL ESTATE

Real estate has long been a risky investment; external factors ranging from warring nations to Mother Nature can and have had an impact on the value of property. The notion of *buying swamp land in Florida* has been used as an acronym for "getting conned."

It is now anticipated, as we head into the new millennium, that the real estate market, which was hot in the '80s and fell off in the '90s, will once again be on the upswing. However, real estate buyers need to do thorough homework before investing so they can avoid that *sinking feeling in the Everglades*.

Among the positive aspects of real estate investment are the potential appreciation of the property or land and the income from rental. You can also borrow 80 to 90 percent of the cost from a lender while putting little money down. And there are certain tax deductions associated with owning property.

On the other side of the coin are the instability of the real estate market, maintaining and managing the property, and real estate taxes. And let's not forget the "fun" of dealing with tenants.

For whatever reason, real estate has always been an attractive investment, possibly because it is tangible. Owning stock means owing a stock certificate, but trees, grass, and buildings are tangible.

One important factor to note is that the real estate business is fraught with unscrupulous characters. It is therefore critical that you buy through a licensed real estate dealer who you know has a good track record. Be aware that there are con artists out there, looking to make money from foreclosures or from various schemes.

The late-night infomercials show companies willing to teach you how to buy houses for "no money down" and make a fortune. Without getting into the

details, doesn't it puzzle you that something that sounds like a sure way to make money is advertised on local television at 2 AM? Not that such a scheme is completely without merit. People can and do succeed in this way. However, they are the exception. There may be many complications, such as foreclosing on the property, evicting the tenants, maintaining the property until you find another tenant, handling legal matters, and red tape with the local government. The companies on the infomercials are most often looking to sell you either tapes, books, or courses on how "you too can become a real estate tycoon!"

Nonetheless, if you are seriously interested in real estate investments, there are some options to think about. One option is to invest in property, residential or business, with the idea of renting it out. This is only feasible for certain individuals. Here is what you need:

1. Investment capital, which can be primarily borrowed
2. A good knowledge of the real estate market, at least in your area of choice
3. Some management skills
4. Some repair skills or the ability to get the right person for the job when necessary
5. People skills

Many landlords lack this last "talent," which leads to confrontations with tenants or poor choices in tenants in the first place. Many judgment calls are needed in regard to dealing with problems presented by tenants (calls that are not spelled out in the lease).

If you purchase property with the idea of renting it out, look at it very carefully and learn as much as you can about the property and the neighborhood in which it is located. Here are some questions to consider:

- Has this property been successfully rented out before?
- How old is the property?
- What condition is it in?
- How much needs to be renovated and how much will this cost?
- What are the current zoning and tax laws?

- What is the economic state of the surrounding area?
- What is the crime rate?
- What are politicians in the area looking to do next in regard to laws, rules, and restrictions concerning landlord/tenant relationships, real estate taxes, changes in the infrastructure, and so forth?
- What is the accessibility to the property?
- How much will you have to spend on maintenance and upkeep?
- What are other properties renting for in that area and how much can you potentially make above and beyond your costs (including mortgage and maintenance costs)?

On the positive side, renting property for commercial or residential use can be very lucrative. If you are sitting on a prime location and can be selective in choosing tenants who will pay their rents in a timely manner, you are in luck. On the other hand, tenants can often be a nuisance and insurance and repairs can be costly. You also run the risk of a bad turn in the real estate market or an over-saturation of the market in the area you choose.

LOCATION, LOCATION, LOCATION!

The old real estate adage "location, location, location" should be your number one concern. A marvelous restaurant in the worst part of town may struggle while a dive in the hottest, most "up-and-coming" section may flourish.

Your best bet is to find a location that is in an area earmarked for revitalization. Seek out areas that will be booming in the next couple of years so that you can get a good price before the market value rises. Sit in on meetings of local government and find out exactly what is being planned for the neighborhood.

People have cashed in on lucrative real estate deals by making the right move at the right time. One gentleman interested in investing in real estate learned from a friend that a major company was relocating to a town in a neighboring state. He quickly confirmed the details, surveyed the neighborhood, and, before word hit the street, bought several empty stores adjacent to where the company was about to set up shop. Those storefronts were quickly rented out as business in the area increased. Over time he was able to raise the rent and keep his tenants, who had successful businesses thanks to the corporate move. In short, a good real estate investment means studying many factors and moving fast.

UNDEVELOPED LAND

Another primary option in the real estate market is to purchase undeveloped land. Often known as raw land, undeveloped land is purchased with the intention of either developing that land at some point or selling it to someone who will develop it.

For most people, the problem with buying such land is that developers have their eyes and ears to the ground (pun intended), just waiting for the right opportunity. The outsider rarely has a chance to step in and buy a tract of land just prior to the big announcement that Great Adventure is opening a theme park down the road. And even if you do get the opportunity, unless you have the means to develop the land or sell it to someone who can, this property, like the swamp land in Florida, can remain worthless.

Be very careful when purchasing raw land. Study the local economy of the area in which you intend to buy to determine the value of the land and which way it is headed. Learn the tax laws, building codes, and zoning regulations that may affect your land should you choose to develop it. Have the land inspected to determine if it can be developed. If the land is deemed wetland, like in our swamp story, it may be virtually worthless.

In short, this is an area where expertise or a great, well-researched bit of inside information is worthwhile. It's a very risky investment unless you are very sure of the land quality and that you can develop it or resell it.

REITs

Real estate investment trusts and mutual funds provide two ways to get involved in the real estate market without having to worry about leaks in the bathroom, late rental payments, or toxic waste discovered on your property. This type of investment also requires a lot less money.

REITs invest in various corporations involved in the real estate market, such as industrial parks, shopping centers, construction companies, equity ownership of properties, and so on. They are listed on the NASDAQ and on the stock exchanges.

Essentially REITs work in the same way as equity and bond mutual funds, except they set up a diversified portfolio only in the real estate market. Some have fared well in recent years. They primarily pay the bulk of their earnings in the form of shareholder dividends.

When looking to invest in real estate mutuals, consider the following:

- The economic conditions where the real estate properties are located
- The past performance of the fund and future projections
- The cash flow of the companies involved
- The ability of the fund to diversify your investment and move your money around if necessary
- The manager of the fund

REITs, as of the mid to late 1990s, have trailed the broader market, according to the S&P 500 index. However, they are now starting to pay higher and higher dividends and to attract new investors as they look forward to a stronger real estate market in the years ahead.

REAL ESTATE PARTNERSHIPS

Also known as limited partnerships, this is another way to invest in real estate. There are both public and private partnerships. They essentially buy into a property, rent it out to various tenants, and watch the value of the property grow until it is very advantageous to sell. There are, however, several drawbacks to this type of arrangement. Partnerships are run by a general partner, and not unlike a fund manager, he or she has a lot of decision-making power in regard to running the partnership. It may not be as easy, however, to chart the general partner's track record. The general partner or partners may also handle things in a manner in which you are not comfortable. Beyond all of that, keep in mind that there are usually numerous costs and fees involved in setting up a partnership.

Ultimately, you hope that when the partnership is liquidated you have made a profit on rental and finally on sale of the property. However, this is not always the case. Unfortunately, for many reasons, properties often do not amount to what the partners had hoped they would. In the '90s, because of the depressed real estate market, partnerships have sold for well below the price investors bought in at. Should you try to get out of the partnership before it is liquidated, you may have a hard time selling. So, until such limited partnerships look extremely promising, this can be a very risky venture for the average investor.

COLLECTIBLES

From fine art to baseball cards to bowling balls, there is a collection for everyone, and nearly everyone collects something. Although no formal statistics have been tabulated, it is estimated that over a hundred million Americans have some type of collection, and the number could be significantly higher. Often the idea of collecting starts in childhood as youngsters collect dolls or trading cards. A collection can serve many valuable lessons in responsibility for a child and can satisfy the need for people of all ages to have a hobby or passion that can help take them away from other day-to-day obligations.

For some, a collection is a way of keeping a connection to the past, to history, or to a loved one. For others collecting a form of art, clothing, or a part of popular culture is simply fun and/or aesthetically pleasing. To each individual, collecting means something special, which explains why such a vast array of collections exist.

Beyond the enjoyment associated with collecting comes the devotion and, in some cases, fanaticism. This devotion has spawned a multibillion-dollar collectibles market. In fact, in the late 1980s and early '90s, the collectibles market outperformed the S&P index. Although it has tapered off, the market is still a big business.

There are two basic types of collectibles: vintage and contemporary.

VINTAGE COLLECTIBLES

Vintage collectibles are items from yesteryear that have grown in value because of their scarcity and/or historical signifi-

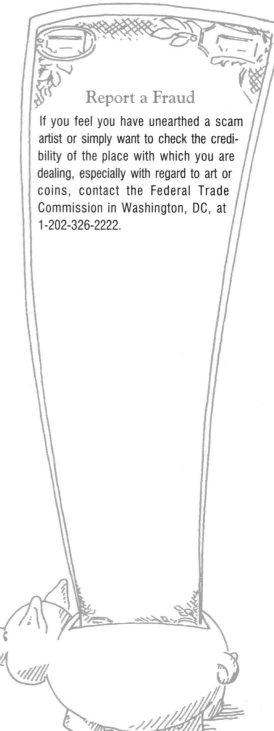

Report a Fraud

If you feel you have unearthed a scam artist or simply want to check the credibility of the place with which you are dealing, especially with regard to art or coins, contact the Federal Trade Commission in Washington, DC, at 1-202-326-2222.

cance. As collecting became more popular in the late '80s, it became more difficult to seek out and purchase such rare items at reasonable prices. More people became aware that an original Superman comic or a Mickey Mantle rookie card had great value. It became much harder to make such a purchase at a garage sale for a couple of dollars. In fact, shops marketing all types of collectibles began overpricing their goods in the hopes of making a killing.

If you have items of potential value from years ago (simply because you don't throw things out), you should have them appraised or at least buy a book on the subject. There are numerous books and magazines on collecting stamps, cards, model trains, automobiles, dolls, comic books, photographs, sports collectibles, and various antiques.

Almost every major type of collectible now has a group or club that will link you up with others who are interested in the same subject. There are over 1,500 major clubs in the United States, with smaller groups meeting unofficially to discuss their passion for collection. Groups can help you determine the value and credibility of your collectibles. They drive the sales of the items because they raise the knowledge level surrounding the particular collectible. They can also help you find the right books, newsletters, and magazines to read and auctions to attend.

Since there are no pricing rules for vintage collectibles, the price is based on how much you can get someone to spend on the item in question. The number of people looking for an item will drive the value up, along with the number of such coins, stamps, dolls, or cards in existence. For example, when baseball card collecting was hot, a Honus Wagner card sold at a Sotheby's auction for around $500,000. Owning a Honus Wagner card was the goal of numerous top baseball card collectors. The card was initially part of a cigarette company's marketing, and since Mr. Wagner did not want to be associated with the company, very few of the cards were printed. Thus, the card sold at Sotheby's was one of a rare few of that initial printing still in existence. It also helped that Honus Wagner was a Hall of Fame baseball player, as his notoriety increased the value of the item. And, finally, the card was in excellent condition—a significant factor with regard to the value of a collectible item.

To help determine the value of a collectible, you might want to call an appraiser. Make sure he or she is reputable. You can contact the Appraisers Association of America or the International Society of Appraisers. But don't stop there. Talk to experts at auctions and shows. Or contact groups or clubs. Make sure of the authenticity of the item. Collectibles such as autographs can be more risky. Good forgers can still create authentic looking Thomas Jefferson signatures. On the other hand, it is more difficult to assemble a brand new 1910 Model T Ford.

Some collections, such as coins, are graded by independent organizations and guidelines are established. The guidelines are not laws or regulations; they simply apply to the world of coin collecting. They also separate the amateurs from the pros.

A vintage collection is usually something that was started in childhood, passed down from generation to generation, or the result of very good, very shrewd hunting to find good prices on valuable items. Collectors are people who will go to great lengths to find such bargains. You have to know your collectible very well and be skilled at dickering and purchasing.

There's nothing wrong with holding onto a collection and enjoying it. In fact, that is what most people do. Some will choose to sell an item or two for the excitement of seeing how it is valued in the marketplace.

If you are going to sell collectibles, unless you are pressed for cash, take your time and get to know the market. Don't sell a three-cent stamp that's been in your family for fifty years to the first person who offers you $100 when, if you do your homework, you'll find out that the stamp, in good condition, could garner you $300. The one thing many sellers do incorrectly is fail to learn the value of their item. The one thing buyers love to do is find those people.

As you might expect, a profit on collectibles needs to be reported in your income tax.

CONTEMPORARY COLLECTIBLES

There are over $9 billion in annual sales of contemporary collectibles, and the industry is growing rapidly, at 11 percent annually. Contemporary collectibles include figurines, porcelain statues, Lladro, cast art, animation art, and other items often sold in limited edition sets. By the year 2001, this industry is expected to be a $17 billion business. From an investment standpoint, these collectibles, in contrast to the vintage items, are being made with collecting in mind and are therefore not yet as intrinsically valuable. They are, however, more accessible, with an average price of around $50.

The limited edition sets may be more valuable depending on their significance. For example, historical items or items related to a specific theme may be more valuable. It's important when buying these items that you get a certificate of authenticity. Specific labels and markings distinguish the legitimate goods from the phonies, so be careful. You can also contact the manufacturer of a specific collectible for a list of authorized dealers. And, not unlike the vintage collectibles, these items lose value if they are not in excellent condition.

Most often people collect contemporary collectibles for the enjoyment of it. They seek out items that they find intrinsically pleasing or have some personal significance in their life. The most popular contemporary collectible items are the Christmas collectibles, including figurines and ornaments.

There are numerous magazines available for collectors in all areas, from vintage wines to china dolls. Libraries have reference directories, such as *Barron's Magazine Directory*, for locating the specific magazine that focuses on your particular interest. The *Writer's Market*, an annual publication designed for writers, also lists many of the magazines for each type of collectible and is available in major bookstores. At www.randomhouse.com you can find an online catalog of over one hundred price guides for antiques, coins, stamps, cards, and other collectibles.

ART

Art has the potential to appreciate tremendously. BUT BE CAREFUL. It's important to work with dealers you trust. People have been duped by unethical dealers.

Naturally, if you have even one painting by a renowned artist, you are dealing with a valuable piece of artwork. Have it appraised and get a rider to cover it on your insurance policy.

When purchasing artwork, it's always recommended that you buy what you like, since art is an aesthetic purchase as well as an investment. Learn as much as you can about the work and the artist from books and galleries (many galleries now have their own Web sites). Buy the best you can afford. The best work of a lessor known artist is often more valuable than a lessor work of a known artist, unless you are talking about a Picasso or one of a few artists that will always command an extremely high price.

The work of young up-and-coming artists may be inexpensive and become valuable very quickly as they become better known. Of course, it's very difficult to find the next great artist, unless you have carefully researched the current art market. Even then you may be wrong, so choose a work you enjoy first and think of the potential value second.

The value of a piece of art depends primarily on the artist and the level of collection interest. You may also want to learn how many prints of the work exist. Limited prints or autographed prints have a market all their own and can also be quite valuable.

When looking to buy, sell, or get the true value of a work that you own, it's best to work with highly reputable galleries and/or auction houses that you feel comfortable dealing with.

And remember, you don't have to sell at the first enticing offer. If you want to hold onto the work, it's yours to enjoy.

LIST OF COLLECTIBLES WORKSHEET

COLLECTIBLE:		COLLECTIBLE:	
PURCHASE PRICE:		PURCHASE PRICE:	
APPRAISED BY:	DATE:	APPRAISED BY:	DATE:
VALUE AT ONE YEAR:		VALUE AT ONE YEAR:	
VALUE AT YEARS:		VALUE AT YEARS:	
VALUE AT YEARS:		VALUE AT YEARS:	

COLLECTIBLE:		COLLECTIBLE:	
PURCHASE PRICE:		PURCHASE PRICE:	
APPRAISED BY:	DATE:	APPRAISED BY:	DATE:
VALUE AT ONE YEAR:		VALUE AT ONE YEAR:	
VALUE AT YEARS:		VALUE AT YEARS:	
VALUE AT YEARS:		VALUE AT YEARS:	

COLLECTIBLE:		COLLECTIBLE:	
PURCHASE PRICE:		PURCHASE PRICE:	
APPRAISED BY:	DATE:	APPRAISED BY:	DATE:
VALUE AT ONE YEAR:		VALUE AT ONE YEAR:	
VALUE AT YEARS:		VALUE AT YEARS:	
VALUE AT YEARS:		VALUE AT YEARS:	

COLLECTIBLE:		COLLECTIBLE:	
PURCHASE PRICE:		PURCHASE PRICE:	
APPRAISED BY:	DATE:	APPRAISED BY:	DATE:
VALUE AT ONE YEAR:		VALUE AT ONE YEAR:	
VALUE AT YEARS:		VALUE AT YEARS:	
VALUE AT YEARS:		VALUE AT YEARS:	

Part III

LONG-TERM PLANNING

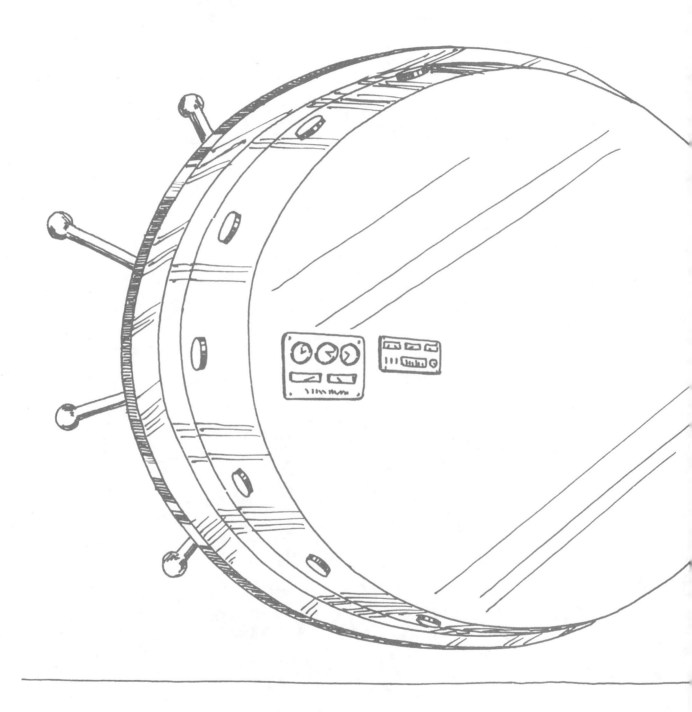

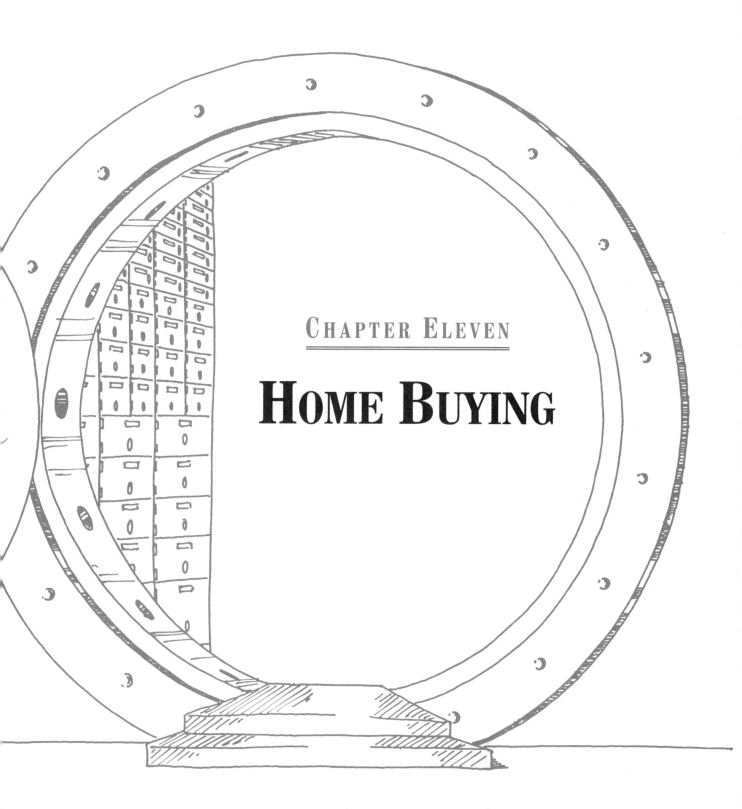

CHAPTER ELEVEN

HOME BUYING

Owning a Home

The nation's home-ownership rate rose to 66 percent in 1997, according to government figures released at the end of that year. That is the highest ever percentage of owners.

I t's rare that someone drives along a street, passes a beautiful home, decides he or she has to have it, pulls over, and then and there writes a check for $1 million on a $500,000 house, so as not to inconvenience the owners too much. Okay, it's more than rare. In fact, it just doesn't happen, except maybe in the movies. Major purchases, for most people, take some time, obviously some money, and some careful planning.

Major purchases such as a home, other real estate, or a car usually require a great deal of involvement with a bank. Therefore, your first order of business is to find a bank that you feel comfortable dealing with and one that feels comfortable dealing with you.

When planning a major purchase, you should review your assets and look over your budget very carefully, since this new purchase will have a long-lasting impact on how and where a portion of your money will be allocated. Usually a major purchase has to fit nicely into the scheme of your life at the time. If you didn't get the raise you were counting on, your son needs braces, you're saving for your daughter's college tuition, or the leaky roof needs repair, you might decide not to purchase that new car you had your eye on.

FIRST-HOME BUYING

Finding the right home and financing it is a major task that takes some time and effort. You must be comfortable both financially and emotionally with the home you choose and the method in which you will pay for it. You also have to consider how much money it will take to maintain the home. If any one of these factors is not thought through carefully, you may be sorry later. There are stories of people who bought the homes they "thought" they wanted, only to learn that upkeep of the property and real estate taxes were more than they had bargained for.

There are many good reasons to buy a home. Here are a few:

- A growing family and a need for more space
- A desire to relocate into another area or neighborhood that you find desirable
- A longtime dream to own a home, ownership of something solid, "equity," and a sense of control

Here are a few bad reasons to buy a home:

- Trying to keep up with the Joneses
- A job relocation (better to rent until you are comfortable in the area and with the new job)
- You just want to get away from where you are now

People often move just to get out of one location, only to make a poor decision on a home somewhere else. Buying a home should not serve as an escape route from other aspects of life. And never buy a home because you just love the color!

THE FIRST STEPS

Buying a home can be an intimidating, even frightening, experience, especially for young couples establishing themselves in careers while building their families. Many people are afraid they simply can't afford a new home and will never be approved for a loan. The Mortgage Bankers Association of America (MBA), a Washington, DC based association representing three thousand organizations dealing in real estate financing, is trying hard to dispel such myths and encourage home buying. Politicians, with supportive tax laws, are also behind the current wave of home ownership.

The MBA suggests that you talk to an accredited real estate loan officer. Usually loan officers will be happy to answer your questions because they want your business. Loan officers can act as consultants, offering help and various plans. People should not be afraid to go in with questions and establish a relationship even before seeking preapproval. Go to more than one bank and don't be discouraged if one paints a less than rosy picture. You should seek out as much information as you can by checking the real estate sections of the newspapers and even by attending seminars.

One common myth regarding home mortgages is that home buyers (especially first-time buyers) need a spotless credit reference. Often people worry if they've missed even a single credit card payment by thirty days. Others worry because they don't have a credit card. In such cases banks look at utility bill payments, water bills, and even rent payments. All you

Fixed Rates Versus ARMs

Fixed-rate loans are advantageous when the interest rate is very low, since you are guaranteed that low rate for the life of the loan. Adjustable-rate Mortgages (ARMs) are usually more attractive when interest rates are high as you expect interest rates to decrease in the future.

have to do is travel across America to see that millions of people, from all walks of life and from all income levels, live in their own homes. So, obviously, finding and financing a home is done every day.

Another myth is that a 20 to 30 percent down payment is required to purchase a home. However many homes are purchased with 10 percent down, some with as little as 5 percent. Naturally, the more money you put down, the less you'll have to pay off in a mortgage.

When planning to purchase a home, there are several areas you must be familiar with. For example, you should know the difference between fixed-rate mortgages and adjustable-rate mortgages, and even "balloon" mortgages. There is also the matter of determining how much you can afford to spend. As a general rule, the theory is that you should anticipate spending two and a half times your annual family income on your home. Thus, a family earning $50,000 a year would consider a home in the $100,000 to $125,000 range. Naturally, this will vary depending on savings and debts. And there are special loan programs available that allow a couple to buy a home at an even higher price.

Help for first-time home buyers is available from the Federal Housing Administration and the Rural Housing and Community Development Service. You may qualify for loans from these two government offices. You may also be eligible for a VA loan if you have been or are currently in the armed forces. Many other groups and organizations offer assistance to first-time home buyers.

THE PROCESS

Once you have decided to go house hunting, you should get what is called preapproval. To determine whether you will be approved for a mortgage once you find the home you like, the bank looks over all of your financial records, including tax returns and income statements. This process is becoming increasingly important because brokers often do not want to start showing you houses until they know that you have a range of prices that you can afford (preapproval will help you determine the amount at which you can buy a house).

Super Software

You know, of course, that there are computer programs that do almost anything these days. That's true in house hunting, too. If you need help beyond this book in securing a mortgage, designing a house, or even landscaping the home you will buy, you can check out where to get a program especially for your needs by consulting the *Real Estate Software Directory*. This annual publication is available in Windows 95 and costs $10 for two 3.5" disks.

It lists over 500 real-estate software packages from some 230 vendors in the United States and Canada. To order your directory, send a check or money order to Real Estate Center, Mail Stop 2115, Texas A&M University, College Station, TX 77843. Or call (800) 244-2144, and charge the directory to your credit card.

According to Fannie Mae (discussed again later in this chapter), no more than 36 percent of your income (before income tax payments) should go to mortgage payments, including interest, and the escrow deposits for real estate tax. This rule is not fixed in stone; however, it is a guideline that many brokers use. Therefore, if you earn a combined income of $100,000, you should be able to spend $36,000 a year, or $3,000 per month, on your mortgage and escrow deposit. Some banks and lenders are more conservative, expecting you to spend only 25 percent of your income on your home expenses.

MORTGAGES

There are several types of mortgages you can get from lenders. It's important that you choose both the lender and the mortgage carefully, since your home mortgage (and the subsequent payments) will be part of your life for a long time, sort of like a guest who comes to visit and never leaves.

In your mortgage search, you will discover several places from which you can borrow. Carefully explore what each one offers before even applying. Direct lenders such as savings banks, commercial banks, and savings and loans (S&Ls) are very popular in the mortgage market. In the '90s, mortgage brokers have become very popular; they serve as intermediaries in obtaining a mortgage for you. They are also helpful for people with credit problems, those who are self-employed, and anyone not having the time to shop around.

15-20-30 (HIKE!)

Do you want a 15-, 20-, or 30-year mortgage? The basic rule of thumb is that the shorter the term of the loan (or mortgage in this case), the lower the amount of interest you'll have to pay. On the other hand, the shorter the term, the higher the monthly payments. The amount of your down payment will enter into your decision regarding the length of term of your mortgage. At present, 10 percent

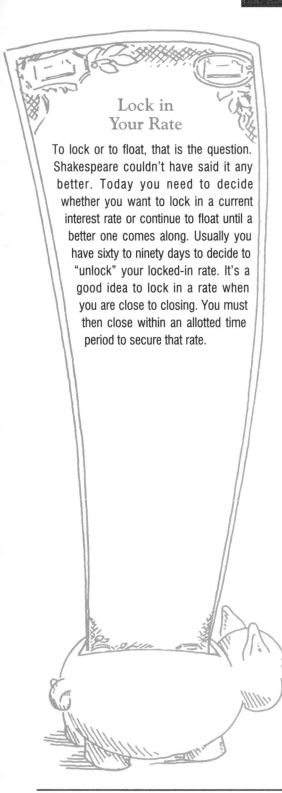

Lock in Your Rate

To lock or to float, that is the question. Shakespeare couldn't have said it any better. Today you need to decide whether you want to lock in a current interest rate or continue to float until a better one comes along. Usually you have sixty to ninety days to decide to "unlock" your locked-in rate. It's a good idea to lock in a rate when you are close to closing. You must then close within an allotted time period to secure that rate.

is a common down payment; however, if you have come into a large lump sum of money, you may elect to put down even more.

TYPES OF MORTGAGE LOANS

Once upon a time there were just fixed-rate and adjustable-rate loans. Now a whole new set of options have come onto the playing field. Thus, like everything else in the modern world, you have more choices than you could possibly need.

Thirty-year fixed-rate mortgages are for those who like stability and plan to stay put a while. It's been *the* loan for millions of home owners. You pay a fixed rate for the thirty years, and when it's all over, you throw a party. Basically, it's the old traditional loan for those who don't want to be bothered following interest rates.

Similar to the thirty-year mortgage is the **fifteen-year fixed-rate mortgage**; it has a lower interest rate but higher monthly payments.

In **adjustable-rate mortgages** (ARMs) the rate is adjusted every year, every three years, five years, or however the ARM is set up. Initially the rates are lower than those of fixed-rate mortgage plans. The rates are compiled from the national mortgage average, which is compiled by the Federal Home Loan Bank, using a number of different sources including the prime lending rate and other factors. Just like with investing, the rates can go either way. For your protection, most ARMs include caps or maximums regarding how high your interest rates can go in a year or during the life of the loan.

Depending on how long you plan to own your home and the interest rate offered for the first several years, you may choose a **10/1, 7/1, 5/1, 5/5, or other fixed-adjustable loan**. These loans are fixed for five, seven, or ten years and adjustable thereafter, either every year or every three or five years, depending on the loan. There are also loans that fluctuate for the initial years and become a fixed rate later on. These loans may be good for those who are not planning to stay in a house for very long.

The huge number of fixed-adjustable combinations are good for people who follow the interest rates and are prepared to refinance if and when necessary. A real estate broker, often doubling as a mortgage broker, can help explain the subtleties of your many options. The key factors include how long you think you will be in the house before moving, the current rate of interest in that market, the state taxes, your short- and long-term plans, and your current financial situation.

For example, those just out of college and not yet near their peak earning potential may want to own a home and pay less money now and more later on when they can afford it, or once their investments in other areas have paid off. They may only be in the home for a while and wish to sell in a few years. Or a couple in their forties, for example, who have a lot of money coming in, may make a large down payment, plus pay higher mortgage payments early on for a fixed rate so as not to have to pay as much once they've retired and their cash flow is less. They may, at a later point in their lives, rather save for other things, like travel. This is the bottom line: You can now look over various loans to choose one that best fits your current lifestyle and future plans.

There are also **balloon mortgage rates**. These are shorter term loans, usually five to ten years, that stipulate a series of equal payments, then balloon into full payment at the end. The interest rate can be much lower (based on the interest only), but you must have plans to refinance at the current rates once the loan is due. This is another option for people who are just getting started, young couples, or someone just out of school. It is also good for someone who is not planning to stay in a home for long. (Home owners average just under eight years in one home.) The loan is then refinanced. Sometimes lenders set up refinancing plans at the time of the loan, but they usually won't lock you in at a particular rate.

A **guaranteed payment mortgage** is often good for young home buyers who expect their earnings to increase over the years. Your payments start low and gradually build over time along with your income level. The drawback of such a loan is that if your income does not increase (or if it does but your expenses increase as well), the rising payments can be difficult.

REO Properties

A bank's mortgage loan officer may tell you that you need a higher down payment, but the REO person in that same institution could say 5 percent is fine. Real-estate owned (REO) properties—properties taken back by lenders in foreclosure—are an albatross for every institution that has them. While they usually resell those homes at or close to market price, lenders can strike a deal on the down-payment requirement and/or interest rate. Check with a lender's REO department.

Shared appreciation loans have a very low interest rate, but in return, the lender receives part of your home appreciation. Therefore, as the value of your home increases, so does the amount that is owned by the lender. These are not as common anymore because lenders aren't as comfortable predicting the real estate market as they were back in the '70s. Also, people don't like the idea of the lender owning part of their home. Said one homeowner, "We have a shared appreciation loan; I let the lender own one bathroom and the basement. That way if we have a flood, it's his problem."

TYPES OF LENDERS

Direct Lenders

The advantage of going to a direct lender is that it eliminates the proverbial middleperson. You get the most information, and you get it straight from the horse's mouth. On the other hand, you are flying solo, without an interpreter. If you've done your homework, researched the lending market, double checked the source you are visiting, and have a grasp of the "loan lingo," you may do just fine. Of course, you still have to qualify for the loan.

Banks usually offer several mortgage possibilities if you qualify. Savings and loans also have their share of mortgage options, which are often easier to qualify for. Mortgage bankers also operate as lenders, usually selling loans to Fannie Mae or Freddie Mac, neither of which is a wealthy financier, but both are government-run loan agencies. Mortgage bankers can be located through the Mortgage Bankers of America (1-202-861-6500).

Mortgage Brokers

One thing you can be sure of in the modern world is that whatever you are looking to do, there is someone out there who can broker it for you. Whether it is a travel agent helping you plan your vacation, a wedding planner helping you prepare for your nuptials, or a financial planner helping you read this book, you can find a specialist. Mortgage brokers are specialists in the mortgage game, and like stockbrokers, they are significant players. In fact, mortgage brokers now generate more than 50 percent of all mortgage loans.

Mortgage brokers act as middlepersons for a variety of sources from which to lend you the money. Oddly enough, they do not cost

Check Rates

Mortgage brokers are an excellent path to a good mortgage. Still, just to check that the specifics of the loan a broker has arranged for you are indeed as they have been presented, call that lender yourself. This is a protection against the very few brokers who might incorporate extra charges into your account, thinking you will never check with the lender.

more money. They work with a number of lenders and, in "volume," can wheel and deal and get you wholesale rates that you would not be offered on your own. In fact, often they deal with wholesale lenders. Since mortgage brokers work on their own and often double as real estate brokers (making your life easier), they can set up their own pricing. They will, because they want your business, be competitive and in some cases cheaper than the companies you look at for your loan.

Lenders appreciate the efforts of such mortgage brokers because the brokers do a lot of the leg work, thus saving lenders a great deal of expense when it comes to finding new customers. Often lenders are more apt to accept you through a broker because they already have an established, solid relationship.

From your perspective, mortgage brokers can save you a lot of time and effort in shopping for loans and comparing rates. They can often get you the best rates, even with their commission factored in (which is paid by the lender). It's important to know that the broker is reputable (see if they belong to the National Association of Mortgage Brokers), that they deal with a wide variety of lenders, and that they are easily accessible. As is always a good shopping suggestion, ask around and see if other people have heard of them and even worked with them.

You can check out mortgages on the Internet at www.mortgage-net.com or search under home mortgages.

Fannie, Freddie, and Ginnie

Fannie Mae is the nation's largest source of home mortgage funds. They do not lend money directly to you, but they make sure lenders have the money they need to provide you with mortgages. Essentially, they act as the "silent backers." However, neither Fannie or Freddie are all that silent. Fannie Mae offers a tremendous amount of information on home buying options and opportunities. They offer an important service by helping to provide homes to low- and moderate-income families and other groups that may face barriers when it comes to owning their own homes. They can also provide you with all the home buying information you'll ever need, including information on

Mortgages Online

Get Smart Mortgage Finder provides free advice to anyone looking for the latest information on home mortgages, loans, and rates. Contact www.getsmart.com

Mortgage Market Information Services, Inc. (MMIS) offers a tremendous amount of real estate and financial information. They provide mortgage information to over three hundred newspapers and radio stations. They can be contacted at 1-888-509-4636. They also offer a weekly faxed newsletter at 1-800-844-4648. Or browse their Web site at www.interest.com or http://interest.com/guidelines.html.

rates, locating lenders, how to close, and more. You can contact them at www.fannie.maecom or www.homepath.com.

Freddie Mac is a stockholder-owned corporation chartered by Congress to help increase the supply of funds that mortgage lenders can make available to those looking to buy homes. Freddie has been around since 1970 and is working hard to provide a continuous and low-cost source of credit to finance America's housing.

Nearly 20 percent of American homes are part of secondary Freddie Mac mortgages. Like Fannie, Freddie deals with the lenders, buying the loans. Like banks, they put the investor capital to work and keep money circulating in the home buying market. Basically, as they put it, they "link Main Street with Wall Street" to make it easier for a greater number people to afford homes. They offer a number of services and publications to perspective home buyers. You can contact them at www.freddiemac.com.

Ginnie Mae is another player in the mortgage game. Ginnie is a government-run agency within HUD and is backed and insured by the Federal Housing Administration. Ginnie works with government and Veterans Administration loans. For more information on government subsidized housing, look for Ginnie at www.ginniemae.gov

Secondary Mortgages

Secondary mortgage companies, like Freddie and Fannie, are the go-betweens linking security investors with lenders. About half of the American home market now involves secondary mortgages. Secondary lenders buy the loans from the lenders, allowing the lenders to have more money for other borrowers. They can help bring mortgage costs down. You as a home buyer do not deal with them directly. However, they broaden your selection of mortgage plans and set up guidelines that lenders follow. Secondary mortgage conduits link investors and lenders to provide the funding so that the lenders can offer you mortgages.

You and Your Credit Scores

If the SATs weren't enough, now *credit scores* are used to evaluate your risk factor in a loan application. Since lenders don't want to rely on their own judgment, they now have a score card to refer to. Actually, it can help remove any bias or prejudice from the decision process.

Since 1995, credit scores have gained momentum—Fannie Mae and Freddie Mac have used them as a guide when evaluating mortgage applications. Although they are not the last word, they are now considered heavily, especially by Freddie and Fannie. This rating system, endorsed by the Federal Reserve, has proven to be a fairly decent indicator of loan performance. However, it's too soon to tell for sure.

REFINANCING

People decide to refinance when mortgage rates have dropped far enough that it is worth going through the hassle of mortgaging all over again. Of course, if you do not intend to stay in a house very long, it may not be worth the trouble to refinance, so consider your future plans. To refinance, you have to reapply, and with any luck, the value of your home will be attractive to a lender. There are a variety of charges associated with refinancing (not unlike getting the initial mortgage), so it is important that you lower your mortgage by enough money to make these fees worthwhile. Do the math: divide the costs of refinancing by the monthly savings to figure out how long it will be until you are saving money. You should also review the tax laws in your state before deciding to refinance (or deciding on your mortgage, for that matter).

It is also advised that you consider lenders other than the one you initially financed with. You may return to the same lender, but it is to your advantage to shop around. The idea that you'll save on paperwork isn't usually valid, because in most cases, the loans have been sold and therefore new paperwork needs to be administered anyway. On the other hand, your original lender doesn't want to lose your business, and if you have been a good customer (made timely payments), they may discount or even forgo certain fees.

You can also "cash out" by refinancing for more than the principal due on your original loan. You get the cash that is left after the original mortgage is paid (less some closing costs), and since it's a loan, it's tax free. You are essentially borrowing on the difference between the value of the house now versus the amount you owe on the original mortgage. This money can serve as a good source of funds for college tuition or for capital to start a business. However, cashing out won't work if the value of the house has decreased or stayed the same.

Mortgage Information a Mouse Click Away

www.mbaa.org
Provider: Mortgage Bankers of America
Mortgage Bankers of America offers a section for consumers on home buying, as well as overall home-buying tips and a glossary.

www.interest.com
Provider: Mortgage Market Information Services
This site gives information on mortgages in your state.

www.hsh.com
Provider: HSH Associates, Financial Publishers
This site offers current rates and statistics from over twenty-five hundred mortgage lenders in the United States and Canada, along with qualification guidelines, mortgage calculators, and lending terms.

www.homeshark.com
Provider: HomeShark
This site takes you through the preparation for applying for a loan and through various loan choices. It takes your financial data and then helps you decide which loan is best for you, encrypting it and promising to keep that information private.

THE MONEY $ GAZETTE

Home Buying Tips

1. Don't be fooled by "low rates." Of course, the lower the better, but not at the expense of an unethical lender you do not trust; make sure there are no extra or hidden fees. You and your lender are going to be in business together for a long time. Make sure you feel confident that they have your best interests in mind.

2. Get everything in writing including rate locks and other details. If you are preapproved for your mortgage, make sure you obtain the bank's conditions that must be fulfilled to obtain the mortgage. AND READ ALL CONTRACTS CAREFULLY.

3. Make sure you and the person selling the home are independently represented. If someone is representing both sides, there may be a conflict of interest.

4. Have an engineer inspect the home, including the roof, basement, grounds, and so forth. Even the most honest of sellers may be unaware of items in need of significant repair. Do not waive a clause by the seller to have the home inspected.

5. Find out the amount of time that homes in the area—including the one you are looking at—have been on the market. You can usually start bidding at 15 percent below the asking price. BUT if the houses in the neighborhood are going fast (say in two or three weeks), you may have to start at 7 or even 5 percent.

HOME EQUITY LOANS

You hear the term *home equity* often; it's part of numerous television commercials. Why? Because it's another way for you to borrow money and pay interest. The interest rate is low because the collateral is your house. The process is similar to that of a second mortgage. Your house needs to be appraised, and there is plenty of other paperwork, plus some expenses, along the way. Usually the reason for taking out a home equity loan is a significant one, such as for home renovations or perhaps paying college tuition. Make sure it's a good reason. Don't use home equity as a credit card, or you can put your home and yourself in jeopardy.

READING MORTGAGE RATE SHEETS

Look for the loan that fits your needs. The 7/1 or other such breakdowns are the fixed-adjustable years in the loan.

MORTGAGE RATE SHEETS	
LOAN PROGRAM	PERCENTAGE
30-yr. Fixed Rate	7.087
15-yr. Fixed Rate	6.893
15-yr. FHA Loans	6.917
30-yr. FHA Loans	7.440
1-yr. ARMs	6.010
3/1-yr. ARMs	6.555
7/1-yr. ARMs	7.091
7/23-yr. Balloon	6.787

The listing will also tell you the date through which the rate is available. Thanks to daily financial pages, the Financial News Network, and the Internet, you should always be able to get the latest rates.

Remember that lenders must follow guidelines. All costs including lock-in, registration, and any other fees must be included in your final quote. You should not be hit with additional closing costs. Get everything in writing ahead of time. You can also check with Mortgage Market Information Services (MMIS).

How long has the house been on the market? The longer the time, the more likely that negotiation will bring down the price.

Have there been any price reductions? Price reductions indicate a need to sell and/or a rethinking of property value.

Have there been any previous offers? Do not be intimidated if offers higher than the one you intend to make have been refused. Time has a way of changing things.

How long have the sellers owned the house? Short-term ownership usually means a smaller profit margin and therefore less negotiating room.

What improvements have the sellers made? Do not feel you need to add the cost of improvements to your fair market evaluation. Many improvements never return their original cost. Some additions (those that disrupt the traffic pattern, for example) actually lower the property's value.

COOPERATIVES

Cooperatives, or co-ops, give you equity. Like owning stock in a company, you own shares of stock in the co-operative corporation that owns the building and, thus, are entitled to the proprietary lease on your apartment. (To purchase a co-op, you still need preapproval by a bank.)

The advantages to owning a co-op are that you are not solely responsible for all repairs, except in your own apartment. You are also not solely responsible for the grounds and other surrounding areas.

On the other hand, co-ops come with co-op boards. Unfortunately, too many of these boards consist of individuals who have an unwarranted desire to wield power or have their own personal agendas. They can make it difficult on anyone trying to buy a co-op. You must be "approved" by the board—a far more daunting experience than being approved by a bank or lender. You may also be at the mercy of a lot of house rules enforced because the board members are acting in their own best interests. Talk with people in the building before attempting to buy a co-op. Real estate agents won't tell you the comfort level of actually living there.

VACATION HOMES

If you can afford one, why not? More importantly, a summer home gives you an escape from your usual dwelling and is particularly nice if you are venturing out of the crowded city to the country. And in the long run, if you choose the right location—one that you'll love to frequent in years to come—you'll spend less money on your vacations.

Should you only be using the home a few weeks a year, you might want to rent it out to others, which will help it pay for itself. If that is your plan, look for a home in a popular area so that you won't have trouble finding renters. You will probably not come out ahead in the end, but the rent money will cover a significant portion of the cost of the house.

While a vacation home sounds like the perfect idea, there can be some drawbacks. As is the case with any home, you should make sure the neighborhood will remain as "delightful" as when you chose to buy into it. A lovely vacation home in a rural area where three shopping malls are about to be built may not seem so lovely when the traffic starts heading down your street. Also, the upkeep and maintenance of the vacation home are your responsibilities. When a kindly neighbor calls to tell you that the roof of your country house has just given way to ten inches of snow, your mountain retreat will seem like anything but paradise. In short, it can be difficult maintaining a property that is a distance away. Being a long-distance landlord can be difficult as well.

Some people buy a vacation home in an area with hopes of moving there when they retire. Again, this is a good idea if the neighborhood is expected to remain the same or blossom into the type of community in which you would want to retire. The chamber of commerce and other local organizations may have a good idea of the plans for the future of the neighborhood.

Vacation homes are not usually strong investment ideas, but they can be terrific on a practical level. Weigh the pros and cons carefully and take your time in making a decision.

TIME SHARES

The popularity of time shares has diminished in recent years. They were popping up everywhere, which meant a glut in the market and lower values. Time shares offered you an annual week or two to vacation at the place of purchase or the option to trade for other vacation locations. Although some people were fortunate to buy into them and have a place to vacation for a week every summer (or to trade for another place), there have been numerous drawbacks.

The key word in time shares is "time," and time means change. Some of the companies selling off time shares in 1987 and 1988 (and promising upkeep and great vacation trading destinations for the next ninety-nine years) sold off their properties and sold the businesses, which are now, some ten years later, in the hands of other owners—or out of business, leaving purchasers without the maintenance they were promised. Time share destinations have also changed. The 200 four-star properties you saw in the seller's glossy portfolio in 1989 are now 165 two-star properties and 35 four-star gems, making it much harder to trade to the few top-quality resorts that are left.

THE WONDERFUL WORLD OF RENTING

Renting a house or apartment has both advantages and disadvantages. First of all, renters are not responsible for repairs. Landlords are responsible for all major repairs, painting, and so on. Unfortunately, many landlords are less than helpful. Thus, sometimes people have hassles and are forced to use government housing agencies and courtrooms to resolve disputes.

The choice to rent usually depends on the home buying market, interest rates, and the lifestyle of the individual. Someone who knows nothing about home maintenance may be in for major headaches owning a home. Renting is also a good idea for families and people who may not be in the same location for more than a few years or for a young family that has not yet determined where they want to settle on a more permanent basis. It's a better "in-between" step than going through the hassle of buying a home and reselling it a few years later. For individuals whose careers have them traveling often or even relocating, renting is ideal.

On the other hand, renters often invest a lot of money into their homes and walk away with nothing. You can't build up equity as a renter. When you move away, you have nothing to show for the rent you've been paying except the receipts.

Here are a few other tips on renting:

1. Find out the background of the building or house. Does prewar mean World War II or the War of 1812?
2. Talk to someone in the building about the landlord and maintenance of the building. You want to be comfortable and not have hassles to get services that are promised in your lease.
3. Read the lease very very carefully. Question anything that is not clear. Read the fine print! Read it twice!
4. Know in advance what you are responsible for when you leave the apartment or house. Get it in writing. Get EVERYTHING in writing.
5. Find out what happens if the house or building is sold.
6. Find out exactly how much your rent can be increased. There are housing guidelines in states, cities, and counties.

Look for government agencies locally that deal with housing and landlords.

7. Find out the policy on sublets. Should you need to be out of town for an extended period of time, you may want to rent out your apartment. There are usually specific policies regarding subletting your apartment.

8. Find out if you can add a roommate, spouse, or child to the lease at a later time and what the rules are for "successors" to the lease should you move out (or die) while a family member or roommate remains in the apartment.

9. Check out the "neighbors" if possible. If a rumba band is going to be practicing nightly upstairs from you, it's a good idea to know this before signing that lease (unless you'd prefer to be dancing instead of sleeping).

10. Be wary of apartments over restaurants, dry cleaners, or other commercial businesses; odors and/or noise may make life unpleasant.

SELLING YOUR HOME

Buyers are becoming more savvy than ever before, which is a good thing, since someone buying a home does not want to wake up to surprise leaks in the roof or other home repair headaches. As a seller, it is now up to you to disclose as much information as possible about the house, or be faced with possible litigation. For the most part, after you sell, you want to have nothing more to do with the house except enjoy the fond memories of having lived there.

There are several steps you need to take before pounding that "For Sale" sign into your front lawn. For example, you need to determine who will be selling the house. Will you be selling it yourself or working through a real estate broker? Many people lean toward brokers because they have sales knowledge plus the ability to drum up many more potential buyers a lot faster. Brokers know where to circulate the information that your house is on the market. In fact, the computer age has made it easier than ever for brokers to "list" your house by

Advice Fron the Pros

Warren King, a real estate broker with the King Group, New York City, had this to say:

Brokers generally do not convince people to buy a house. Houses sell themselves. The person looking at the house will either feel that they could be comfortable living there or not. Brokers basically sell their services and try to best understand the needs of their clients. They should be trying to show you, as a buyer, homes that meet your parameters. As a seller, they should be bringing in people who can afford your house and are looking for the type of property you own. A good broker wastes no one's valuable time.

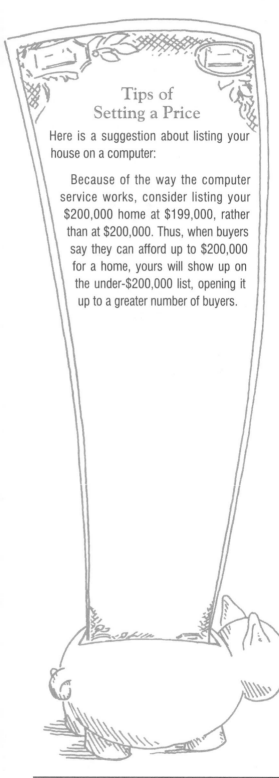

using the Multiple Listing System (MLS), which is a computerized network of homes nationwide. Brokers in most states use this system; it allows both seller and buyer information to be entered and can be used to find potential matches very quickly. There are also MLS books listing homes with photos, operating costs, property taxes, and so on. The modern broker, therefore, has a lot of information at his or her fingertips.

On the other hand, selling it yourself will cut the cost (brokers around the country generally get 5 to 8 percent of the final sale) and can be more attractive to buyers who don't want to have to go through brokers. Don't be fooled, however, into thinking the broker is the only cost. Paying for ads, an appraisal, a real estate attorney, and other services will still enter into the home selling equation.

PRICING

You can hire an appraiser to appraise the value of your house. However, since the bank is going to do this when there's a buyer, it may be unnecessary. A broker can give you a fair price opinion based on what are called "comparables," which is essentially comparing the property to a similar home that has sold in the immediate area in the last six months. The broker looks for a house that has the same number of rooms, including bathrooms, and is as similar as possible to yours. They then take into account other specifics such as new windows, marble counters, granite counter tops in the kitchen, a swimming pool, a finished basement, new electrical wiring, and so on.

The additions you've made to your home and the repairs will add points and subsequently influence the value and asking price. However, the age of the house, condition, and location will be prime concerns. The "comparable" gives the agent a good starting price to work with and the bank can also use it as a guide.

Once the value has been determined, you and your broker will set the asking price. Aim higher and expect 10 percent less than you are asking. For instance, if the house is valued at $300,000 and you ask for $315,000, you will probably end up selling at around $285,000.

Prior to working with a real estate agent, you should check to see that the agent is properly licensed. There are numerous people claiming to be in the real estate business, so make sure whomever you are working with is fully accredited. The Department of State (licensing division) in whichever state the dealer says he or she is licensed can answer questions regarding said license. Next, you should get in writing the arrangement you have with the broker, including all expenses you need to pay and the commission and fees that will go to the broker.

Good real estate agents know the neighborhood and are aware of the value of homes in that area. They also can apprise you of the various places in which they will have your home listed. The better brokers will list your home in as many key places as possible. The more exposure your home has on the market, the more likely you are to get the asking price, or within 10 percent of that price.

THE CLOSING

The closing is the final step in the buying/selling transaction. Once a buyer and seller, with or without a real estate agent, come to an agreement on the price, the attorney for each side—a real estate attorney—draws up the contracts for both sides to sign. The buyer gives the seller a down payment, usually around 10 percent, which is put into an escrow account. Generally, the contract provides that the seller retains the deposit if the buyer cancels the contract, unless it is due to inability to obtain a mortgage. The buyer, who has been preapproved for the mortgage, then takes the con-tract back to the bank or to the mortgage broker, where the underwriter will review the paperwork and pertinent details. Then the bank sends their appraiser to make sure that the house is valued properly. Once this has been approved, the bank issues a commitment letter stating that they will issue a check for the amount of money the buyer needs to borrow (the mortgage). And within two weeks, all the papers can be legally signed, sealed, and delivered.

FEATURES CHECKLIST

ADDRESS:		
	YOUR IDEAL	ACTUAL FEATURES
View/ Landscaping		
Siting		
Style		
Driveway/Garage		
Deck, Porch, Patio		
Windows		
Entraceways		
Floor plan and traffic pattern		
Kitchen		
Bathroom		
Laundry facilities		
Closets		
Number of Bedrooms		
Family room		
Living room		
Dining room		
Attic/Basement		

FEATURES CHECKLIST

ADDRESS:		
	YOUR IDEAL	ACTUAL FEATURES
View/ Landscaping		
Siting		
Style		
Driveway/Garage		
Deck, Porch, Patio		
Windows		
Entraceways		
Floor plan and traffic pattern		
Kitchen		
Bathroom		
Laundry facilities		
Closets		
Number of Bedrooms		
Family room		
Living room		
Dining room		
Attic/Basement		

MORTGAGE CALCULATOR

LOAN AMOUNT	6%	6.5%	7%	7.5%	8%	8.5%	9%	9.5%	10%
$50,000	$300	$316	$333	$350	$367	$384	$402	$420	$439
$60,000	$360	$379	$399	$420	$440	$461	$483	$505	$527
$70,000	$420	$442	$466	$489	$514	$538	$563	$589	$614
$80,000	$480	$506	$532	$559	$587	$615	$644	$673	$702
$90,000	$540	$569	$599	$629	$660	$692	$724	$757	$790
$100,000	$600	$632	$665	$699	$734	$769	$805	$841	$878
$110,000	$660	$695	$732	$769	$807	$846	$885	$925	$965
$120,000	$719	$758	$798	$839	$880	$923	$966	$1,009	$1,053
$130,000	$780	$822	$865	$909	$954	$1,000	$1,046	$1,093	$1,141
$140,000	$839	$885	$931	$979	$1,027	$1,076	$1,126	$1,177	$1,229
$150,000	$899	$948	$998	$1,049	$1,101	$1,153	$1,207	$1,261	$1,316
$175,000	$1,049	$1,106	$1,164	$1,223	$1,284	$1,345	$1,408	$1,471	$1,535
$200,000	$1,199	$1,264	$1,330	$1,398	$1,467	$1,537	$1,609	$1,681	$1,755
$225,000	$1,348	$1,422	$1,496	$1,573	$1,650	$1,730	$1,810	$1,891	$1,974
$250,000	$1,498	$1,580	$1,663	$1,748	$1,834	$1,922	$2,011	$2,102	$2,193
$275,000	$1,649	$1,738	$1,830	$1,923	$2,018	$2,155	$2,213	$2,312	$2,413
$300,000	$1,799	$1,896	$1,996	$2,098	$2,201	$2,307	$2,414	$2,523	$2,633
$325,000	$1,949	$2,054	$2,162	$2,272	$2,385	$2,499	$2,615	$2,733	$2,852
$350,000	$2,098	$2,212	$2,329	$2,447	$2,568	$2,691	$2,816	$2,943	$3,072
$375,000	$2,248	$2,370	$2,495	$2,622	$2,752	$2,883	$3,017	$3,153	$3,291
$400,000	$2,398	$2,528	$2,661	$2,797	$2,935	$3,076	$3,218	$3,363	$3,510
$425,000	$2,548	$2,686	$2,828	$2,971	$3,119	$3,268	$3,420	$3,574	$3,730
$450,000	$2,698	$2,844	$2,994	$3,146	$3,302	$3,460	$3,621	$3,784	$3,949
$475,000	$2,848	$3,002	$3,160	$3,321	$3,485	$3,652	$3,822	$3,994	$4,168
$500,000	$2,998	$3,160	$3,327	$3,496	$3,699	$3,845	$4,023	$4,204	$4,388

10.5%	11%	11.5%	12%	12.5%	13%	13.5%	14%	14.5%	15%
$457	$476	$495	$514	$534	$553	$573	$592	$612	$632
$549	$571	$594	$617	$640	$664	$687	$711	$735	$759
$640	$667	$693	$720	$747	$774	$802	$829	$857	$885
$732	$762	$792	$823	$854	$885	$916	$948	$980	$1,012
$823	$857	$891	$926	$961	$996	$1,031	$1,066	$1,102	$1,138
$915	$952	$990	$1,029	$1,067	$1,106	$1,145	$1,185	$1,225	$1,264
$1,006	$1,048	$1,089	$1,131	$1,153	$1,174	$1,260	$1,303	$1,347	$1,391
$1,098	$1,143	$1,188	$1,234	$1,281	$1,327	$1,374	$1,422	$1,469	$1,517
$1,189	$1,238	$1,287	$1,337	$1,387	$1,438	$1,489	$1,540	$1,592	$1,644
$1,281	$1,333	$1,386	$1,440	$1,494	$1,549	$1,604	$1,659	$1,714	$1,770
$1,372	$1,428	$1,485	$1,543	$1,601	$1,659	$1,718	$1,777	$1,837	$1,897
$1,601	$1,667	$1,733	$1,800	$1,868	$1,936	$2,004	$2,074	$2,143	$2,213
$1,829	$1,905	$1,981	$2,057	$2,135	$2,212	$2,291	$2,370	$2,449	$2,529
$2,058	$2,143	$2,228	$2,314	$2,401	$2,489	$2,577	$2,666	$2,755	$2,845
$2,287	$2,381	$2,476	$2,572	$2,668	$2,765	$2,864	$2,962	$3,061	$3,161
$2,516	$2,618	$2,723	$2,829	$2,935	$3,042	$3,150	$3,258	$3,368	$3,477
$2,744	$2,857	$2,971	$3,086	$3,202	$3,319	$3,436	$3,555	$3,674	$3,793
$2,973	$3,095	$3,218	$3,343	$3,469	$3,595	$3,723	$3,851	$3,980	$4,109
$3,202	$3,333	$3,466	$3,600	$3,735	$3,872	$4,009	$4,147	$4,286	$4,426
$3,430	$3,571	$3,714	$3,857	$4,002	$4,148	$4,295	$4,443	$4,592	$4,742
$3,659	$3,809	$3,961	$4,114	$4,269	$4,425	$4,582	$4,739	$4,898	$5,058
$3,888	$4,047	$4,209	$4,372	$4,536	$4,701	$4,868	$5,036	$5,204	$5,374
$4,116	$4,285	$4,456	$4,629	$4,803	$4,978	$5,154	$5,332	$5,511	$5,690
$4,345	$4,524	$4,704	$4,886	$4,978	$5,254	$5,441	$5,628	$5,817	$6,006
$4,574	$4,762	$4,951	$5,143	$5,336	$5,531	$5,727	$5,924	$6,123	$6,322

LENDER	PHONE
ADDRESS	FAX
Types of financing	
Current interest rates	
Term	
Minimum down payment	
Limit on loan amount	
Loan qualification guidelines	
Points	
Loan origination fee	
Application fee	
Appraisal fee	
Credit check fee	
Other fees (list)	
Prepayment penalty	
Preferred customer benefits	
Time needed for lender's decision	
Length of loan commitment (number of days)	
Renewable?	
Rate guarantee on commitment (if any)	
Late payment penalty	
Notes:	
The best offering for us seems to be:	
Cost of obtaining the loan: (add all the fees payable at the closing) $ $ $ $	
Monthly cost of carrying the loan: $ $ $ $	
Use the mortgage tables to find the principal and interest payment at the named rate of interest for the named term. Or enter the lender's figure for fixed payments on an adjustable loan. Add mortgage insurance premiums, if any.)	

LENDER COMPARISON WORKSHEET

	COST OF SECURING THE LOAN	MONTHLY CARRYING COSTS
LENDER 1		
Loan	$	$
Loan	$	$
Loan	$	$
LENDER 2		
Loan	$	$
Loan	$	$
Loan	$	$
LENDER 3		
Loan	$	$
Loan	$	$
Loan	$	$
LENDER 4		
Loan	$	$
Loan	$	$
Loan	$	$
LENDER 5		
Loan	$	$
Loan	$	$
Loan	$	$

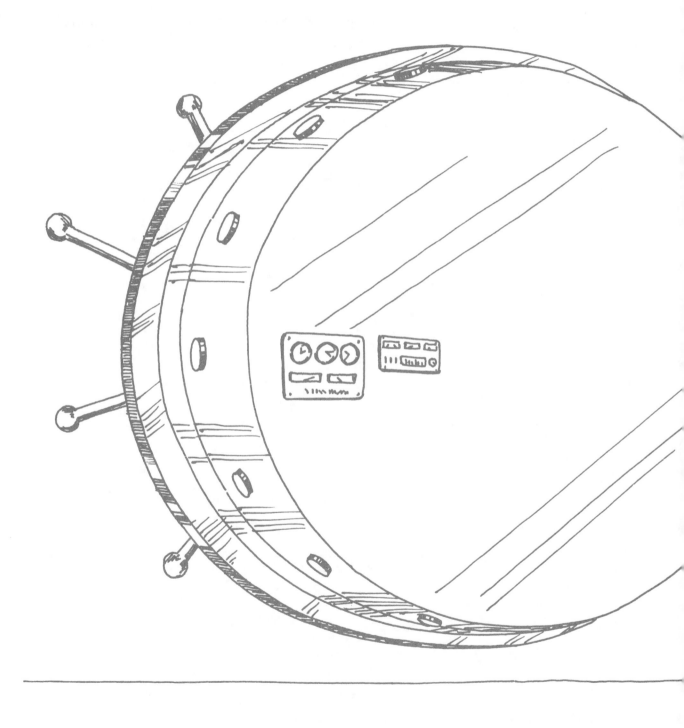

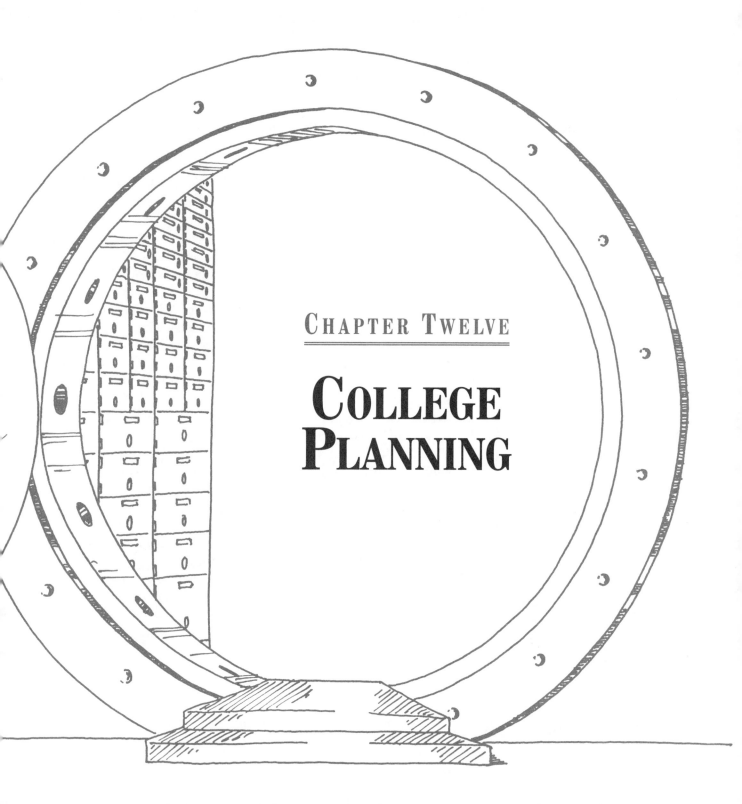

CHAPTER TWELVE

COLLEGE PLANNING

In 1998 the average annual cost of a four-year private college passed the $21,000 mark, and four-year public colleges approached $9,000 a year, including room and board. At an annual increase of 5 percent per year, which has been the rate since the late '80s, college tuition for a child currently in kindergarten may be $50,000 per year for a private college and over $21,000 for a public university.

These numbers, however, are somewhat exaggerated because of certain high-priced institutions. More than 75 percent of students entering college in 1997 were still paying less than $8,000 per year for tuition, not including expenses, or around $12,000, with housing, books, and other expenses factored in. There are many good institutions that turn out numerous success stories in many fields. Today, college is only half the battle; many fields, including technical and computer-related areas, require other types of special training or graduate work. We won't get into those costs. Hopefully your college student will find a way to pay for postgraduate work on his or her own.

Meanwhile, no matter how you slice it, college costs money. On the positive side, financial assistance to students over the past two years has exceeded $55 billion. On the other hand, only 50 percent of students receive such funding, including money from grants, funds, student loans, and scholarships.

The idea of sending a child to college is becoming, in a word, frightening. Scholarships are not easy to get; financial assistance is available, but you may not qualify. So unless you have a rich relative about to leave you a fortune, you better start thinking about a savings plan early on.

Not unlike a retirement plan, a college savings plan needs to build over a period of time and should be invested in regularly. It is important to make a serious, committed effort to such a plan for it to work in the long run.

PROJECTING COLLEGE COSTS

Many books, magazines, and even financial planners and "experts" suggest that you try first to assess what type of school your child will attend before starting your savings plan. They ask questions such as these:

- Is your child likely to attend a public or private university?
- Is your child likely to attend an Ivy League school?
- Would your child be happy with a junior or state college?
- Is he or she likely to go away to school or attend college locally?

These are tough questions to answer when you look at your three-year-old son, who is watching cartoons and building with his blocks. In fact, if you start to think about college when your child is 3, 4, 5, or even 10 years old, you won't be able to answer these questions.

Try to save at least 75 percent of what the cost of the better schools will be when your child is ready to attend. You want the best for your child, so go for it. If you have a seven-year-old, she would go to college in 2010. Based on projected costs for college (according to the College Board's Independent College 500 Index), four years at a private institution would weigh in at around $200,000. Wow! Therefore, if you're looking to accumulate 75 percent of the tuition in your portfolio, you'll need about $155,850—tough but attainable.

WHERE TO INVEST

You will need to set up an account earmarked for college. To your advantage (no matter where you invest) is *time*. The earlier you start, the more risky your investments can be. Over time "riskier" investments in the stock market are not high risk at all. History shows that despite the daily newscasts that start with "the Dow Jones took a beating today," if you invest in stocks over a longer period of time, say ten to fifteen years, you will make money. The amount of time you have before your children are ready for college will determine your investment flexibility. If you start when your child is three, you can utilize the long-term potential of the stock market and stock mutual funds. If your child is ten or eleven, you will need to think more in terms of bond funds and other low-risk means of building a portfolio.

Spread Your Investments

As mentioned earlier, it is advantageous to put your money in more than one place. Keep some money in various pots—that is, diversify. One reason mutual funds earmarked for college tuition are a good investment is that they do the diversifying for you.

Whatever your plan, as your child nears college, you may progressively move more of your money into safer investments After all, if you've worked hard to build a college account, you don't want to jeopardize it in the end.

Whatever way you choose to build your child's tuition account, be proactive. Keep looking for the better options and always keep your goal in mind: to give your child a good education.

SAVINGS BONDS FOR TUITION

Series EE U.S. savings bonds can be cashed in and used for college tuition tax free, if done in the same year. There are several requirements including income restrictions before the tax-free part comes into play. For example, the bond must be in the name of one or both parents, not in the child's name. However, even without the tax breaks, EE bonds are safe investments. Although they tie up your money for at least five years, they are always purchased at a discount from the face value of the bond. The rate of interest varies, but it is currently around 6 percent, if you hold the bond for five or more years. (For more on bonds, see Chapter 9.)

Some federally tax-exempt college bonds are offered by individual states to increase state college enrollment. These bonds pay a fixed interest rate that is set when you purchase them. The advantage is that colleges in these states offer a tuition discount based on redeeming these bonds. If your son or daughter, however, chooses to go to an out-of-state school, you will still be cashing in a viable bond, but you won't receive the discount.

MUTUAL FUNDS FOR TUITION

If your child is under ten, which gives you at least seven years until college, you can start off more aggressively by playing the popular mutual fund game with some of (but not all of) your college tuition plan. Choose a solid growth-oriented mutual fund (see Chapter 8) and let the stock market work for you. Again, as your student gets into his or her second or third year of high school, start moving more of this money into shorter term, safer investment plans. Balanced mutual funds will diversify some of that money between stocks and bonds, providing you with an even safer investment.

ZERO COUPON BONDS FOR TUITION

If you have the money, you might opt to buy zero coupon bonds. A $10,000 bond bought when your child is five years old (earning in the neighborhood of 7 to 8 percent with twelve years to maturity) will be worth about $22,000 when it matures and he or she is ready for college.

Zero coupon bonds are issued by the U.S. government, private companies, or municipalities. The *zero* indicates that you are receiving zero interest until the bond matures, at which point you receive all the accumulated interest at one time at a rate set when you purchase it. This can help alleviate your concern about fluctuating interest rates or reinvesting interest. In essence you know when you buy a zero coupon bond exactly how much it will pay at the time it matures, and these rates are fairly good, since banks don't have to worry about paying you interest along the road to maturity. Other bonds can also work for you. Just keep track of the bond rates (see more on bonds in Chapter 9).

CASH VALUE LIFE INSURANCE PLANS FOR TUITION

Some cash value life insurance plans allow you to cash them in for money. This is generally not a good way to build up the kind of funds needed to help defer the high costs of college. You can do much better with mutual funds, bonds, or other investment plans.

PREPAID TUITION PLANS

Several states allow you to start paying for your children's college when they are very young, usually under five years old. Although there are great discounts offered, this is a long-term risk, as your child may not be thrilled with having had these choices made before he or she was old enough to speak. If this happens, you will get a refund but it may not be 100 percent of the amount you spent. Also, you could invest the same money elsewhere, and it would grow (which is in actuality what the college is doing).

College Savings Bank

Cashing in on the need to save money for college, the College Savings Bank, in Princeton, New Jersey (member FDIC), offers the CollegeSure CD to help you in your college planning strategy. CollegeSure CDs are available in maturities of one to twenty-five years. You can invest in the CD at the maturity you choose, starting with a $1,000 minimum.

The investments, while conservative, work well for college planning. They are indexed to college costs and, according to College Savings Bank, are guaranteed to cover those costs at 100 percent. What more can you ask for? The CollegeSure CD pays an annual rate equal to the average increase in college costs, with no ceiling and no floor rate added.

You can call College Savings Bank at 1-800-888-2723, look for them online at www.collegesavings.com, or e-mail questions to info@collegesavings.com. Also, check with other banks and financial planning services to see what plans they may offer and recommend for college tuition.

Prepaid tuition plans can also be risky because the top ranked school today may not be the best school in 5, 10, or 15 years. Also, the school might not have the program that suits your child's needs. So be careful.

WHOSE NAME DO WE USE ANYWAY?

This can be a Catch-22. There are two sides to giving your child money in his or her name for college. On the plus side, each parent can give up to $10,000 each year to a child under the age of eighteen, without having to pay gift taxes on that money. The Uniform Gift to Minors Act is a way to gift money to your child by opening a custodial account in which both the parent's and the child's names appear with the child's social security number included. If invested in mutual funds, these accounts (you can open several of them) generally produce little taxable income annually, but can over time provide long-term capital gains.

On the negative side, if the child applies for financial aid, the assets that are in the child's name will be weighed against the family; the child will be required to use a significant amount of that money before the family will be considered eligible. On the other hand, if the money is in your account, you are expected to spend only a small percentage of it for tuition before you are eligible to receive assistance. Also, money in your child's name becomes his or hers at age eighteen, and if he or she decides to travel across the country with the money, there is nothing you can do about it.

Most financial experts agree that you should keep the bulk of the college savings in your name and invest wisely. In short, the decision of whose name to put on the accounts may weigh on a few key factors. Ask yourself these questions:

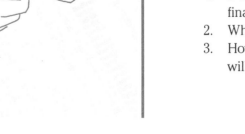

1. Do you expect that your child may want to apply for financial aid?
2. What tax bracket are you in?
3. How much money are you talking about and at what rate will this money be going into the account?

FINANCIAL AID FOR COLLEGE

The question is, Do you qualify? First, you need to pick up the appropriate forms and apply. The forms are then sent by the college to one of a few major agencies who determine whether you qualify. A *needs analysis* determines where you stand. This is a calculation made based on your assets and income in conjunction with about 70 percent of the tuition costs of the school (for the rest, you're on your own). Essentially, they will report to the college and the college will then do their own evaluations; in the end they will tell you how much, if anything, you are eligible to receive. Money earmarked for college in your child's name will be weighed more heavily and a higher percentage will be expected to go toward the tuition payments. Therefore, as noted earlier, money in a child's name can work against him or her when applying for financial aid.

Assistance can come from a number of sources, including the federal government (through Pell grants), the state government, the military, or the school itself. It is to your advantage, when your son or daughter is applying to college, to obtain all of the appropriate forms, fill them out accurately, and submit them on time. Use your tax returns as a guide for filling out the forms.

SCHOLARSHIPS, GRANTS, AND LOANS

From an academic scholarship to a cheerleading scholarship, there are a vast number of college scholarships offered. Every year billions of dollars are doled out from groups, companies, organizations, or individuals to students to pay part or all of their college tuition. AND, believe it or not, billions of dollars go unused. The trick is to learn about them, get the application forms, and APPLY.

Sallie Mae also offers a listing of scholarships (there's more on Sallie Mae later in the chapter). Searching the Internet can also help you find scholarships offered that may not be prominently known. The more obscure the scholarship, the fewer people who apply. And don't stop at one or two; go for several to improve your chances. Check out a wide variety of organizations, fraternal groups, associations, an so on, to find out who offers a college scholarship program. Be careful not to spend money on so called "scholarship finding experts or services," which are often a rip-off.

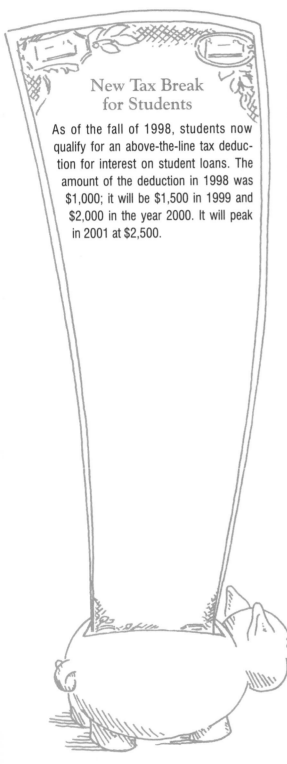

There are also grants that you can apply for. The Pell grant is a federal grant given to lower-income families; it can provide you with up to $3,000 a year. Other grants (and scholarships) are offered by colleges, based on academic success, athletic abilities, or other skills.

Student loans from the federal government still exist, despite cutbacks. Loans are usually based on the interest rate posted on July 1st (the rate changes annually).

The Stafford loan program is a subsidized federal program that is based on need. You begin repayment six months after graduation; you usually have up to ten years to pay it off. An unsubsidized Stafford loan is also available, regardless of need.

Subsidized Stafford loans allow you to borrow up to $2,625 for freshmen, $3,500 for sophomores, and $5,500 for juniors and seniors. You can take out an additional unsubsidized loan for $4,000 for freshmen and sophomores and $5,000 for juniors and seniors. In your last two years of college, you could have a total of $10,500 in loans per year through Stafford. Interest rates, currently around 8.25 percent, will apply.

Perkins loans are provided by the government and administered by the college. They allow you to borrow up to $3,000 per year, and you need not start paying it back until nine months after you've graduated. You then have up to ten years to pay it off. These loans are based on need and usually administered by the school.

PLUS loans are not based on financial need. These are personal loans for the parents and are set up through your local bank. They can be for up to the full amount of tuition, but you need a good credit rating to receive one. The amount of the loan includes housing, transportation, books, and other student needs. The loans are federally backed, and the Federal Student Financial Aid Information Center can provide you with more information (call 1-800-4-FED-AID). You can also write to the National Education Lending Center, 824 Market Street, Wilmington, DE, 19801.

Keep in mind that Perkins loans, Stafford loans (both subsidized and unsubsidized), and PLUS loans are all available for both undergraduate and graduate school programs.

QUESTIONS TO ASK WHEN TAKING OUT A LOAN

Since there are a variety of loans available, it's important to look at a few key areas. Some of the terms will be spelled out, but you should double check the information. Ask these questions:

1. What is the interest rate? How is it determined? Is it fixed or varied?
2. How often is interest added to the loan?
3. Are there any stipulations regarding scholarships or other money you may be receiving for college?
4. Can the loan be consolidated with other loans?
5. What fees are there? (Origination fees are common.)
6. How long is the grace period?
7. How long do you have to pay back the loan?
8. What repayment plans are available?

CONSOLIDATING YOUR LOANS

Since you may need more than one loan source for your education, you may choose to take advantage of federal consolidation, or consolidating your loans from various lenders or programs into "one big loan." On the plus side, you'll have just one payment to make, instead of having to spend your time making payments to twelve different places. Also, it could take up to thirty years to pay back the loan, depending on how much money you actually owe, and you may get a more user friendly, income sensitive repayment plan, one that could make it easier for you to establish a good credit rating.

On the other hand, you may get a higher interest rate, depending on the rate available when you decide to consolidate. Choosing an extended period to pay off any loan can mean that you pay more because you'll pay interest that much longer. And you could lose a deferred status on other loans, meaning you'll have to start paying them off sooner, not later.

EDUCATION LOAN CHARACTERISTICS CHART

PROGRAM	FEDERAL PERKINS LOAN	SUBSIDIZED STAFFORD LOAN*	UNSUBSIDIZED STAFFORD LOAN*	FEDERAL PLUS LOAN*	SALLIE MAE'S SIGNATURE EDUCATION™ LOANS**
DESCRIPTION	A loan for students. A low-interest loan funded by the federal government and administered by the college.	A loan for students. A low-interest loan funded and administered by a lender. For FFELP, the lender is a financial institution or the college. For FDSLP, the lender is the federal government.	A loan for students. A low-interest loan funded and administered by a lender. For FFELP, the lender is a financial institution or the college. For FDSLP, the lender is the federal government.	A loan for parents. A loan to parents to pay for a student's education. Funded and administered by a lender. For FFELP, the lender is a financial institution or the college. For FDSLP, the lender is the federal government.	Three loan programs for students. Private supplemenal loans available from Sallie Mae and a nationwide network of lenders. For details call 1-888-888-3461.
ELIGIBILITY	U.S. citizen or permanent resident. Full or part-time undergraduate or graduate students. Priority is offered to Pell Grant recipients. Need basis.	U.S. citizen or permanent resident. Full or part-time undergraduate or graduate students. Need basis.	U.S. citizen or permanent resident. Full or part-time undergraduate or graduate students. Non-need basis.	U.S. citizen or permanent resident. Full or part-time undergraduate or graduate students. No adverse credit history.	Undergraduate and graduate students in eligible schools and graduale students in eligible health professions programs. Enrolled at least half-time in participating colleges. Based on credit criteria.
AMOUNT	Undergraduate: $3,000 per year to $15,000 maximum. Graduate: $5,000 per year to $30,000 maximum	Year 1 $2,625 Year 2 $3,500 Year 3 & 4 $5,500 Graduate $8,500	Dependent Independent Year 1 $2,625 $6,625 Year 2 $3,500 $7,500 Year 3 & 4 $5,500 $10,500 Graduate NA $18,500 (less amount of subsidized Stafford)	Up to the total cost of the student's education, less other aid received.	Annual cost of education less other aid. Aggregate limit $100,000 in private loans.
INTEREST RATE	5%	Varies Annually Interest rage is variable as established by federal statute. The maximum interest rate is 8.25%.	Varies Annually Interest rage is variable as established by federal statute. The maximum interest rate is 8.25%.	Varies Annually Interest rage is variable as established by federal statute. The maximum interest rate is 9%.	Varies by program.
REPAYMENT TERM	Up to 10 years	Up to 10 years	Up to 10 years	Up to 10 years	15 or 25 years*** depending on loan type
MINIMUM REPAYMENT	$480 per year ($40 per month)	$600 per year ($50 per month)	$600 per year ($50 per month)	$600 per year ($50 per month)	$600 per year ($50 per month)
INTEREST SUBSIDY	Student pays no interest while in school or during any grace period.	Student pays no interest while in school or during any grace or deferment period.	None.	None.	None.
REPAYMENT BEGINS	Following 9 months grace period after leaving school.	Following 6 months grace period after leaving school.	Following 6 months grace period after leaving school.	60 days after funds are disbursed.	Following 6 month grace period after leaving school.
TOTAL ORIGINATION OR INSURANCE FEES	None.	Up to 4%	Up to 4%	Up to 4%	Varies by program.

*   Characteristics of Federal Family Education Loans (FFELP) and Federal Direct Student Loans (FDSLP) are essentially the same, though the repayment terms differ slightly.

** The Signature Education Loan Programs is an example of a supplemental program that offeres privately insured loans.
Other private loan programs are available. Contact you college financial aid office for information on available programs.

*** Annual Percentage Rate (APR) Examples—If the student were to borrow $5,000 with a cosigner, have a 48-month in-school period followed by a 6-month grace period, and if the variable rate remained constant at 8.375%, with a supplemental fee of 6%, the interim APR would be 8.831%. If the student maintained a constant variable rate of 8.375% during a 15 year repayment period, the monthly payment under the Standard Repayment Plan would be $67.29 over 180 months, and the APR during repayment would be 8.375%.

Printed by permission of Sallie Mae

THE PAYBACK

Although filling out forms is a genuine nuisance, you'll be thrilled when you receive your college loan money. Unlike a scholarship, this money will need to be paid back when you graduate or leave school. With any luck at all, college will prepare you for the real world, where a job and a steady source of income can make paying back loans more palatable.

College loans may vary in terms of how long you have to pay them back. Generally, payment begins six months after you are out of school and will extend anywhere from ten to fifteen years.

There are also several ways in which you will be able to repay your loan. Standard repayment plans usually involve a monthly payment of principal plus interest. Other methods include plans in which you start with reduced payments of interest only and graduate to higher payments including the principal. You end up paying higher total interest, but at least you have lower payments for the first several years after school when your earning potential is at its lowest.

There are also income sensitive payback plans that vary, depending on your income level. Talk with the lender about the types of payback plans. Often students are so excited that their loan applications have been approved that they forget about the repayment process. If you set up this aspect of the loan carefully, in advance, you will save yourself headaches later.

PLACES TO TURN FOR GUIDANCE

Not unlike Ginny Mae, Freddie Mac, and the rest of the home-buying secondary mortgage organizations, Sallie Mae is a privately based corporation in the business of buying student loans from lending institutions and passing on savings and other incentives to you. Working with several different loans, primarily Stafford and PLUS, Sallie, who just passed her twenty-fifth birthday, has several ways to make paying off loans easier. It's worthwhile for you, therefore, to look for lenders who work with Sallie. Programs designed to make your payments a little easier include Great Rewards, which lowers your interest rate if you've made the first forty-eight payments on time, and Direct Repay. The Elect Step Program allows you to pay only interest charges for the first two to four years.

There are various other incentives offered by Sallie Mae that you can learn about. Because of their strong presence in the student loan market, they are worth investigating. They offer a brochure called *Paying for College*, which outlines the variety of loans offered. They also offer help with the financial aid process through a college answering unit at 1-800-891-4599; and they have a brochure called *Borrowing for College*, outlining the financial planning process.

There is also a private loan program (the Signature loan) offered by Sallie Mae through participating schools; it operates much the same way as the PLUS loans for parents. Contact Sallie Mae at 1-800-524-9100 or through their Web site at www.salliemae.com.

Now celebrating their 100th anniversary, the nonprofit association known as *The College Board* is still among the leading sources of information available for sending kids to college. Their *College Board Scholarship Handbook* offers in-depth information on more than 2,800 scholarships, grants, internships, and loans for undergraduates and graduate students.

The board also provides information on traditional programs to help people take the first steps in identifying appropriate investment vehicles. There are state-sponsored initiatives to help students—the criteria of which vary from state to state—such as prepaid tuition plans, college savings plans, and various investment possibilities. The board provides information on these plans for over three thousand institutions in their *College Costs and Financial Aid Handbook*.

The College Board software includes *Fund Finder*, which lets students match their characteristics with the requirements of over 2,800 federal, state, and private sectors who can provide financial assistance for those who meet the eligibility guidelines. The software also includes the costs of colleges throughout the country, plus a worksheet for estimating how the family will fund the tuition.

ExPan is another program available that helps students with the difficult task of choosing, applying to, and paying for college.

You can reach College Board at 45 Columbus Avenue, New York, NY, 10023-6992 (1-212-713-8000). Or visit their Web site at www.collegeboard.org.

You need not be from the Lone Star State to take advantage of *Texas Guaranteed Student Loan Corporation*'s wealth of college payment information. From career planning to finding a school to payment possibilities, this nonprofit organization has a lot of material at your disposal. TGS has a wealth of newsletters and other written material, plus very thorough Web sites. If you want to talk to a support specialist, they can hook you up with one of their staffers to help guide you through the process of finding loans or other financial assistance, filling out the applications, determining repayment plans, and so on.

They can be reached at P.O. Box 201725, Austin, TX, 78720-1725 (1-800-252-9743). Or visit their Web sites at http://adventuresineducation.org or www.e-hound.org

A LITTLE HELP FROM THE STUDENT

Part of a college education is learning to be part of the real world. One way modern college students can accrue some life lessons is by helping to pay their own way. Summer jobs or part-time jobs during the school year, either on or off campus, can help students pay for a lot of their daily expenses. Many colleges waive tuition fees, or at least reduce them, in exchange for work on campus.

Students can also help themselves by learning how to handle their money wisely. Sharing expenses with roommates, buying used textbooks, and cutting corners are among the many ways students can cut down on expenses. But the key to managing money wisely throughout the college years is to stick to a realistic budget.

A simple budget should list income from part-time money and "gifts" from Mom and Dad on one side of the ledger and anticipated semester expenses on the other. By the second or third semester, students should have the knack of sticking to a budget. Expenses may include tuition payments, board or rent, meals, books, equipment and supplies, travel, parking, clothing, laundry, dues for clubs or organizations, entertainment, and miscellaneous. The toughest part for the student is trying to keep up with the "gang," some of whom can simply afford more. Unfortunately, trying to keep up with the Joneses too often carries well beyond the college years.

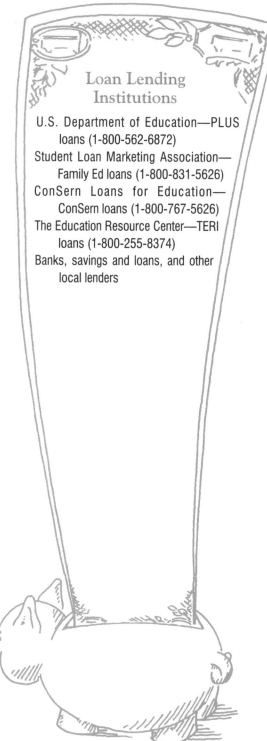

Loan Lending Institutions

U.S. Department of Education—PLUS loans (1-800-562-6872)
Student Loan Marketing Association—Family Ed loans (1-800-831-5626)
ConSern Loans for Education—ConSern loans (1-800-767-5626)
The Education Resource Center—TERI loans (1-800-255-8374)
Banks, savings and loans, and other local lenders

LIST OF SCHOLARSHIPS APPLIED FOR

NAME OF SCHOLARSHIP	SPONSOR	AMOUNT OFFERED	DATE APPLIED	TERMS OF SCHOLARSHIPS	RESPONSE DATE

STUDENT LOAN LIST

NAME OF LENDER	NAME OF LOAN	DATE APPLIED	TERMS OF LOAN	INTEREST RATE	ORGANIZATION FEES	REPAYMENT TERMS

FINANCIAL RESOURCES FOR A COLLEGE STUDENT WORKSHEET

	FAIR MARKET VALUE
SAVINGS IN PARENTS' NAMES	
Bank Accounts	
Mutual Funds	
Brokerage Accounts	
SAVINGS IN STUDENT'S NAME	
Bank Accounts	
Mutual Funds	
Brokerage Accounts	
COLLEGE LOANS (ANNUAL AMOUNT)	
SCHOLARSHIPS (ANNUAL AMOUNT)	
ESTIMATED ANNUAL EARNINGS FROM WORK	
TOTAL AVAILABLE FOR SCHOOL YEAR	

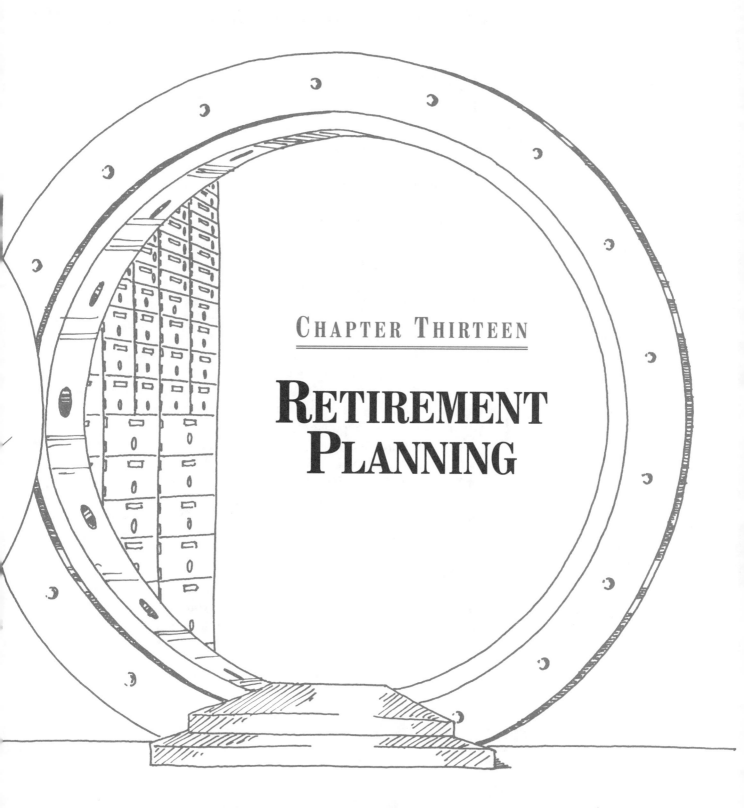

CHAPTER THIRTEEN

RETIREMENT PLANNING

E very year millions of people call it quits. They leave the daily grind and opt for the life of leisure they have long planned for. It's called retirement. It's a time of life in which many people catch up with the things they never had time to do. The trick to a successful retirement is to put aside enough money over the years so that when you decide to go around the world in eighty days (to celebrate your eightieth birthday), you can afford it. The reason for putting money aside now for later is so that it will grow, presumably at a rate faster than inflation.

SOCIAL SECURITY

Before venturing into the various ways in which you can set up retirement plans, it might be worth taking a quick look at the plan that the government has set up for you. It's called Social Security.

The Social Security Act of 1935 followed the insecurity of the Great Depression. It was created to ensure that seniors were taken care of. Today, over sixty years later, some forty-eight million people collect Social Security benefits. Although some politicians may try to confuse the issue and restructure the rules, Social Security will remain as long as the public demands it.

Social Security is relatively simple to understand. The FICA payment deducted from your paycheck is earmarked by the government for Social Security and Medicare at a rate of 7.65 percent. Of that percentage, 6.2 percent (of up to $68,400 of earned income) goes to Social Security, and the remaining 1.45 percent (of unlimited earnings) goes to Medicare. The amount is matched by your employer (by law).

If you are self-employed, you pay your own Social Security taxes when you pay your income taxes. The IRS then reports your earnings to Social Security. You have to pay both your own rate and the employer share so in essence you pay twice as much. However, there is a tax deduction you can take on the employer share.

Social Security is calculated on a "credit" basis. There are variations on this theme for part-time employees or people who do not work the full year. The general rule, however (as of 1998), is that for every $700 in income earned per quarter, you earn a credit. This amount rises gradually as the average income levels increase, but it is still a low amount. Anyone born after 1929 needs 40 credits to qualify for retirement benefits. If you were born prior to 1929, you need 1 credit less per year. For example, if you were born in 1928, it would be 39 credits; 1927, 38; and so on.

The money taken out of your pay is accrued and determines your benefit amount. In 1999, an insured worker will receive full benefits at age 65, but beginning in 2000, the age will gradually rise. Those born after 1959 will need to be age 67 to obtain full benefits. Early retirement at age 62 is available for workers with sufficient credits, but benefits will be reduced by 20 to 30 percent for life.

A spouse of a retiree may also be eligible to receive family benefits if he or she is over sixty-two years of age. Widows or widowers may be eligible to receive survivor's benefits if at least sixty years old. Unmarried widows or widowers raising a child entitled to child's benefits may receive mother's or father's benefits. People of any age, who have had a steady income of at least $500 per month or a certain number of credits accrued depending on age, can receive Social Security disability payments if they become unable to work for an extended period of time. Contact the Social Security Administration if you think you qualify for benefits.

It's nearly impossible to live on Social Security retirement benefits alone. The program was designed to help. However, supplemental Social Security benefits are available for people who have a low income and few assets.

People today are living longer and need more money as they get older. Therefore, there is a lot of controversy regarding how to manage the Social Security system and subsequent benefits. It is important that you keep an eye out for any sweeping changes that are proposed. Although the growing number of individuals over sixty-five and their families will make sure Social Security remains, there may be other changes forthcoming.

MEDICARE

Your Social Security office can provide you with Medicare information as well. Medicare provides basic health insurance to

How to Reach Social Security

For information, contact the Social Security Administration. Request form SSA-7004 to receive a copy of your Personal Earnings and Benefit Estimate Statement.

Request this information every three or four years to double check that the records are current and accurate. It's your money, so you have a right to know that it is being handled correctly. If your employer is not taking out money for Social Security, let them know that as well. Employers are required by law to deduct Social Security. Don't wait until you're about to retire to check on your Social Security benefits.

Their address is P.O. Box 17743, Baltimore, MD, 21235, 1-800-772-1213, or you can get information online at www.ssa.gov.

Retirement Tips

1. Take advantage of tax benefits for those over sixty-five.

2. Take advantage of senior citizen benefits.

3. Don't let a financial planner or anyone else talk you into anything you don't want to do. It's still your money. Deal only with advisors (including planners) that you trust.

4. Keep a budget.

5. Keep busy. The worst fear of people looking at retirement is that they won't have things to do. Plan ahead.

6. Enjoy the rest of your life— family, friends, travel, activities, hobbies, the early bird special—whatever you choose. Don't forget that the average life expectancy is rising, so retirement at sixty-five may mean twenty to twenty-five more healthy years. Go for the gusto!

people age 65 or over who are *entitled* to Social Security benefits (even though they may not be receiving them), and to disabled people receiving Social Security disability payments for at least two years. People who require kidney dialysis or a kidney transplant may be eligible for Medicare at any age.

Medicare covers both medical and hospital insurance. The medical insurance (Part B) primarily covers doctor's fees, physical therapy, x-rays, and diagnostic tests. The hospital insurance portion (Part A) is for stays in the hospital or in a skilled nursing facility following a hospital stay.

You can, if you choose, have the Medicare portion of your Social Security sent directly to a health maintenance organization (HMO), if you choose to use them as your service provider. Some HMOs offer you more options, such as more hospital days, choice of a doctor, and no deductible. But be careful. If an offer looks too good, there may be a catch. HMOs have their own rules and regulations. They may not cover certain procedures and may require that you see a primary physician before seeing the specialist you need. Check them out carefully.

Various MEDIGAP insurance plans are available to supplement Medicare coverage. The plan must accept you if you apply within 90 days of applying for Medicare Part B Medical Insurance.

You can get Medicare (and Social Security) questions answered by calling 1-800-772-1213. Medicare information may also be obtained at www.medicare.gov and www.hcfa.gov.

PENSIONS

The government and various unions offer pension plans in which your employer puts money aside for you based on a percentage of your income. Check to see whether your company or union offers a pension plan. You may have to meet certain requirements, such as a certain number of years or hours per year, in order to become eligible.

Pension plan reforms occur often; acts affecting pension law were passed in 1993, 1994, and 1996. If you work for a company that offers a pension plan, you have certain rights.

Once you become 100 percent vested, you have the right to your money upon retirement. The amount you receive is based on the number of years you've worked for the company and your salary during the last few years of employment. Your employee benefits department can apprise you of where you stand in regard to your pension benefits.

Some companies offer pension payment options. You might, for example, elect to take a lump sum payment, which you can then roll over into your IRA. Or you might elect to receive a monthly benefit upon retirement. Should you die, your beneficiary receives the pension payments.

EARLY RETIREMENT PLAN

Companies forced to cut back on hiring sometimes offer employees an early retirement package, particularly if the employees are in a union. If you are offered an early retirement package, review it carefully to determine how much money you need presently and how much you will need in upcoming years. Some companies will allow you to draw an annuity from the company for life, and others will give you the lump sum in your pension plan. You should also evaluate what you will be doing after your retirement. Do you want to keep working? Is a retirement lifestyle right for you at fifty-three?

Determine what happens if you do not accept a retirement package. Can you keep your present job? Can your hours be cut down because the company is downsizing? What would it be like to stay with the company? Will you be treated differently?

Should you receive a retirement package, get as many details as possible. It is very important to find out if you can remain on the medical plan and how it affects your pension or retirement plan.

Get the details in writing. A verbal statement of intent on the part of the employer can lead to trouble. For example, people have taken an early retirement package at the age of fifty-five with a verbal agreement that their medical coverage would continue indefinitely. Then, five or ten years down the road, the company, either under different management or in financial

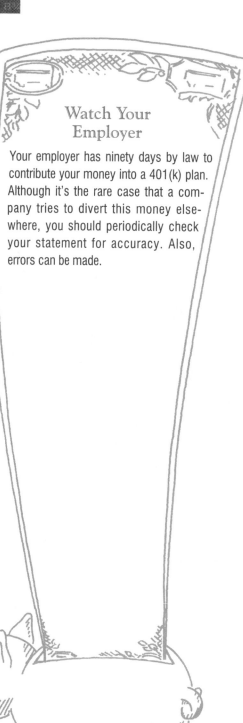

Watch Your Employer

Your employer has ninety days by law to contribute your money into a 401(k) plan. Although it's the rare case that a company tries to divert this money elsewhere, you should periodically check your statement for accuracy. Also, errors can be made.

trouble, looked for an area to cut back. One area they cut back on was medical insurance to former employees. Therefore, those who had been given this early retirement package found themselves without medical coverage when they needed it the most.

YOUR RETIREMENT PLAN

The majority of Americans, even those with a pension plan, must take responsibility for the bulk of their retirement. Do not despair, however, because the investment possibilities offered today allow for substantial savings for your "golden years." It's not that hard to save a sizable amount of money for your senior years. For example, if someone at age 30 decides to start putting money aside in a qualified retirement plan at $5,000 a year for each of the next 10 years at 8 percent annual return, at age sixty-five, he or she will have $496,000.

How much money you need depends on your lifestyle, age of retirement, future plans, and other investments. It is estimated that you will need about 75 percent of your average income in your peak earning years, traditionally your forties and fifties. Naturally, this also depends on what you do for a living. The bottom line in determining your retirement expenses is to look at your current budget and see how much you need to cover your expenses at present. Evaluate what expenses you will have at the age in which you plan to retire. Don't forget to increase the amount slightly in conjunction with the inflation rate.

It is not hard to set up a budget for your senior years if you look at what your current budget is and make appropriate adjustments. For example, you won't be paying for daily transportation to and from work, but you may need more money for weekly commuting for medical visits. Likewise, family expenses for children may be much less, but you may need money for travel expenses to visit your grandchildren. Try to estimate your expenses. Then, take your total and multiply by the inflation factor.

Start to save for retirement sooner rather than later. The primary options when it comes to setting up retirement accounts include 401(k), IRA, SEP-IRA, and Keogh accounts. Then there are defined benefit plans, profit sharing, and other lesser known plans.

401(K) PLANS

Since their inception in 1981, the 401(k) plans have made saving for retirement particularly easy; your employer sets up the account for you, and (if you choose to participate) your money is automatically transferred into it. Also, since you never see the money (contributions are usually made through salary deduction), you don't miss it, and you don't pay income taxes on it. Each employer may set up 401(k) plans differently, with some kicking in immediately and others going into effect after you've worked for the company six months or one year. There are also stipulations regarding the number of hours you need to work.

As of 1998 you may be able to contribute up to a maximum of $10,000 of your salary into your 401(k). The plan providers can set up other specifications in conjunction with the company. In over 80 percent of companies with such plans, employers match a portion of the amount you put in by 25, 40, 50, or even (although rarely) 100 percent. Some plans are vested, meaning that you need to stay for x amount of years before you can benefit from the company-matched portion of the plan. Thus, companies are saying that they will help you save up for your retirement provided you stay with them for a little while.

The 401(k) also gives you flexibility. You can choose how you want your money invested. Plans generally offer a few options including money market accounts, general growth or equity stock funds, or even stock in your own company. Different plans offer different options. Most of the time you can change these investments or the percentage of money allocated to each area.

Since 401(k) plans are for retirement, the one major restriction is that you leave the money in the account until you are $59\frac{1}{2}$ years of age or face a penalty upon withdrawal. However, in the case of some hardship situations, you can withdraw the money sooner without paying a penalty.

All in all, if a 401(k) plan is offered, you should take it. Reports show that in offices where such a plan is set up more than half of the employees utilize it, and the number should be higher. You do not pay tax on your 401(k) contributions, so if your company is matching your contribution at 50 percent, it's like getting at least a 50 percent return on your investment.

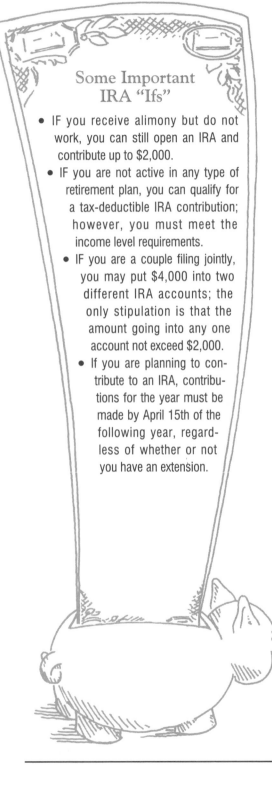

Some Important IRA "Ifs"

- IF you receive alimony but do not work, you can still open an IRA and contribute up to $2,000.
- IF you are not active in any type of retirement plan, you can qualify for a tax-deductible IRA contribution; however, you must meet the income level requirements.
- IF you are a couple filing jointly, you may put $4,000 into two different IRA accounts; the only stipulation is that the amount going into any one account not exceed $2,000.
- If you are planning to contribute to an IRA, contributions for the year must be made by April 15th of the following year, regardless of whether or not you have an extension.

For nonprofit organizations such as schools and hospitals, a 403(b) plan is available. Although this tax-sheltered plan is more limited in its investment options, it works on a similar basis to the 401(k) plan. Local and state governments offer a 457 plan. Roll overs on 457 plans may be restricted under state laws.

ROLL OVER

If you change jobs (by choice or not), you can roll over your 401(k) plan into the new company's plan; by law the employer has to allow you to do so. Or, you can roll the money into a rollover IRA account. It is to your advantage to have the money rolled over by a direct trustee-to-trustee transfer, thus avoiding any taxes. If you have the money sent directly to you, prior to putting it into another account, the company has to withhold 20 percent in a new account or the entire amount will be considered taxable income. If you can compensate for the 20 percent withheld for taxes when you open the new account, then none of the roll over will be taxable, thereby allowing the 20 percent that was withheld to be returned to you.

For example, if you receive $50,000, a withholding tax of $10,000 will be taken out, and you will receive a Form 1099 from the plan, showing the $50,000 distribution, with $10,000 withheld. If you then invest the remaining $40,000 into a rollover IRA within sixty days, only the $10,000 withheld (from the original $50,000) will be taxed. You will, therefore, pay a tax on $10,000 based on your income tax bracket (and a 10% penalty, if you are under age 59 ½) and receive the balance as a refund. If, however, you deposit another $10,000 into the rollover IRA, to bring your total back up to $50,000 (within sixty days), there will be no taxable income and no tax. Upon filing your tax return with Form 1099 attached, you will be refunded the $10,000 that was withheld.

IRAs

For those who do not have 401(k) or 403(b) plans at their disposal, IRAs are the fashionable retirement plan of the nineties. IRAs, or Individual Retirement Accounts, come in many configurations. The bottom line is that you can contribute up to $2,000 a year; a nonworking spouse may contribute an additional $2,000.

Banks, mutual fund companies, and brokerage houses are among the places from which you can obtain an IRA. You simply need to ask for an application form. The choice largely depends on your comfort level in the institution and their investment possibilities. Mutual fund families traditionally have more options, but banks, because of the competition, are now also offering a great number of ways in which you can invest. Brokerage houses can be the best places to turn because they can move your IRA from one fund to another very easily, without other fees; and they often get good rates.

ROTH IRA

A popular new type of IRA today is the Roth IRA. The Roth is not unlike the traditional IRA in terms of getting a plan started. However, you cannot take a tax deduction on a Roth as you can with the traditional IRA. On the other hand, there are advantages on the withdrawal end that are significant (to be discussed later in the chapter). The maximum contribution on a Roth IRA is phased out for a single individual if the adjusted gross income (AGI) is between $95,000 and $110,000 and for a married couple if the AGI is between $150,000 and $160,000 (as of 1998).

If your AGI is under $100,000, you may be able to roll over your money from your traditional IRA into a Roth IRA, but you will be taxed on the rollover. If you recently opened a traditional IRA and the amount is low, you may wish to pay the tax so that you can have the advantages on the withdrawal end of the Roth IRA. However, if you have had an IRA for years, the tax may be too high to make a rollover worthwhile. Also, as

IRA Tax Tip

To get the most out of your IRA, make your contribution early in the year so that you have the money working for you in a tax-free account for the full year.

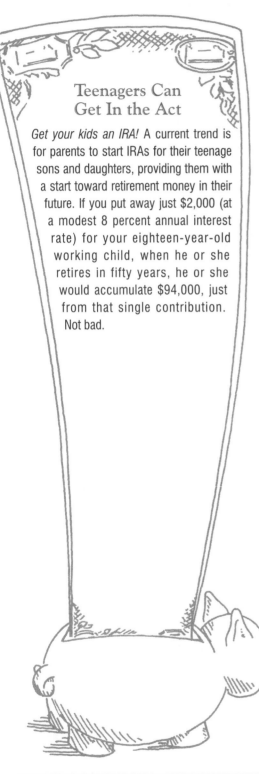

taxes are evaluated and debated in Congress over the ensuing years, it might be advantageous to wait and see what changes are made. Just as the new Roth IRA recently appeared, you may find a newer model without rollover tax rates.

The Roth stipulates that the money remain in the plan until you are 59½; however, after five years, you can withdraw money without a penalty if you are disabled, if you use the distribution to pay up to $10,000 of qualifying first-time home buying expenses, or if the distribution is to the beneficiary following the death of the account owner.

The primary difference between a traditional IRA and a Roth IRA boils down to a question of now or later. Would you prefer to take a tax deduction now and to pay taxes later upon withdrawal, or would you prefer no deduction now but no taxes later? Evaluate this by your current income level and tax bracket. Also consider what your income will be upon retirement. All in all, a traditional or a Roth IRA is a strong retirement vehicle.

SEP and Simple IRAs

Two other IRAs are the SEP-IRA for people who are self-employed and the Simple IRA for small businesses with income under $60,000. The SEP allows you to contribute 15 percent of your earned income up to $30,000; the Simple allows you to contribute up to the first $6,000 of earned income. These accounts are both light in paperwork. SEP-IRA plans may be established and contributions made for a tax year up until the return is filed, which may be until October 15th for a return on extension.

IRA Inertia

The vast majority of IRA holders do little, if anything, with their IRAs, beyond the annual contribution. The thinking is that once the money is earmarked for retirement, worry about it later. This isn't necessarily a bad thing. If you're earning a good rate of interest, you need not take the time and effort to seek out a tenth of a point higher interest in some other type of account. Often people find themselves chasing returns based on reading an article or hearing about a hot fund that may have been a bigger winner last year. Unfortunately, the hot fund one year may not be the next year's winner. If you're going to take an active interest in your IRA or in your finances in general, do your homework and don't be impulsive. Study the trends over a period of time and don't jump at the latest return. Return chasing can be like chasing tornadoes—hazardous.

On the other hand, don't let your IRA languish if you are getting a low rate of return or have money in cash accounts that won't help you reach your ultimate financial goals. You can keep an eye out for better interest rates and move your IRA accordingly. The same holds true with your level of risk. If you are more comfortable taking a greater risk than you were when you started the IRA or if you now need to save for your newborn son or daughter's college tuition in eighteen years, you might want to take a higher risk approach.

WITHDRAWING MONEY FROM A TRADITIONAL IRA

You cannot withdraw money from an IRA without penalty until you reach the age of $59^1/_2$. Like everything else in life, there are exceptions. These exceptions include money used for qualifying higher education, first-time home buying expenses, or substantial medical costs. Also, if you inherit the IRA from your spouse and maintain the distribution schedule of the deceased spouse or if you have certain disabilities that can be expected to last indefinitely, you can withdraw money without a penalty.

Once you hit $59^1/_2$, it's up to you to withdraw your money as you see fit. It helps to have a plan for withdrawing the money. Traditionally, once you hit $70^1/_2$ it is mandatory that you start withdrawing your money, or you will face a stiff penalty.

Should you be holding an IRA (not a ROTH IRA), the required annual withdrawal will be based on life expectancy depending on your age as determined by a government table (beginning at $70^1/_2$ years of age). You need the total of the fair market value of all plan assets on the last day of the year and the appropriate divisor (based on age) from the government life expectancy table to calculate the amount of withdrawal for the current calendar year. If you do not meet the annual

Taxing Your IRA

Except for the Roth IRA, your IRAs are deductible (subject to income limitations), but the proceeds will be taxable when you withdraw the money. However, if your income level during retirement is low, the taxes will be low as well.

IRA Withdrawal for First-Time Home Buying

Another first time? First-time home buying usually refers to not having owned a home or primary residence for *two* years. Always check the definition on this when you see the phrase "*first-time*" home buyer. You may still qualify as a first-time buyer, even if you owned a home once before!

withdrawal minimum amount, you will pay a penalty of 50 percent of the amount you failed to withdraw.

If you are married, you can use a joint life expectancy table, which has a longer life expectancy than if you calculate for one person. If you use this double life expectancy, you have a higher divisor and lesser amount that you have to take out than if you use the single table.

If a person passes away, the spouse can roll over the IRA as the beneficiary. He or she may then continue taking the money out utilizing his or her own life expectancy or the joint life expectancy table if a "time certain" method of calculation was elected prior to the first withdrawal. A "time certain" method defines the number of years you are going to be making withdrawals in accordance with the government table.

KEOGH PLANS

In a Keogh plan, employers set aside money for themselves and their employees. After three years of work, at one thousand hours or more per year, employees must be deemed eligible for coverage. Keogh plans, however, are most popular with those who are self-employed. You are allowed a maximum contribution as a self-employed individual of $30,000 per year. There are three types of Keogh plans, and additional constraints may be imposed depending on the type of plan.

In a profit sharing Keogh, annual contributions are limited to 15 percent but can be as low as 0 percent in a given year. In a money purchase Keogh, contributions are limited to 1 to 25 percent of compensation (but once set, they must continue for the life of the plan). A paired Keogh combines the terms of the profit sharing and money purchase plans. Keogh plans must be established by December 31st of the year for which you want to start making contributions, although you have until you file your tax return (which can be October 15th if on an extension) to make the contribution.

Like IRA and 401(k) plans, Keoghs have penalties for early withdrawal, or money taken out of the account before the age of 59½. Once you retire, you can have the money paid to you in monthly amounts (which are taxable) or in one lump sum (which is also taxable). Also, like the other plans, distributions must start by age 70¹/₂.

Since self-employment or any employment situation may change, you can roll over the money into an IRA. The roll over rules are similar to those of the 401(k) plan; a direct trustee-to-trustee transfer is recommended to avoid having to pay taxes.

The SEP (which was discussed earlier) is a variation on the Keogh; it can be easier to administer than the typical pension plan and beneficial to small businesses. Employers and employees both put money into this plan.

DEFINED BENEFIT PLAN

A defined benefit plan is usually used by a small business when the principal is older, within ten years of retirement. You fund the benefit plan by figuring out what benefit would be payable on retirement, as if you were buying an annuity for someone at 65. You are essentially planning backward, looking at what income you'll need later, and trying to figure out how you'll get there.

If you want to accumulate $200,000 in a finite number of years, you work backward and figure out how much you can put away each year and what additional return or interest you'll receive on your savings. There are actuarial factors that are used to work out what you will need to contribute to the plan each year to reach your goal. The actuary uses a formula to come up with the rate based on federal government regulations and their tables. It's a complex formula, but it is a solid way for older people and self-employed people to start saving for retirement and to put away more significant amounts and watch them grow quickly.

The annual contribution is not limited like it is in a profit sharing or a defined contribution plan. Benefits, however, are limited to $130,000, which is the government-imposed annual limit as of 1998.

You need to have your own documents and file with the IRS and the Department of Labor. Some banks sponsor defined benefit plans, as do brokerage houses. You would probably, however, go to a pension attorney or an actuary to set up such a plan.

SUMMARY OF RETIREMENT PLAN FEATURES CHART

PLAN TYPE	CONTRIBUTION LIMIT	INVESTMENT OPTIONS	SUITABILITY FOR EMPLOYEES	ADMINISTRATIVE REQUIREMENTS	KEY ADVANTAGE	KEY DISADVANTAGE	WHO SHOULD CONSIDER
IRA	Up to $2,000	Annuities, Mutal Funds, Stocks, CDs, No life Insurance	Personal Plan: Not Designed for Employee Benefit Purposes	NONE	Completely Your Own Plan	$2,000 Contribution Limit ($4,000 with spouse)	Almost Everyone's "First" Plan
SEP	15% of Earned Income or $30,000, Whichever Is Less	Same as IRA	Limited by Restricted Options	Simple Document, No Annual Filing Fee	Employee Plan with Least Paperwork	Must include Part-time Employees	Employer with Maximum IRA and No Employees
SIMPLE	Up to First $6,000 of Earned Income	Same as IRA	Best for Small Business under $60,000 Income	Document, Annual Meeting, Some Tracking	Largest Deduction of Owners with Limited Income	Must Match Employee Contribution up to 3%	Smaller Employer with Low Income or Employer with "Side Income"
PROFIT SHARING	15% of Overall Pay up to $30,000 Individually	Any Prudent Investment, Including Life Insurance	Vey Good for Work Incentive; Appeals to Younger Employees	Document, Annual Gov't Filing, Employee Reports	Flexible Contributions	Provides Limited Benefits for Older Participants	Employer with Young Employees and Variable Income
AGE WEIGHTED PLAN	15% of Overall Pay up to $30,000 Individually	Any Prudent Investment, Including Life Insurance	Appeals to Older Owners and Operators	Document, Annual Gov't Filing, Employee Reports	Flexible Contributions and High Allocation to Older Worker	High Installation Costs	Older Owner of Closely Held Corporation
401(K)	$10,000 Employee Contributions or 15%—the Lessor of the Two	Any Prudent Investment, Including Life Insurance	Best for Younger Employees If Maximum Contribution Made	Document, Annual Gov't Filing, Employee Reports	Employee Investment Direction; Positive Employee Perception	Complex Administrative Requirements	Larger Stable Company Who Want to Retain Employees
MONEY PURCHASE PLAN	25% of Pay or $30,000, Whichever Is Less	Any Prudent Investment, Including Life Insurance	Best for Younger Employees If Maximum Contribution Made	Document, Annual Gov't Filing, Employee Reports	Larger Contribution Limit Than Other Defined Benefit Plans	No Contribution Flexibility	Employer with Young Employees and Stable Income
DEFINED BENEFIT PLAN	Maximum Benefit Is 100% of Pay up to $130,000	Any Prudent Investment, Including Life Insurance	Best for Older Employees Due to Guaranteed Benefit	Document, Annual Gov't Filing, Employee Reports	Favors Older Participants	Complex Administrative Requirements	Older Employer with Stable Income

Reprinted by permission of Barry Kilzer and Kilzer Financial Group

OTHER PLANS

In a profit sharing plan, the company for whom you work pools an amount of its profits and distributes them annually according to a set formula. If the company does not show a profit or shows very little profit, less money is put into the plan.

A money purchase plan works in a similar manner, only the amount is not based on profits but on your salary. These plans are less common because if the company does not show a profit, it still must make the same contribution to its employees.

Retirement plans are generally tax deferred, which makes them attractive. Unless you are self-employed or are an employer, you will have little say about which plan your company offers. However, you should participate if such a retirement plan is available.

Financial planner Barry Kilzer of the Kilzer Financial Group in Carmel, California, is a fee-only advisor who has been helping to set up retirement plans for over twenty years. The chart on page 208, compiled by Kilzer, gives a solid basis for comparison between the various IRAs and other retirement plans.

EQUITY

Unless you are an antique dealer or a collector of some type of valuable art, you probably do not make purchases with the idea of selling them off in your retirement years. In fact, many such valuables are generally earmarked for grandchildren.

However, it is not far fetched that you own a home worth perhaps $300,000. If there are two of you rattling around in a nine-room house, you might decide to sell and buy a retirement condo in Florida or Arizona for $150,000. If you do, you will have gained an extra $150,000 for your retirement years. The new government home equity tax laws allow you to sell your home and not pay tax on up to $250,000 profit as a single individual or $500,000 if you're married. You had to have lived in the house for a minimum of two years. (For more on this subject, see Chapter 16.)

This scenario is not uncommon. Often couples, as well as widows or widowers, find that they are happier in another

Double Your Money, Double Your Fun!

In case you are wondering how long it will take your investment to double, there is a simple formula. Remember the number 72 and divide the interest rate by that number. For example, at 8 percent interest, your money will double in 9 years (72 divided by 8 = 9); at 6 percent, 12 years (72 divided by 6 = 12); and at 4 percent, 18 years (72 divided by 4 = 18).

Naturally this won't work if your principal can be lost or depleted. But $5,000, left alone, will become $10,000 by using the above principle, whether it is in a retirement or other type of bank account. It's a matter of the interest rate and the magic number 72.

setting during their retirement years and that they no longer need a large house. They may, in fact, no longer need two cars. It's not a matter of cutting back but a matter of being comfortable and practical. Larger houses mean more to take care of and more to clean. Two cars mean more money for maintenance and for insurance payments. For many people reaching retirement age, it's a matter of practicality. Your home is, therefore, a major asset that you might use to your advantage.

HANDLING MONEY DURING RETIREMENT

If you've done some proper planning in advance, you should be able to enjoy your retirement years while resting assured that you have money available. While it is likely that your living expenses will be lower, you will still need to have a steady income. You've worked long and hard to get to this point; you should not have financial headaches during retirement.

You need to set up a budget in advance, as you did prior to retirement—the difference being that during retirement your income will be derived from money withdrawn from those retirement plans that you set up, plus Social Security and any pension you are entitled to. You might also think about part-time work to remain busy as well as to make some money. If you are able to equal 75 percent of your income prior to retirement, you should do okay.

During the five to ten years approaching retirement, you should set up your retirement plan. Think about these questions:

1. What do you want to be doing during retirement?
2. Where do you want to be living?
3. What finances will be available?

Your anticipated lifestyle will have a lot to do with planning your financial future. The couple that wants to spend a great deal of time traveling might want a smaller permanent location. They may want to spend more money on airline tickets and other such travel expenses and less money on home

Investment Strategies

It's suggested that you move money from higher risk to lower risk investments as you approach retirement. To determine what percentage of your investments should be in stocks or equity funds, subtract your age from 110. In other words, if you're 71, 110 minus 71 = 39, or a maximum of 39 percent of your investments should be in individual stocks or mutual funds.

repair and maintenance. Such a couple might also start looking for credit cards that offer frequent flier mileage.

The couple that wants to maintain their home and have their children and grandchild there often to visit, might look for local activities to become involved in to stay active. It's long been theorized that people who stay active live longer, more enriched lives.

FIVE RETIREMENT OPTIONS TO CONSIDER

Many of the financial magazines, the planners, and the "experts" offer a host of new and inventive ways to invest your money. If you've worked many years to save up for retirement or you are trying to get by on a more limited amount of income/savings, this is not the time to get caught up in anything risky. However, with inflation, an approach that is too safe and conservative may have you falling behind.

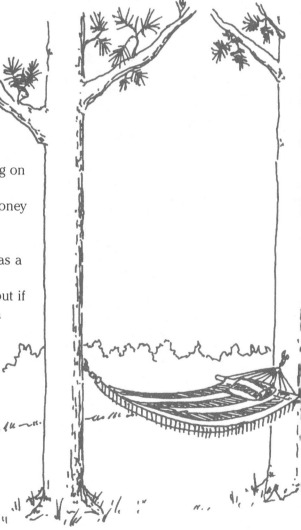

Here are some suggestions you should consider, depending on how much money you are dealing with, your age, and your lifestyle. Remember, your goal is to be comfortable with the money you have coming in.

1. Keep at least the first $30,000 in a safe place, such as a bank CD, Treasury note, money market account, or other cash instrument. Yes, this may sound boring, but if this is your cushion, you need to hold onto it with a tight grasp.

2. Invest a high percentage of your portfolio in bond funds (through a broker or planner). If you want a steady stream of income, investing in high yield bond funds is one way to achieve it. These funds can provide a cushion you won't find with more high-risk equity funds.

3. Sell off the house, buy a condo, and put your money toward travel, grandchildren, and other things you desire. Many retirees appreciate not having to pay real estate taxes and maintenance

on a house that is way too large for them. Put the rest of the money into investments, starting with safe ones and expanding to more risky ones based on your needs and how much money you have to work with.

4. Convert cash value life insurance into an annuity plan that pays monthly income. The money that built up during your working years when your family needed to be supported can now be better invested.

5. Keep an active portfolio. Again, this depends on your income and amount saved. However, if you have had a retirement plan—401(k) or pension—or accumulated any significant savings, you can maintain a diversified portfolio, only hedge toward the more conservative side. Equities can work in your favor, particularly those paying dividends; just maintain the percentage of your money in stock funds or individual equities that makes you feel comfortable.

FINANCIAL RESOURCES FOR RETIREES WORKSHEET

	MONTHLY INCOME
Annuities:	
Pensions:	
Social Security:	
Employment Income:	
Interest Income (bank accounts, bonds):	
Dividend Income (stocks, mutual funds):	
Retirement Plan Distributions (IRAs, 401(k)s, Keogh Plans, etc.): (if distributions are taken annually, divide by 12)	
Rental Income:	
Other Income:	
TOTAL:	

BUDGET FOR RETIREMENT WORKSHEET

SOURCES OF INCOME	$	EXPENSES	$
Former employer benefit plans (includes pensions & profit sharing)	$	Rent or monthly mortgage payments	$
IRA withdrawals	$	Food	$
Net income from real estate	$	Medical, including insurance premiums	$
Social Security	$	Local travel	$
Dividend income from stocks	$	Vacation travel & hotels	$
Interest from banks, bonds, mortgages	$	Entertainment (theater, movies, home, etc.)	$
Income from part-time work	$	Newspapers, magazine subscriptions	$
Annuities: A	$	Gifts	$
B		Charitable contributions	$
C		Automobile expenses	$
D		Property & other insurance	$
E		Alimony and/or child support	$
Other	$	Membership dues	$
		Domestic help or home care	$
		Home maintenance	$
		Other	$
		Total expenses	$

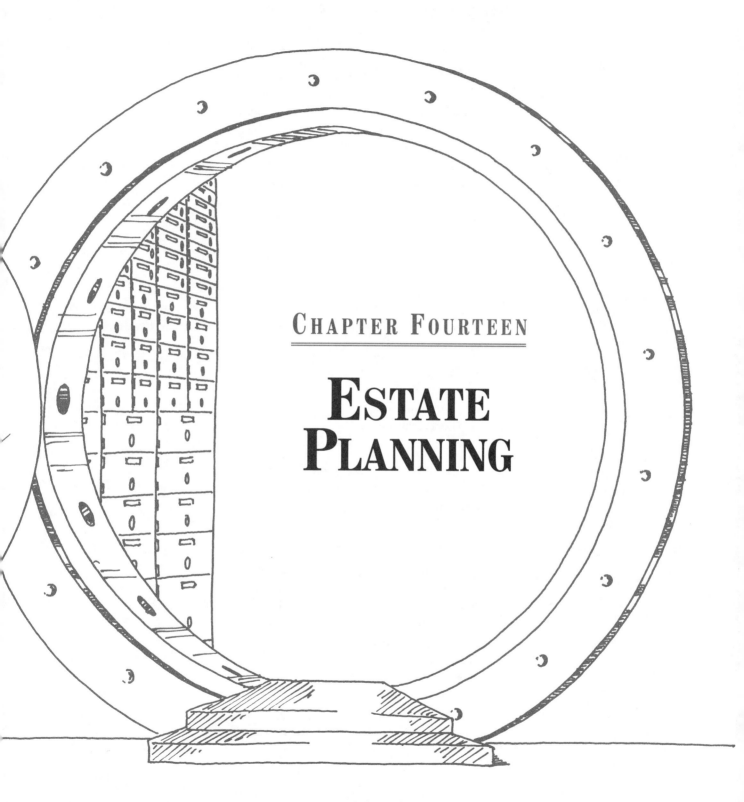

CHAPTER FOURTEEN

ESTATE PLANNING

E state planning is not something that most people look forward to. However, it is a way to make sure that all you have worked hard to attain ends up in the right places after you die. It gives you a sense of how your estate will be distributed, plus some control over that process. If you neglect estate planning entirely, you will be leaving the process up to the courts, who will not necessarily distribute the assets as you would have wished.

People often shy away from estate planning because it makes them uncomfortable. This, however, can have repercussions on those whom you love. Amazingly, less than half of adult Americans have wills, and a smaller number have made further plans regarding their estates.

The first two steps in the process of estate planning are to evaluate what assets you have and to evaluate what assets you anticipate having in the future. You will then be faced with working through issues such as these:

Legal issues
Financial issues
Emotional issues
Logistical issues
Tax issues

By planning and covering these issues during your lifetime, you are reassuring yourself that your loved ones will be taken care of after you die.

PROFESSIONAL HELP

Yes, there are do-it-yourself computer programs and books for preparing your will. If your assets are under $100,000 and are primarily in a few areas such as a life insurance policy, bonds, and some cash accounts, plus a few personal items of value, you might get away with these quicky modern methods of planning your will. However, in today's world, for most people estate planning is much more complicated.

Estate planning becomes more complex when there is more than one beneficiary, when you're talking about the demise of both people, or when someone has a *second to die* insurance policy.

There are also second marriages, children from prior marriages, step children, same sex couples, and numerous other lifestyles that make estate planning more difficult.

Therefore, it's to your advantage to talk to an estate planning attorney or a professional financial planner. Planning strategy, often using credit shelter trusts and other methods of moving money around (such as gifting), can save a family hundreds of thousands of dollars in estate taxes.

SUIT YOURSELF

It's important that you plan your estate to suit your wishes. After all, they're *your* assets. Some people do not want to gift out their money, wishing to retain a cushion to cover their living expenses. They are not concerned about whether the government takes a bite after they are gone. Other people want to move as much money as possible out of the grasp of Uncle Sam. For some, it's not a matter of the government getting money in taxes but a concern over how the money will be distributed and even spent by those who will receive it.

Comprehensive planners look at the overall situation of each person individually. Although planners and lawyers will cost you money, they can plan your estate in a manner that affords your heirs far greater protection.

THE WILL

The legal document that determines how your assets will be divided for after your death is your will. The document should cover all assets including these:

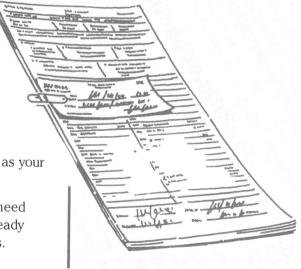

1. Bank accounts
2. Stocks, bonds, mutual funds, and your investments
3. Real estate you own, including your home
4. Any and all other tangible property you own, such as your car, boat, furniture, jewelry, art, and so on.

The will stipulates to whom these assets will be given. It need not, however, bequeath anything in which a beneficiary is already named, such as life insurance policies, IRAs, or pension plans.

There are several types of wills that can be drawn up. A simple will has assets distributed outright to the beneficiaries. A young couple who draws up a will and bequeaths everything to each other have what is often termed a "sweetheart" will. A more complicated will may have testamentary trusts established to receive assets from the estate, or may "pour over" (transfer) assets to a "pour over" trust created by another document.

As your family and your assets grow, your will may become more complex. This is why it pays to have an estate planning professional counselor to help you account for all situations. It is also advisable to look over your will when family situations change and make the appropriate alterations for second marriages, children from each marriage, and so on. Your will reflects your life, so it should be updated as your life changes.

It also should be mentioned that some people today are filing what is called a *living will*. Such wills provide medical and health care instructions to be carried out should you, for example, become physically incapacitated and require a life support system to stay alive. A health care power of attorney should be named in conjunction with a living will.

PROBATE...

The scene in many old movies showed the judge and the family seated in the courtroom. As the will was read, the family members waited impatiently to see what each of them would receive.

Probate is essentially the administering of the will by the court. The probate process first establishes whether there is a will. If a will exists, probate issues letters in conjunction with the document, appointing the executor(s). The executor then follows the wishes outlined by the deceased in his or her will. This is not always easy, as taxes may need to be paid and the money may not be there to pay them. In such a case, the executor may have to sell off some of the assets to raise the money to cover the taxes. There may also be challenges to the will by relatives of the deceased. Furthermore, property has to be valued correctly, which may require obtaining appraisals. In short, there may be any number of headaches associated with being the executor of a will. Probate can take a long time, and whatever the executor does must be reviewed by the court.

...OR NOT

Probate is something that many people seek to avoid for several reasons:

1. It is public record, and individuals with considerable wealth often want to keep the administration of their estate private. They also do not want people coming after their heirs looking for money (owed or otherwise).
2. Probate is often a long, slow, tedious process that can drag on for years.
3. Probate fees to an attorney and sometimes to the executor can mount over time.
4. If you own homes or property in different states, there will be ancillary probate, which means probate will take place in those states as well.

AVOIDING ESTATE TAXES

While probate and estate taxes are separate, they are similar in that there are several reasons to avoid them, or minimize their effect. First and foremost, estate taxes can take a big bite (sometimes as much as 55 percent) after a certain amount is reached in the value of the estate. As of 1998, that amount went up to $625,000. Essentially, this means that your estate can be valued at fair market value up to $625,000 before federal taxes kick in. This amount is rising and by the year 2007 will be $1 million. HOWEVER, if you are gifting, you may deplete some of this $625,000 exemption during your lifetime.

According to the Federal Gift Act, you are allowed to give $10,000 per year to as many people as you wish, free of gift taxes. But, if you give more than that amount to one person in one year, you will utilize part of that $625,000 exemption. In other words, if you gave someone a $50,000 gift in one year, the first $10,000 would be exempt from taxes, and the next $40,000 would come off of your lifetime $625,000 exemption. Your estate would then be taxed on the amount over $585,000. (For more in regard to avoiding estate taxes, see the section on gifting, in this chapter.)

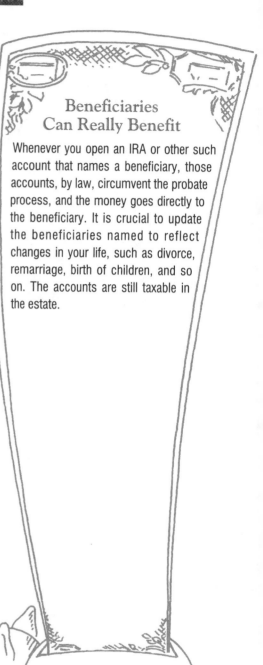

Beneficiaries Can Really Benefit

Whenever you open an IRA or other such account that names a beneficiary, those accounts, by law, circumvent the probate process, and the money goes directly to the beneficiary. It is crucial to update the beneficiaries named to reflect changes in your life, such as divorce, remarriage, birth of children, and so on. The accounts are still taxable in the estate.

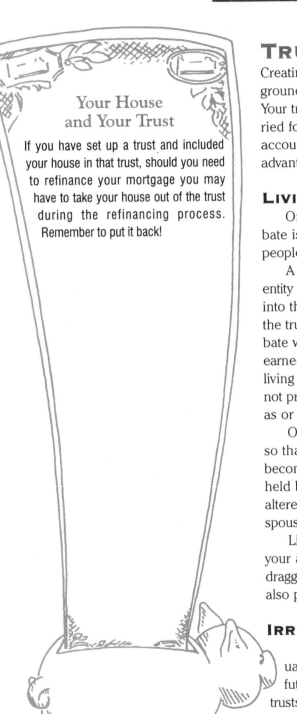

Your House and Your Trust

If you have set up a trust and included your house in that trust, should you need to refinance your mortgage you may have to take your house out of the trust during the refinancing process. Remember to put it back!

TRUSTS

Creating a trust is like building a house. You start from the ground up, adding as many doors and windows as you need. Your trust ultimately allows for your plans and wishes to be carried forth more specifically and privately than just a will. A good accountant can show you various ways to use trusts to your advantage from a tax paying standpoint.

LIVING TRUSTS

One of the most commonly used methods of avoiding probate is to put assets into a living trust. Such trusts name the people (or trusts) who will receive the assets upon your death.

A living trust, also known as a revocable living trust, is an entity unto itself. By placing your assets, including your house, into the trust, you maintain control while you are still living (as the trustee and beneficiary) and keep the assets outside of probate when you die. You will have to pay taxes on any income earned by the trust during your lifetime, and the assets held by a living will are included in your estate for federal tax purposes. If not properly set up, the administrative expenses can be as high as or higher than if the assets went through probate.

Often a husband and wife open a jointly held revocable trust so that when one spouse dies, his or her half of the estate becomes irrevocable and goes to the remaining spouse. The part held by the remaining spouse is then revocable and can be altered. There is also a successor trustee named, should the spouse die or become incapacitated.

Living trusts can be advantageous because they allow for your assets to be distributed as you wish, without the long, dragged out (sometimes contested) probate process. They are also private and offer various options.

IRREVOCABLE LIFE INSURANCE TRUSTS

These trusts purchase life insurance policies on individuals. The premiums are paid directly by the trust or by the future beneficiaries on behalf of the trust. Other insurance trusts include "Crummey trusts," in which gifts are made, to the trust, that utilize up to the $10,000 per person gift exclusion for each beneficiary, so that the premiums can be paid. The million dollars in a life insurance policy held by an insurance trust bypasses probate and is not taxed in the individual's estate. You can stipulate how and when the money will be dispensed to the beneficiaries, when forming the trust. The key factor is that it must be irrevocable.

SUPPORT TRUSTS

Support trusts are designed to support your children and your spouse. They can be set up in any number of ways, detailing exactly how the income and trust principal should be distributed. The trustee can be given flexibility, or not, depending on the situation. This is also called a discretionary trust. The trust may give basic parameters and allow the trustee to use his or her judgment. For example, a person could set up a five-by-five plan allowing for $5,000 per month for needs and $5,000 per month for wants. In a spendthrift trust, a variation of the discretionary trust, the trustee is told to keep a tighter reign over the spending of the beneficiaries.

Support trusts and living trusts can provide creditor and predator protection for your spouse or children. For example, the money can be protected if your daughter is a professional such as a doctor, who could be sued, or if your son's fiancée tries, after the wedding, to get at that money set aside for your son. People have, unfortunately, seen their trust funds squandered at the hands of a spouse, who ends up leaving when the money is spent.

CREDIT SHELTER TRUSTS

A credit shelter trust is a trust for those estates that go over the $625,000 exemption. As of 1998, federal estate taxes on $750,000 stood at $46,250, and the amount on $1 million was $143,750. An estate worth $2 million would pay $578,750 in federal estate taxes, and an estate worth $5 million would pay over $2.1 million. That's a lot of tax to pay!

Therefore, credit shelter trusts allow you to leave the highest amount of money that can go free of taxes (currently $625,000 as of

1998) to the trust when you die so that it doesn't go to the spouse and thus avoids taxation in the spouse's estate. If a couple has $1,250,000 in assets divided equally into both of their names, when the husband dies, he could have his $625,000 go into the trust. His widow would then be able to use the income from the $625,000 for her living expenses. Then, when she passes away, the $625,000 in the trust would bypass estate taxes (this is also called a bypass trust), and she would only have her own $625,000 in assets in her estate, which would not be taxed.

QUALIFIED TERMINAL INTEREST PROPERTY TRUSTS

A qualified terminal interest property trust, also known as a Q-tip trust, is used often by people who have children from previous marriages and want to be sure that they are taken care of along with their second spouse and subsequent family. This is a form of bypass trust set up under the provisions of the Internal Revenue Code that will prevent the second husband or wife from stepping in and taking the money that is deemed for your children. You set up a trust in the will in which you give the executor the power to elect that the property will qualify for a marital deduction. (Property left to a spouse who is a U.S. Citizen is exempt from estate tax under the marital deduction.) The spouse receives income for life. You can also allow for the spouse to receive distributions of principal. This trust property is included in the spouse's estate and is taxable, but it is distributed according to the trust.

DYNASTY TRUSTS

A dynasty trust can continue for generations. It is often established as a generation-skipping trust, which uses the exemption from the tax on transfers that "skip over" a generation. It takes a skilled estate planner, perhaps working with a CPA, to put this together to avoid tax ramifications.

Basically, if there's a scenario you want covered, there is probably a way to set it up. Gay and lesbian couples, people who are living together but not married, and other lifestyles create more elaborate challenges for estate planners. However, where there's a "will," or in this case a trust, there's usually a way.

GIFTING

The old television show *The Millionaire* was about a wealthy man who gave away million-dollar checks to unsuspecting strangers. Imagine the tax ramifications! Gifting is a more civil, more practical approach to giving money away. In fact, all transfers between spouses are tax free, other than transfers to a nonresident alien spouse (or trust transfers of mortgaged properties or U.S. savings bonds.) Therefore, you are free to transfer significant amounts of money to your spouse without worrying about Uncle Sam butting in.

People with significant estates often want to get money out of the estate to bring the total under the (current) $625,000 magic number. One way of doing this is to set up a system of "gifting" in which you give to each of those you choose $10,000 or less annually, the amount that can be given tax free. If you are married, you can elect to gift-split with your spouse, and raise that tax-free limit to $20,000, with half of the gift being attributed to each spouse. (If you let it be known that you are gifting money away, you may be surprised how many friends and long-lost relatives will show up that you never knew you had.)

Depleting the estate can be very difficult for an older person who is not working. People in this situation may find it hard to write out a series of $10,000 checks and give away $50,000 a year. They may fear that by giving up assets, they may not have enough left over to stay afloat.

Often a parent will give a gift to a child, knowing that the child would not ever let him or her become impoverished. It is a matter of the size of the estate, the amount a person chooses to gift away, their comfort level in so doing, and the relationship with the people to whom they are gifting.

You can also establish irrevocable trusts to which you make annual gifts in the name of your children or grandchildren. The appreciation of the trust assets will no longer be part of your estate. It is necessary to consult a qualified estate attorney to draft the trust documents.

Another gift giving strategy is for a grandparent to make tax-free educational gifts to his or her grandchild by paying the tuition directly to the private school or college. As you can see,

Estate Taxes

Although $625,000, the cut-off point where estate taxes begin, sounds like a high number to a lot of people and although that number will rise over the next several years, keep in mind that in the 1990s, the value of a house and a good retirement plan can build up to that number more easily than you think. Also keep in mind that if you've ever surpassed the $10,000 per person gifting exclusion in one year, your $625,000 exemption will be lowered. It is a high number, but many people, by the time they retire, have accrued more assets than they anticipated.

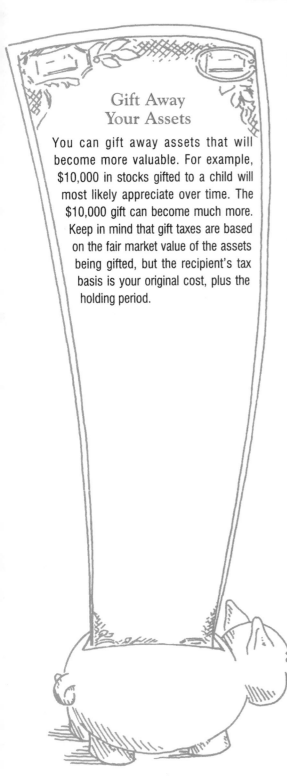

Gift Away Your Assets

You can gift away assets that will become more valuable. For example, $10,000 in stocks gifted to a child will most likely appreciate over time. The $10,000 gift can become much more. Keep in mind that gift taxes are based on the fair market value of the assets being gifted, but the recipient's tax basis is your original cost, plus the holding period.

gifting can be an effective way to distribute your assets and avoid high federal estate taxes.

JOINT TENANCY WITH RIGHTS OF SURVIVORSHIP

Joint tenancy with rights of survivorship means that the asset is held jointly. When one joint tenant dies, the property automatically transfers through survivorship to the surviving joint tenant. How the asset was acquired and the relationship between the joint tenants determines the basis of the asset and whether it is taxable in the estate of the decedent.

When spouses are the only joint tenants, then upon the death of one spouse, the asset automatically passes to the surviving spouse. For spousal joint tenancies created after 1977, 50 percent of the fair market value of the asset is reported on the decedent's estate tax return, regardless of who paid for the asset. The spouse's basis in the property becomes one half of the original cost, plus the value of the estate's one-half share, which is known as a "step-up" basis.

If your joint spousal estate will exceed the amount exempt from estate tax, currently $625,000 (as of 1998), it is recommended that you hold assets, such as securities, in your individual names. In that way, through estate planning, the estate of the first spouse to die can utilize trusts in his or her will to shelter the $625,000 from being taxed in the surviving spouse's estate.

TENANCY IN COMMON

Another form of ownership is tenancy in common, which can be used by two or more people. This is frequently used for real estate and allows several people to share ownership of property. The interest of a tenant can be transferred and can be inherited by a beneficiary named in a will. The new owner then shares ownership with the others. An estate planner can help utilize this form of ownership in establishing a gifting program to transfer title to other people, such as children, and hence remove from or decrease the value of the assets in your estate.

PLANNING FOR A WILL WORKSHEET

NAMES OF EXECUTORS (TO ADMINISTER THE ESTATE):	
NAMES OF GUARDIANS (AND ALTERNATES) OF MINOR CHILDREN: (can have a Guardian over the child himself, and a Guardian over the child's property)	
PROVISIONS FOR PAYMENTS OF DEBTS AND TAXES:	
SPECIFIC BEQUESTS OF MONEY AND TANGIBLE PROPERTY:	
NAME OF PERSON OR ORGANIZATION	AMOUNT OR ITEM
DISPOSITION OF THE REMAINDER OF THE PROPERTY:	
NAMES OF PRIMARY BENEFICIARIES (INCLUDING TRUSTS)	PERCENT
NAMES OF CONTINGENT BENEFICIARIES	PERCENT
Attach a list of assets (see Chapter 16) and insurance policies (see Chapter 15)	

Part IV

The
Inevitables

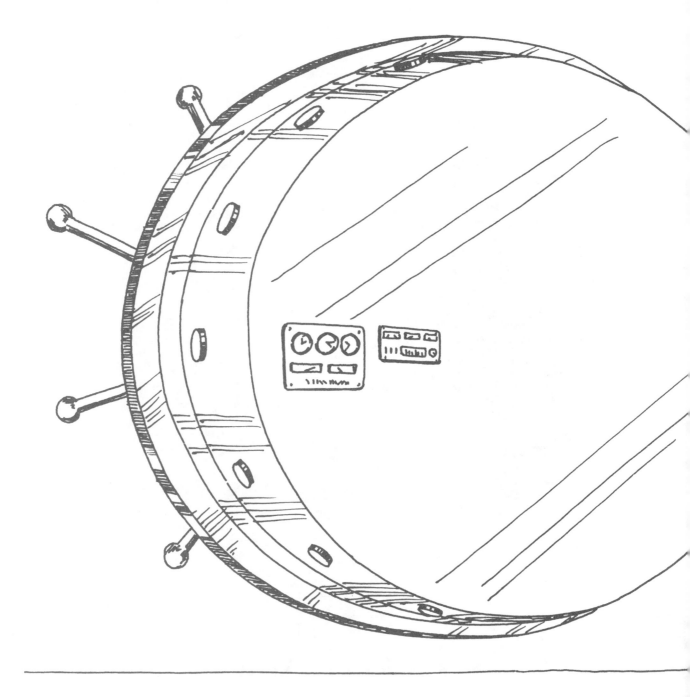

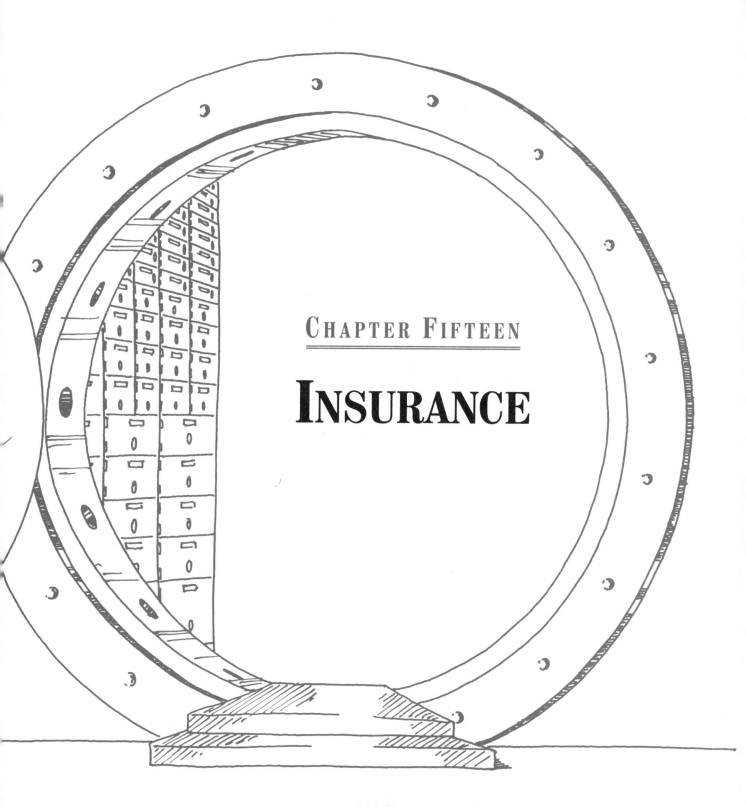

CHAPTER FIFTEEN

INSURANCE

The subject of insurance has long been thought of as dry and tedious. Those who aren't in the field are often at a loss for understanding the jargon and details associated with insurance. Nonetheless, although insurance, like medicine, may not conjure up images of "fun," it is important.

Insurance is a safeguard against the future. If psychics were right with their predictions even 50 percent of the time, insurance companies would suffer, because we would know our future predicaments. For now, however, insurance is a way of protecting yourself financially against certain future occurrences.

For the most part, five significant forms of insurance will cover you: life, health, auto, home, and disability. Occasionally, you may need a rider on an additional item. But don't become a sucker for a lot of additional insurance on every little thing.

In a most simple example, the basis of insurance was exemplified by ten softball players in Kentucky, each of whom put in $10 per game in case any one of them got injured and needed to go to the doctor. In the sixth inning of the first game, one player got spiked on a play at home plate, so they allocated $60 of the $100 collected to take care of his injury/doctor visit. The other $40 went to the ever-increasing pool, which grew faster than the injuries occurred. If, however, this had been a team consisting of the most injury- and accident-prone guys in town, the likelihood of an injury would have increased, and they would have had to put in $20 a piece to cover the greater medical costs.

This is the basis of insurance: pooling money from many individuals to cover the misfortunes or disasters of a few. And because we cannot tell the future, we can't know which among us will be the ones to sprain an ankle sliding into second base.

In the case of the Kentucky softball team, when the season ended, they took the remaining money, which totaled $600, and threw a season-ending party. This extra money is known in the insurance company as a dividend, although most of it now goes to the insurance company.

Currently, there are thousands of types of insurance options covering everything from your life to your baseball card collection. The trick is to determine the type and the amount of coverage you need. Sifting through the multitude of insurance companies and policies can be a tiresome task. The vast majority of people have little time to compare and contrast insurance companies, so they buy from the first agent that comes along. Since this is what you may do anyway, at least take a few minutes to read through the insurance basics and perhaps get some referrals from others who have already purchased insurance. You might also go online and look at what a few top insurance companies have to offer.

Keep in mind, before signing up, that the more reputable, better established insurance companies can offer you stability, which is something you need when looking toward the future. You want a sense of confidence that the company will be around to pay potential claims, even after a merger.

LIFE INSURANCE

The first and foremost type of insurance is life insurance. People will traditionally start thinking about life insurance when they get married and when they have children. Once you have others dependent on you financially, insurance becomes increasingly significant.

Once this happens, you need to determine the type and amount of coverage to purchase. Factors that determine how much you can afford to buy and what type of insurance is best for you will include your age, health, family situation, and income. One rule of thumb is that you buy three to five and a half times your annual income in life insurance coverage.

Remember that above and beyond everything else, insurance is a numbers game run by large companies who have a penchant for figuring out all sorts of risks and probabilities. It is important that YOU be the determining factor when calculating which of these numerical equations is right for your specific situation.

TERM, WHOLE LIFE, AND VARIABLE UNIVERSAL

There are three primary forms of life insurance: term, whole life, and variable universal life. *Term insurance* is bought for a set amount of time, starting at 1-year renewable and ranging up to 5, 10, 20, and even 30 years. It is the simplest

Term Versus Cash Value Policies

Judge for yourself whether you want a term or a cash value policy. Life insurance sales people make higher commissions on the latter, which is why it's best that you know what you want beforehand. Do your homework and never let anyone talk you into buying a policy that does not suit your needs or financial situation.

and least expensive form of insurance. It is, therefore, very popular today, particularly with younger buyers who can't afford more complex plans. Term basically says that if you die in such and such a time period, your beneficiary collects. Period. There are no other investments, no other hassles.

Since there is so much competition in the marketplace today, term insurance can be relatively inexpensive. Term insurance, however, gets increasingly more expensive as you get older. You may start off paying $200 in premiums when you're in your twenties but be paying $4,000 in premiums at the age of sixty-five, when you can't really afford it. For that reason, many people switch to cash value policies as they get older. Some people, however, work with other investments and stop buying life insurance entirely once the kids are out of college and on their own. If you plan your retirement and set up a sufficient estate, you may not need to continue holding life insurance past a certain point in life.

You can also buy a convertible policy, which allows you to make the conversion from a term policy to a whole life policy. Since whole life policies, or any policies for that matter, depend on your age, many companies allow you to convert after five years but still use the rate at which you originally bought the policy five years earlier.

A traditional *whole life* policy is one that builds guaranteed cash value, provides lifetime protection, and, in most cases, pays an annual dividend. The dividend is based on current dividend scales. It can accelerate the amount of cash that's available in the policy, or it can be used to buy more insurance. There are usually six or seven options available with annual dividends.

Whole life is more expensive than term. If you pay your premiums, however, the value of the policy will continue to grow over the years. A whole life policy will also pay a lump-sum benefit to your beneficiary. If you do not keep up with your premiums, however, you could find yourself without coverage.

There are various types of policies you can buy, depending on your financial situation, that let you pay either higher premiums later on, all the money up front, premiums that increase over the years, and so on. Don't worry, whatever you may need, some insurance company has figured it out, and there's a policy waiting with your name on it.

The third form of life insurance is *variable universal life*. This is becoming a very trendy type of insurance because it is both insurance and an investment vehicle. Basically, you take the risk of the guarantees off of the insurance company and put it on yourself by investing this money internally in the policy. There is flexibility, as you have a choice of different funds you can pick from. A part of your premium goes into your investment; the rest goes to your insurance costs. You can also borrow or withdraw money from the account. You can vary the premium amount that you will pay and, therefore, give yourself more control than in other types of cash value insurance. However, you need to stay on top of the account and manage it. This does not always work well if the premiums are small because the money goes into both the insurance and the investment, and you need to be able to cover both.

If the insurance market continues to do in the next ten years what it has done in the past, you will probably have more cash in this kind of policy than in any other. But the word *guarantee* does not appear in these policies, as it does in whole life, because the risk is taken on by the insurer and not the insurance company.

Since all growth in insurance policies is tax deferred, you do not pay taxes on the growth on a cash value policy, whether it is a traditional whole life or the variable universal. This is one of the advantages of variable universal life—your capital gains from a mutual fund, which would normally be taxable income, are inside the protection of the insurance policy.

Insurance policies are one of the few tax-deferred cash value investments left on the face of the earth. The question is, Are you better off investing elsewhere? If you do the math and find that you would do better with tax deferral than other investments, then variable universal might be best for you.

LIFE INSURANCE FLEXIBILITY

Policies are usually not set in stone. Depending on the changes you decide to make, different types of insurance allow you varying flexibility. Consider the following:

Insurance Carriers

Among the leading insurance companies to choose from are Allstate, Electric Insurance, John Hancock, Lincoln Benefit Life, Metlife, Phoenix Home Life, Ohio National, State Farm, Transamerica, Traveler's, Aetna US Healthcare, Prudential, Paul Revere, and Blue Cross Blue Shield. There are many more.

There are also many insurance Web sites. A number of them can be reached at www plus the name of the company. Quicken has a good Web site at www.insuremarket.com; it has access to information about a number of the leading companies.

Other sites include www.insure.com, www.autoinsure.com, and www.homefair.com (which offers you "the insurance professor" to help you with your insurance needs).

Dividends

Dividends, where do they come from? There are three basic ways insurance companies are able to afford to pay dividends. At the end of year, insurance companies take the following three factors into consideration and can issue increased dividends or pay the same as in previous years. (Ultimately, it's a pool of different sources that make up your dividend.)

1. A lower mortality at the end of the year than was predicted at the beginning of the year, which creates a surplus in the death benefit payouts
2. A return on investments that is higher than anticipated at the end of the year
3. Lower operating costs than anticipated at the beginning of the year

1. Look for account flexibility of investment vehicles.
2. Look for premium flexibility, which means you can change the premium.
3. Look for face value flexibility, which means you can change the face value of the policy.
4. All insurance will have you name a beneficiary—that name can be changed in the event of divorce or death. Don't forget to make the change if necessary.

HOMEOWNERS INSURANCE

Unfortunately, there are a number of catastrophes that can occur, most at the hands of Mother Nature, that can jeopardize your home and set you back financially. Homeowners insurance is designed to protect you in case of any number of "disasters," including lawsuits by individuals injured within your home. It is, however, set up with numerous guidelines and many factors taken into account.

Factors include the age of the home, its condition, how well it meets safety requirements, and its location. Houses in areas with higher frequency of hurricanes or on fault lines will obviously be more costly to insure than a home in an area that hasn't seen a natural disaster since, say, 1823.

Homeowners insurance covers the value of your home if it is whisked away, as in the *Wizard of Oz*, and you have to rebuild from the ground up. You can and should seek out a policy that has a guaranteed replacement cost included so that no matter what the assessment, the home can be rebuilt.

Generally, policies also cover the land the house sits on, plus other structures, such as a dog house, tree house, garage, patio—or anything not directly attached to the structure you call "home." It's important that your property conforms to any building and zoning codes and laws that are applicable.

Homeowners insurance should include liability. Liability insurance is important because it protects you if your "sure-footed" neighbor falls down the back stairs and does an accidental half gainer from the patio into your swimming pool, and then decides to sue you.

Your "stuff" is also covered by the policy, usually at around 50 percent, which takes into account the wear and tear. "Stuff" includes almost anything from jewelry to stuffed animals. If something is included in the policy, you are given a value on it known as an actual cash value, which takes into account the depreciation of the item. You can select a policy that will give you the full replacement value of this item as though you were buying it brand new. Though nothing can make up for losing an item of sentimental value, at least you can get a new item in its place. When it comes to sentimentality, you cannot ever be fully covered.

It is suggested that you have a list or, in the modern era, a video-tape of the "stuff" in your home. You can even do a "guided tour" on videotape, announcing what the items are. Some people choose to buy additional coverage on jewelry or other key home items. This should depend on the value of the items. Often it's not worthwhile to pay more for things that are easily replaceable. Antiques or truly valuable works of art or jewelry may be worth the extra coverage.

If, for any reason, you are forced to stay outside of your home for any length of time, a homeowners policy usually gives you some money toward hotel and other living expenses, until you can return to your house.

When buying a home, you will hear the term *mortgage insurance*, also known as private mortgage insurance (PMI). This insurance may be required by your lender. It covers the lender in the event that you default on your mortgage payments. If you make a down payment of 15 to 20 percent, you should not have to buy this insurance. The cost is about .65 percent of your original loan balance, so if you borrow $200,000, you'll pay an additional $1,300 a year. Mortgage insurance is no longer a requirement after a certain period, but you may have to remind the lender to cancel it. Otherwise, it can become one of those extra expenses that people notice but fail to fully understand and just continue to pay, even when they should not have to.

There is also title insurance. It is usually recommended when buying an older house, particularly one that has changed hands several times over the years. It is to your benefit to have this insurance in case the title is ever challenged in court. The title or deed to the property could be invalid, meaning you do not actually own the house. If a developer seeks to buy the land, you could find yourself in big trouble. Therefore, this insurance is usually bought for the sakes of the homeowner (at least you hope you own it) and the lender. Order the policy during the mortgage application process. It's not expensive and may be very worthwhile. You'd hate to find out after all those years of mowing the lawn and doing home repairs that the house isn't yours.

IN REVIEW

Ultimately, you want coverage that protects your home against as many catastrophes as are valid. Liability is important because something could happen to a friend, neighbor, or relative in your house, and (no matter how well you think you know them) they could sue the pants off you. Homeowner policies offer either replacement cost coverage (more expensive) or cash value coverage (less expensive and recommended for older homes). Either way, you want as close to 100 percent coverage of the value as possible. Find out how much it would cost at today's rates to replace your home, and you will have an idea of how much coverage you need. Local contractors, builders, and others in your community can give you approximate costs for your home. You can then gauge how much the additions you've made over the years would cost in today's market. Update your policy to meet the changing costs of building, and if you add on a room or two, a new roof, an indoor activity center, or a gymnasium, amend the policy accordingly.

Then, do your inventory and get a good idea of what the value is of your important possessions. Carry riders only when necessary. A good policy should cover as much as possible. If you don't see it included, ask why!

Renters insurance is similar to homeowners insurance in that it protects what is in your home or apartment. Replacement cost coverage, which costs a little more, covers items in full. Cash value coverage, which costs less, allows for depreciation (wear and tear) on your possessions. Once again, make sure liability is included.

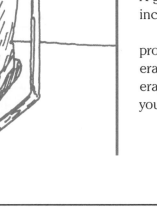

AUTO INSURANCE

Most states require drivers to have auto insurance. But even if it's not required, it's strongly advised.

Automobile insurance is divided into three areas of coverage: collision, comprehensive, and liability. Of the three, liability can have the strongest impact: Someone without collision insurance risks losing the cost of his or her car, but someone without liability could lose much much more than that in a lawsuit.

Liability protects you against bodily injury or property damages caused by a third party in an accident; it also covers your legal bills. In this era of increased lawsuits, liability insurance is absolutely necessary to protect your assets. Some states have established minimal levels of liability coverage that you must purchase. If you have assets totaling more than $300,000, you might consider additional liability coverage (on your car and home) or umbrella liability coverage to protect you against any accident for which you could be held responsible.

Collision insurance pays for damages to your vehicle. The maximum amount is limited to the depreciation value of your car, which is not the same as the car's replacement cost. It's a good idea to check the *Official Used Car Guide* once a year to determine the value of your car. You can usually find this guide in your local library. Over time, you may drop collision, as reimbursement for repairs may be less than the book value of the car. At some point, they may not be worth making at all.

Comprehensive insurance pays for noncollision expenses, including theft, vandalism, and natural disasters. Since you won't get more than the book value of your car, this too can become less worthwhile as the car gets older. After all, why pay $1,000 in premiums for a car that is only worth $750?

No-fault insurance eliminates finger-pointing and the long process of trying to determine who was at fault. Some states require it. The downside is that someone else's recklessness can drive up your premiums. Thus, good drivers are not big fans of "no-fault" insurance.

Uninsured and/or underinsured motorist coverage is important if you are hit by a vehicle driven by someone who is, as the name implies, uninsured or underinsured. This insurance costs little and in some states is required. Without this coverage, you could get stuck with a lot of out-of-pocket expenses. It covers you and your passengers, who also may not have adequate insurance.

New Insurances

There are new types of insurance that cover numerous expanding areas of technology. In fact, you can even buy a form of "biological insurance," which isn't really an insurance policy but a preventative form of health care for newborn babies. Their umbilical cord blood is stored, and if ever necessary, it can be used in place of a (far more costly) bone marrow transplant to fight any number of diseases, such as leukemia. A company by the name of CorCell provides cord blood collection, testing, and storage. Families wishing to explore this new kind of "insurance" can contact CorCell at 1-888-3CORCEL or www.corcell.com.

As to the three areas of coverage—collision, comprehensive, and liability—shop around and find out exactly what is included under each premium. Rental cars are covered under many policies, despite what the people at the rental counters tell you. There are also many little extras that can be added, such as towing insurance. Most of these extras, however, are unnecessary. Shop around and shop wisely. Look for discounts and deals. Sometimes a company will offer a discount on your auto insurance if you have another insurance policy with them. You may also get discounts if you insure two or more cars, install antitheft devices, and have a clean driving record (i.e., no accidents).

There are a number of factors that insurance companies take into account when determining your auto insurance costs. This may explain why (as with airline fares) no two salespeople will quote the same rates. Some factors, like age and sex, you can't control. However, others you can control, to some extent. For example, air bags and other similar features can bring down insurance costs. Also, you could buy a car in a lower risk category in regard to theft. If you could interview a car thief, you might get a good idea of the more likely targets. Short of that, check police statistics to find out which cars are most commonly stolen. We do know that trendy cars are more at risk than less popular cars. And color can make a difference—red cars are stolen more than gray. Go figure!

The bottom line with car insurance is to get what you need. Don't overlook liability coverage—in addition to collision and comprehensive—and don't buy a lot of unnecessary extras. Also, as is always the case, read the contract carefully and make sure you understand exactly what is and isn't included. If you are concerned about something, don't be afraid to ask questions. "If I stop at a red light and a tree falls on my car, am I covered?" No question is too stupid if it's a matter of your money and your potential savings.

HEALTH INSURANCE

One of the most heated issues in recent years has centered around health insurance. HMOs have come into prominence to the dismay of many doctors and to the delight of many companies that can now spend less to insure their employees. Unfortunately, the consumer has been caught somewhere in between.

Since health insurance is important for everyone, it's an issue that concerns us all. Those who go without health insurance by choice are either quite wealthy or taking a big risk.

Most workers are covered by their employers and most employers are signed up with either health management organizations (HMOs) or preferred provider organizations (PPOs).

HMOs traditionally limit you to the doctors in their plan. You can choose your primary physician from their plan, but you can't be referred to a specialist unless you see your primary physician first. Then you have to see a referral doctor before seeing the specialist, and sometimes this can be a long, drawn out process. In response to complaints about referrals to referrals to referrals and limitations on whom people can see, POS, point of service dual options, have arisen to limit the gatekeeper approach.

PPOs cost more, but they cover more, and they allow you to see doctors outside of the plan, covering as much as 80 percent of the cost. They usually have a deductible you must meet. (Managed care plans do not.)

Basically, the more options a plan offers, the more you need to spend. And choice in medical plans can be overrated. Having lots of choices doesn't necessarily mean you're better off. HMO doctors are most often just as qualified as any doctor you may select on your own. And, in those instances that you truly need a specialist, the specialist is just that, someone who has worked long and hard to build up a reputation as an expert in a particular field.

When seeking health insurance on your own, look for the larger companies, who do not rule you out for not meeting a certain medical profile. If you're self-employed or a freelancer (or an independent contractor), find out if there are plans you can join in conjunction with associations you may belong to. Usually unions have medical benefits.

If you should lose your job, or choose to leave, by law—the Congressional Omnibus Budget Reconciliation Act (also known as COBRA)—the company must offer you the opportunity to keep your medical benefits for up to eighteen months, at your own expense. This is advantageous because the company has a group plan, so the premiums are lower than those you would have to pay on your own.

Defining Pre-existing Conditions

The least favorite two words in the English language today are *pre-existing condition*. In many cases, you can be denied coverage, or have to wait to collect payment, for conditions that existed prior to signing up with that plan. This is the insurance company's way of denying a lot of people coverage for a wide variety of illnesses. Short of signing up for a plan shortly after birth, it's hard not to have some "pre-existing" condition if you're an adult. Look for plans that don't use this to get out of things like "covering you for an allergy because prior to joining the plan you were already breathing." Legislators are working to restrict and possibly eliminate this popular coverage loophole.

DISABILITY INSURANCE

The risk of being disabled is greater than that of dying prematurely. Since people are living longer, there are more people who become unable to earn a full living because of a disability. Therefore, disability insurance is becoming as significant as life insurance.

You may think, "Why bother? I'm covered by workman's compensation at my job." Coverage at your job is fine, but what happens if you get injured horseback riding while on vacation? Your employer will say, "Sorry, it's not an injury sustained at work, or work related."

This doesn't mean you don't want disability coverage on the job; it just means you may want additional insurance on your own. Companies may limit the amount of the benefit, but it is recommended to try to get at least 60 to 70 percent of your monthly income covered.

When purchasing disability insurance, follow these guidelines:

1. Notice how *disability* is defined in the policy.
2. Look for *occupation coverage*, which covers partial disability that affects YOUR profession. A serious injury to a finger can be the end of a surgeon's livelihood; a similar injury to a toe might not affect the surgeon but might end the career of a dancer.
3. Look for built-in inflation protection.
4. Look for a policy that is noncancelable and guaranteed renewable. Be sure you don't need physical exams to keep the policy. With regard to company policies, check to see what happens if you lose your job. Can you stay covered and at what cost?
5. How long will you need to wait before the policy goes into affect? Some policies might not kick in for thirty days, but the wait can be longer. A few months is reasonable, but a lengthy waiting period can leave you uncovered for too long.
6. Don't let a deductible scare you off, even if it's a 20 percent out-of-pocket expense. Companies will usually set a maximum and then pay 100 percent if medical costs become exorbitant.

LIFE INSURANCE POLICY COMPARISON WORKSHEET

INSURANCE COMPANIES	A.	B.	C.
TERM			
Annual Premium			
at $50,000	$	$	$
at $100,000	$	$	$
at $500,000	$	$	$
WHOLE LIFE			
Annual Premium			
at $50,000	$	$	$
at $100,000	$	$	$
at $500,000	$	$	$
Annual Dividend			
at $50,000	$	$	$
at $100,000	$	$	$
at $500,000	$	$	$
VARIABLE UNIVERSAL LIFE			
Annual Premium			
at $50,000	$	$	$
at $100,000	$	$	$
at $500,000	$	$	$

CURRENT INSURANCE POLICIES LIST

LIFE INSURANCE					
PERSON COVERED	CARRIER	POLICY NUMBER	FACE VALUE	PREMIUM	PAYMENT FREQUENCY (MO./QUART./ET)

PROPERTY & LIABILITY INSURANCE					
PROPERTY COVERED	CARRIER	POLICY NUMBER	COVERAGE	PREMIUM	PAYMENT FREQUENCY (MO./QUART./ET)

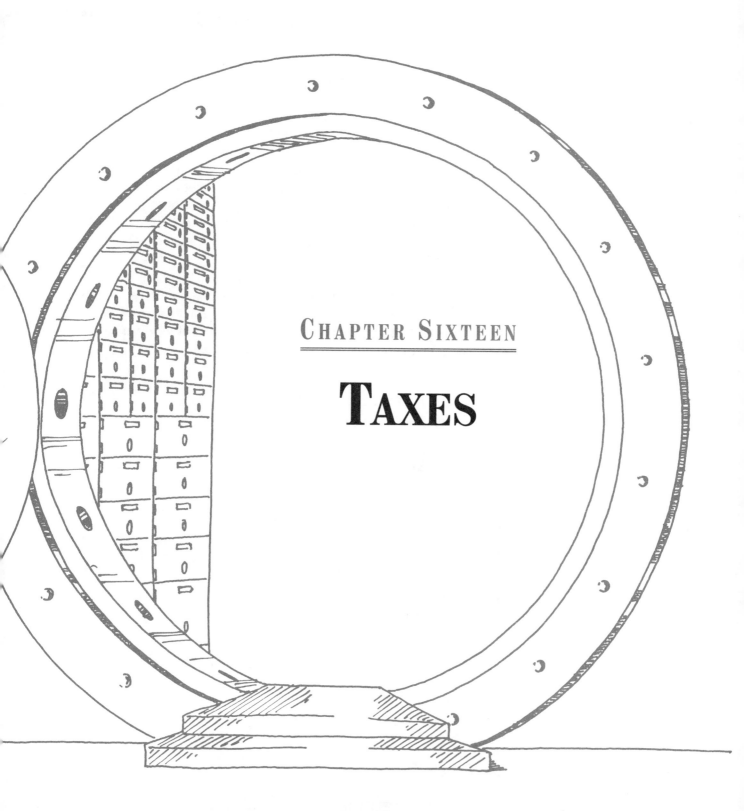

CHAPTER SIXTEEN

TAXES

Income tax, one of the two inevitables in life, is a staple in America and has been for generations. Your tax return is due April 15th. That's the easy part. Figuring out how much you owe and how you can owe less is the hard part.

The tax system in the United States has been under fire in recent years for being antiquated. Politicians continue to discuss and debate ways to amend, revise, and redraft a method of taxation that would be less complicated and fair to all. But, while sweeping tax reforms remain part and parcel of political rhetoric, the overall tax structure remains in place, with just enough annual changes to affect some and confuse many.

While the overall structure is complicated, there are also millions of details that make up the current system. Here is a brief overview of the current tax system. It's important to get a basic understanding so that you'll have a better idea of *why* you hate paying taxes so much.

TAXABLE INCOME

Your taxable income includes the following:

Wages
Commissions
Compensation for services, including tips
Bonuses
Interest
Dividends
Capital gains
Unemployment compensation
Alimony
Annuities
Royalties
Rent collected
Profits from self-employment or a partnership
Social Security (with limits)
Pensions and income from other retirement plans
Gambling winnings

The current tax rates are at 15, 28, 31, 36, and 39.6 percent. The table in your annual tax guide will tell you the exact amount of income tax you owe for up to $100,000 of taxable income. Over that amount, you will need another table and have to do some calculating.

Along with federal income tax, in most states, you pay state income tax. Currently there are seven states that do not have a state income tax: Alaska, Florida, Nevada, South Dakota, Texas, Washington, and Wyoming. Florida, however, has an intangibles tax on the value of your investments.

The forms, supplied by the IRS, include the 1040, which is the most commonly used tax form. Tax forms can be obtained from the IRS, your local library or post office, some banks, or by calling 1-800-Tax-Form. You can now download most tax forms through the Internet at www.irs.ustreas.gov . You can also get forms by fax. Or check the tax booklet for the number of the form you need and call 1-703-368-9694.

FILLING OUT THE FORMS

Following the instructions is not always easy, which is why each year more and more Americans turn to H&R Block and other tax preparers for much needed assistance. If you do choose to tackle the return yourself, it's suggested that you use last year's return as your guide.

Proceed slowly and, if necessary, recheck your backup information (sales receipts, statements from banks or brokers, trade slips, etc.) to be sure your entries on the tax forms are correct. You need to compute your total income, then your adjusted gross income, or AGI, which is the number you will use most often while calculating itemized deductions. The AGI is calculated by deducting from your income certain expenses, also known as above-the-line expenses, including deductible IRA contributions, the medical savings account deduction, moving expenses, half of the self-employment tax, the self-employed health insurance deduction, contributions to Keogh and self-employed SEP and Simple plans, penalty paid on early withdrawal from savings accounts, and alimony paid.

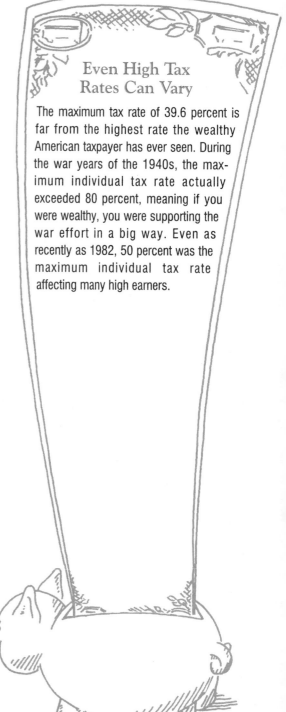

Even High Tax Rates Can Vary

The maximum tax rate of 39.6 percent is far from the highest rate the wealthy American taxpayer has ever seen. During the war years of the 1940s, the maximum individual tax rate actually exceeded 80 percent, meaning if you were wealthy, you were supporting the war effort in a big way. Even as recently as 1982, 50 percent was the maximum individual tax rate affecting many high earners.

Once you have calculated the AGI, you can then either take the standard deduction or your itemized deductions from schedule A in your tax booklet. Determine which method is in your favor. These are the standard deductions for 1998 tax returns, by category:

Single	$ 4,250
Married filing jointly	$ 7,100
Head of household	$ 6,250
Married filing separately	$ 3,550

ITEMIZED DEDUCTIONS

If your itemized deductions amount to more than the standard deductions, by all means use the itemized total. These are among the schedule A itemized deductions:

- Medical deductions (beyond the first 7.5 percent of your AGI)
- State and local income taxes and real estate taxes paid
- Home mortgage and investment interest paid
- Gifts to charity (receipts are required for contributions of $250 or more)
- Casualty or loss from theft
- Unreimbursed business expenses and investment expenses (over 2 percent of your AGI)

Regarding the second item, if you are in a state with significant state taxes, this can be an important deduction. In fact, you may even prepay state taxes in the fourth quarter by December 31st to get the itemized deduction.

There are many stipulations and even more gray areas that can limit some of these deductions. The tax form can explain them more closely; so can calling the IRS or a tax preparer. And yes, the tax preparer's fee is one of the deductions you can take on schedule A.

Carefully review any deductions, making sure they fit the parameters. Also make sure you keep backup material in case this information is questioned. Use the previous year's deductions as a guide.

Glaring changes, such as $2,000 in unreimbursed business expenses one year and $22,000 the next, will attract attention, so be especially careful to have documented evidence of any major changes in your deductions.

One recent catch is that there is now a limit on total deductions. As of 1998, you need to reduce your deductions by 3 percent of any AGI over $124,500. In other words, if your AGI is $154,500, you need to look at that extra $30,000 above the limit of $124,500 and take 3 percent or $900 (3 percent of the $30,000 is $900). Then subtract that from your deductions. Thus, $9,900 in deductions is reduced to $9,000.

Once you've completed your deductions, subtract your personal exemptions and compute your taxable income. The tax calculation formula would look like this:

1. Gross income minus adjustments or above the line deductions equals adjusted gross income (AGI).
2. AGI minus itemized or standard deductions minus personal exemptions equals taxable income

CREDITS

After the tax is computed, additional credits can reduce the tax. They are listed on Form 1040 and include a credit for child and dependent care expenses, a credit for the elderly or the disabled, an adoption credit (for expenses), and a foreign tax credit. Also, as of 1998 there is a credit for each child under age seventeen.

REDUCING AND AVOIDING TAXES

For years baseball has been called the great American pastime. But year round, millions of Americans (over two hundred million) play the real American pastime, that is, trying to figure out how to reduce taxes. There are three primary ways to reduce taxes:

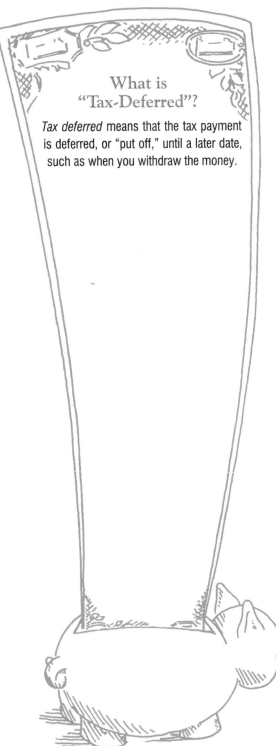

What is "Tax-Deferred"?

Tax deferred means that the tax payment is deferred, or "put off," until a later date, such as when you withdraw the money.

1. Minimize what would be your gross annual income by finding tax-free investments in which to put your money.
2. Take as many itemized deductions as allowable.
3. Earn less money and fall into a lower tax bracket.

Although the last choice doesn't sound very practical, if you are on the verge of receiving a large amount of ordinary income and it's December 19th, you might try to defer receiving that money for two weeks to keep it out of a particular calendar year, thus avoiding a higher tax bracket.

TAX-FREE INVESTMENTS

There are a number of legal ways (some of which are mentioned in various sections of the book) to defer taxes or to avoid taxes altogether. Both 401(k) and 403(b) retirement plans, as well as some IRAs, allow you to put away some of your income before paying taxes on it. Depending on the plan, however, you may have to pay taxes when you withdraw the money. This isn't necessarily a bad thing, since your income level during retirement may be less than it is now. U.S. Treasury bills and U.S. Treasury bonds are places to invest money to avoid state taxes, and municipal bonds are tax exempt for federal purposes, and for state purposes in the states in which they are issued.

Compensation that is paid in the form of benefits by your employer for hospitalization, group life insurance, other health plans, or dependent care is not taxable, subject to certain limitations. Furthermore, if you are reimbursed for money spent in direct relation to your employment (e.g., if you are reimbursed for dinner expenses incurred because you had to work late), such payments are not taxable. Also, under flexible spending plans, you can reduce your taxable income by making tax-free salary contributions to plans for reimbursement of expenses for medical or dependent care.

SOME RECENT LAWS

While the overall concept of taxes remains a constant, the laws that surround them are constantly changing. New laws are often to your advantage; however, discerning them is not always easy.

Family, children, education, and owning a home are the principles around which many of the changing tax laws are centered. The tax credit for each child increased from $400 in 1998 to $500 in 1999, with special provisions made for taxpayers who have three or more children who qualify (dependents under the age of seventeen). However, if your modified adjusted gross income level exceeds $110,000 for a married couple or $75,000 for a single individual, these provisions begin to phase out.

Families formed by the adoption of a child can benefit with a tax credit of up to $5,000 for expenses within the calendar year in which the adoption was finalized (adoption costs average $15,000 to $20,000).

Education tax breaks include the Hope Tax credit. It consists of a 100 percent credit per student for the first $1,000 of tuition expenses and a 50 percent credit for the next $1,000 for each of the first two years (i.e., a $1,500 credit each year) of postsecondary schooling for payments made after 1997. As of June 28, 1998, there is a 20 percent credit for the third and fourth years of college, per taxpayer; it's called a lifetime learning credit and is for up to $5,000 (or $10,000 after the year 2002). The phaseout on this credit begins at $80,000 for couples and $40,000 for singles. There are also deductions now available for interest on student loans.

In an effort to encourage home buying, first-time home buyers are now allowed to draw up to $10,000 from their IRAs without penalties, provided they use it toward the purchase of a new home in the subsequent 120 days. (As mentioned in Chapter 13, "first-time" *usually* refers to not having owned a home or primary residence for the previous two years.)

Home sellers can now receive up to $500,000 in nontaxable profits as married couples or $250,000 as single individuals for selling their homes, provided they owned the homes and lived there for at least two of the last five years. It's important to keep records of how much you paid for the house plus any improvements and of the sales transaction.

Also, there's help for those working from home. As of 1999, self-employed individuals who work from home offices will be eligible for deductions if they use their home offices for administrative and/or managerial tasks and do not have another fixed location for doing such activities.

QUARTERLY VERSUS YEARLY PAYMENTS

Filing your tax return and paying taxes are two different things. Many people think that "April 15th" is the only day in the year that taxes are due. Wrong! April 15th is when the tax RETURN is due. Companies, self-employed individuals, and anyone who has money coming in (that would result in $1,000 or more in taxes) should pay quarterly estimated taxes. Otherwise they pay interest and penalties, which explains why some people find the taxes they owe (on April 15th) to be higher than they anticipated.

If your paycheck is your only source of income, then your employer is withholding taxes for you, in which case you can skip this section. However, if you receive dividends, interest, capital gains, and other income, you, too, should be paying estimated taxes, unless the total tax liability is within $1,000 of the taxes withheld by your employer.

Estimated taxes for the current year are based on the actual tax from the previous year, less the withholdings. If you paid $12,000 in taxes last year, you can pay quarterly taxes at that same amount for the present year, or $3,000 per quarter. This can be helpful if in the second quarter of the year you suddenly make an extra $100,000. For that quarter, you can still pay $3,000 in estimated taxes, as you are protected from penalties by equaling or exceeding one fourth of last year's tax. Make sure you pay on time. Any tax balance due on the $100,000 can be paid by April 15th (when your tax return is due) without incurring a penalty.

Quarterly estimated taxes are paid for the period ending March 31st, with the tax payment due April 15th; May 31st, with the tax payment due June 15th; August 31st, with the tax payment due September 15th; and December 31st, with the tax payment due January 15th. Often people neglect to pay quarterly taxes and save all their income taxes for the following April 15th. They are then surprised to find that they have incurred penalties for not paying on time.

ANNUALIZED INCOME

When paying quarterly taxes, you can also compute an annualized taxable income each quarter and pay the tax based on that amount. For example, if you have $10,000 of taxable net income in the first quarter of the year, you could pay that quarterly payment based on making $40,000 for the whole year. If you have an income that is seasonal and is higher in the latter part of the year, you might choose to do this. You can do this for each quarterly payment.

For example, if in the first quarter you earn $10,000 and in the second quarter you earn $5,000, you can then annualize for your second payment based on $15,000. Keep in mind, however, that the quarterly breakdown of tax payments is not even; the breakdown, as listed previously, falls after 3, 5, 8, and 12 months. Therefore, you would calculate your second "quarterly" payment based on 5 months. So, $15,000, annualized for your June 15th (second quarter) payment, would be taxed based on an annualized income of $36,000. An easy way to calculate this is to see how much one month would be and then multiply by the number of months you are up to at the end of that quarter (3, 5, 8, or 12). For example, $15,000 in five months is $3,000 per month or annualized at $36,000, from which you would base your second estimated tax payment. Compute your total annual tax on $36,000. Calculate $5/12$ of that amount, which is your total cumulative liability to that point. Then subtract the amount you paid in your prior payment, and you will arrive at your current amount due. Take your time and double check your calculations.

EXTENSIONS

Anyone can get a six-month extension to file their form. Contrary to popular belief, this does not mean you don't have to pay the approximate balance of tax due by the April 15th filing date, plus quarterly tax estimates due for the current year. It just means that you can delay filing the return. To avoid a penalty when you file your return, you are still expected to have paid 90 percent of your taxes for the year.

Too many people think an extension, like postponing jury duty, means you can forget about the situation entirely. This is not true, since you're still expected to pay. Therefore, don't utilize an extension unless it is absolutely necessary (e.g., to gather or locate more information—sometimes investors can't get information on their earnings from an investment in time—illness, or being out of the country). Otherwise, it's best to get your return over with by April 15th.

STATE AND LOCAL TAXES

The general rule of thumb is to do your federal return first and then use most of the same information for your state return. BUT, before the tax year ends, estimate your full state tax liability and arrange for payment by December 31st if you can use "state taxes paid" as an itemized deduction.

Each state has a Department of Revenue, usually located in the state capital, that can answer your questions regarding state taxes and provide you with any paperwork you may need, plus information in the form of brochures. If you are a resident of more than one state, are working in one state while living in another, move from one state to another, or work or receive income from more than one state, you may have to figure out several sets of state tax laws. Good luck.

One of the best places to seek out individual state-by-state information is at www.taxweb.com. This Web site can provide you with easy access to information. Just click on the particular state you choose.

TAX PREPARING

Tax preparation should not begin in January, unless you have a relatively simple, straightforward financial picture. The more income you have, beyond that from an employer, the more organized you should be throughout the year. Keep paid bills, receipts, brokerage statements, home mortgage forms, and any other transactions filed and clearly marked throughout the year. Make sure to keep your W-2 form(s) on hand as well as any 1099s that are sent to you. If you are self-employed, you should receive a Form 1099 from each payor for any money you earned over $600.

If you don't have many sources of income but can't figure out the tax forms or if you simply want someone else to prepare them (for your own peace of mind and comfort level), then you can go to a tax preparer. H&R Block prepares returns for millions of Americans, as do other companies. They are less expensive than CPAs and may be all you need to sort out your return.

However, if your financial picture is more complicated (i.e., if you have capital gains, self-employment income, numerous interest and dividends, investments galore, a partnership), consider hiring a certified public accountant (CPA) to do your return for you. Base your decision on how complex your return is and how many questions you need answered. A CPA can do the following:

- Determine quarterly estimated tax payments
- Decipher which additional forms and schedules are needed for more complicated financial situations
- Make recommendations and suggestions that can help you better plan and structure your tax and financial situation

When working with an accountant, provide him or her with last year's return (as a basis to start with) as well as all your income information. Then go over your deductions carefully. If you are not sure about a deduction, ask; and if necessary, bring in the financial records to help determine the answer. Have everything well organized before your visit so that you won't have to pay an hourly rate to help your CPA sort through your papers. Give him or her sufficient time to prepare a return or even file for an extension. In other words, don't show up at his or her doorstep on April 14th.

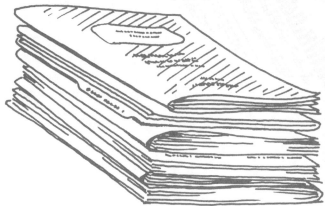

DEADLINES

It's important to pay quarterly taxes and file your income tax return on time. The postmark must meet the deadline. You can also file electronically by e-mail. Your tax return booklet will provide you with the information. The IRS Web site (www.irs.ustreas.gov) can also help you figure out how to file electronically. If you mail in your return, you can now use these designated private delivery services:

- Airbourne Express (overnight air express service, next afternoon service, 2nd day service)
- DHL Worldwide Express (same day, DHL USA overnight)
- Federal Express (priority overnight by 11 AM, standard overnight by 3 PM, 2nd day)
- UPS (next day air, next day air saver, 2nd day air, 2nd day air AM)

WORKING WITH THE IRS

The Internal Revenue Service, no matter what you think of it, does provide explanations, several free publications, and other information about the tax returns you will be filling out. If your return is not very complicated and you have a grasp of what the IRS is actually talking about, you can use the guidelines and file your own return.

The IRS will answer questions (call 1-800-TAX-FORM or go online at www.irs.ustreas.gov). Be careful when asking tax questions, however, because often there is a communication breakdown when trying to explain a specific tax situation and decipher an answer correctly. If it's not a straightforward question, you may be better off requesting that a booklet or pamphlet on the subject be sent to you.

Should you be called in for an audit, you need to organize your paperwork. You should also call your accountant, if you have one. The IRS will inform you of when they want to see you and specify what part of your return (and what year or years) they want to audit.

You need to be prepared, organized, and cooperative. What this means is that finding all the paperwork is only half the battle. The other half is making sure you can clearly explain your deductions and exactly what each receipt is for. Give yourself some time to prepare, in case you need to track down certain documents. AND MAKE SURE YOU HAVE COPIES OF EVERYTHING.

Contrary to popular belief, IRS agents are people too. Thus, if you are cooperative and helpful, the process should run smoothly. The IRS is looking for solid reasons and backup for your deductions, as well as for explanations and documentation for everything. An audit that moves along smoothly can benefit you in the end. Auditors are very aware that you don't want to see them. Nonetheless, they have a job to do; so it's in your best interest to leave any hostility outside the room. Hit a bucket of golf balls or do some other activity to relieve stress before the actual audit.

Prior to an audit, you should put yourself in the place of the auditor and try to determine what he or she wants to see to validate your deductions. Besides talking with an accountant, you might contact someone you know who has been audited to discuss some of the questions you may be asked. Although every audit is different, you should get an idea of what to expect. Online you can check www.taxchecker.com, a site that helps review your return and a possible audit.

An audit is not something you can't survive, if you work within the system. If you have valid proof that you have been treated unfairly, you can appeal to the auditor's supervisor. Many times, settlements are reached at the supervisor's level. If you still feel you have been treated unfairly, you can appeal the decision to the U.S. Tax Court. This can be costly, time consuming, and a very difficult battle to win—which is why it's not often that anyone takes on the IRS.

BUDGETING TO PAY YOUR TAX BILL

Always set aside a percentage of your income for paying taxes, not unlike an employer withholding a portion of your

Filing Electronically

You can now file your tax return through the Internet, which means you can work on it up until the last minute. Since 1997, electronically filed returns are up some 20 percent. The IRS is happy about such electronic returns, as they take only six to eight days to process, involve less paperwork, and have 19% fewer mathematical errors. Remember, your computer can do the math and help make the chore of doing your taxes easier and faster, but you still need to enter all the pertinent information. So be careful!

income for taxes. Put aside a percentage on a monthly basis. If there's a large capital gain, put aside money for the taxes incurred. If you are self-employed, don't forget to set aside money to pay self-employment tax as well as income tax.

Be ready to pay quarterly. However, if you do find yourself unable to pay due to some financial emergency, you can work out a payment plan with the IRS. You will, however, pay interest and, possibly, penalties.

SOME RESOURCES

Some places to seek help, besides tax books in the library, include a couple of leading tax software programs: Turbo Tax Deluxe from Intuit (MacInTax for Mac users) and TaxCut Deluxe from *Kiplingers*. There are numerous other tax programs available, but many are geared for professional tax preparers and may only serve to confuse you. Look for material geared towards taxpayers like yourself.

Besides the IRS Web site, you can go online and get information from www.hrblock.com/tax . The H&R Block site includes new tax laws, ways to itemize, and a calculator for determining your refund.

One of the more interesting books, although not easy reading, is Jeff Schnepper's annual *How to Pay Zero Taxes*. Contrary to the title, you won't get away without paying taxes. However, if you study the book carefully, it can help you pay as little as allowable by law.

Probably the most thorough book you can buy is J. K. Lasser's *Your Income Tax* guide, which comes out annually. J. K. Lasser also offers a monthly tax newsletter. You can contact them at 1-815-734-1104.

FAIR MARKET VALUE OF ASSESTS WORKSHEET

Checking Accounts

Bank Money Market Accounts

Certificates of Deposit

Mutual Funds

Brokerage Account/Stocks & Bonds

Retirement Plans (IRAs, 401(k)s, Keogh Plans, etc.)

Cash Value of Life Insurance

Real Estate, including Residences

Partnerships and Other Investments

Tangible Personal Property (autos, collectibles, jewelry, art, etc.)

Total

PERSONAL INCOME TAX DEDUCTION WORKSHEET PRIOR TO LIMITATIONS

ADJUSTED GROSS INCOME	
Early withdrawal penalties	$
Traditional IRA	$
Moving expenses	$
Alimony	$
Self-employment health insurance	$
Medical & dental expenses	$
ITEMIZED DEDUCTIONS	
Taxes paid	$
a. state & local income	$
b. real estate	$
c. personal property	$
d. investment	$
Interest	$
a. mortgage	$
b. home equity loan	$
c. student loans (limited)	$
Gifts to charities	$
Casualty & theft losses	$
Unreimbursed employee expenses	$
Union dues	$
Tax preparation fees	$
Job hunting expenses	$
Gambling losses	$
Uniforms or special clothing	$
Education expenses to improve skills	$
TOTAL DEDUCTIONS PRIOR TO LIMITATIONS	$

BUSINESS DEDUCTIONS WORKSHEET

Cost of goods sold	$
Returns & allowances	$
Advertising	$
Business gifts	$
Car & truck expenses	$
Commissions & fees	$
Depreciation expense	$
Dues to professional organizations	$
Employee benefit programs	$
Insurance	$
Interest	$
Legal & professional services	$
Office expenses	$
Office supplies	$
Rent	$
Repairs & maintenance	$
Payroll taxes & licenses	$
Travel (local & out of town)	$
Meals & entertainment (enter 50% of total)	$
Subscriptions	$
Seminars & professional development	$
Utilities & telephone	$
Wages paid	$
TOTAL:	$
List equipment purchases below (subject to depreciation)	
PURCHASE DATES	COSTS

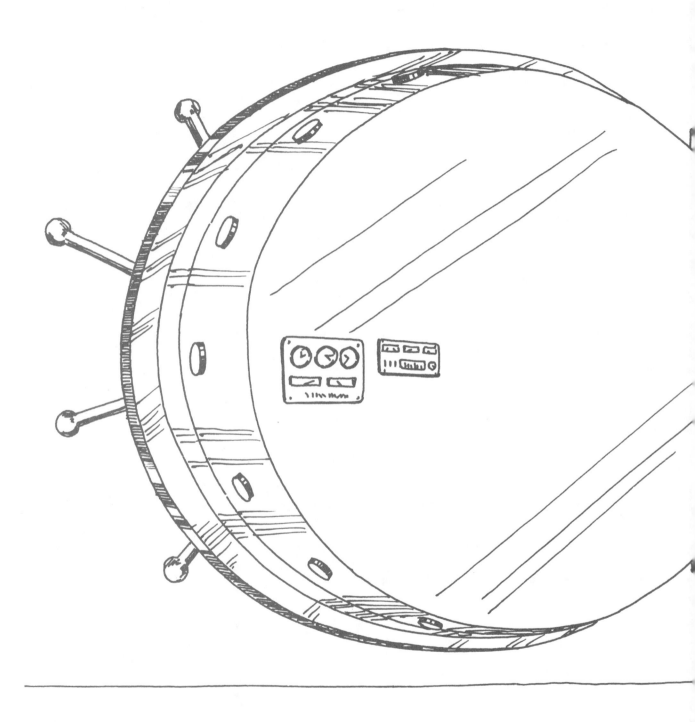

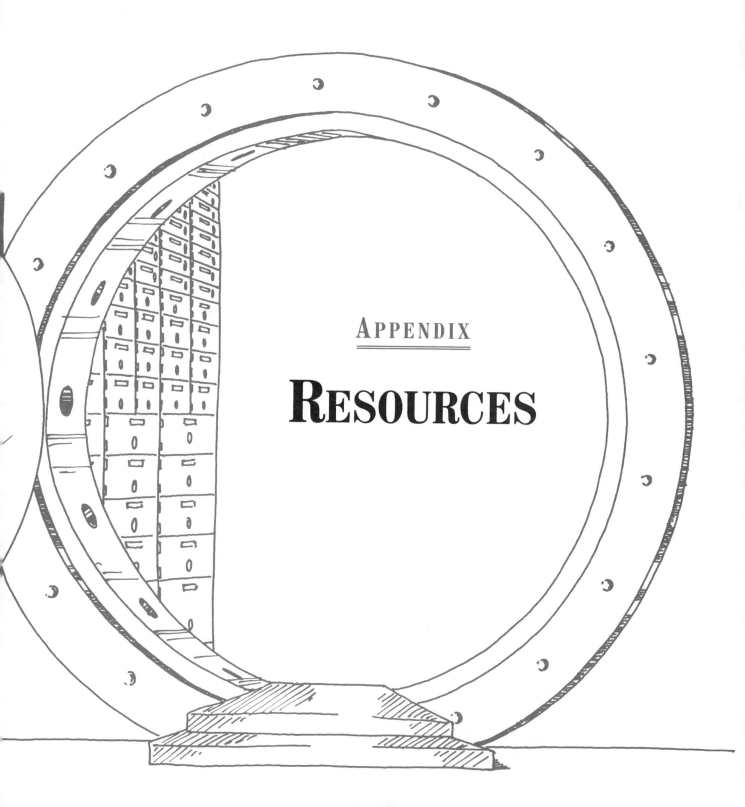

APPENDIX

RESOURCES

The Best Magazines and Newspapers for Investors

Barron's
200 Liberty Street
New York, NY 10281
1-800-544-0422
www.barrons.com

Bloomberg Personal Finance
P.O. Box 888
Princeton, NJ 08542-0888
1-888-432-5820
e-mail personal@bloomberg.com
www.bloomberg.com

Craines
1400 Woodbridge Avenue
Detroit, MI 48207
1-800-678-9595
www.craines.com

Financial World
1328 Broadway, 3rd Floor
New York, NY 10020
1-800-666-6639;
In-state 1-212-594-5030

Forbes
60 Fifth Avenue
New York, NY 10011
1-800-888-9896
www.forbes.com

Investor's Business Daily
12655 Beatrice Street
Los Angeles, CA 90066
1-800-831-2525
www.investors.com

Kiplingers
1729 H. Street NW
Washington, DC 20006
1-800-544-0155
www.kiplinger.com

Money
1271 Avenue of the Americas
New York, NY 10029
1-800-633-9970
www.money.com

The New York Times
(Business Section)
229 W 43rd Street
New York, NY 10036
1-800-698-4637
www.nytimes.com

Smart Money
(Dow Jones & Company, Inc.)
1755 Broadway
New York, NY 10019
1-800-444-4204
www.smartmoney.com

Technical Analysis of Stocks and Commodities
4757 California Way, SW
Seattle, WA 98116-4499
1-800-832-4642
www.traders.com

USA Today (Money Section)
1000 Wilson Boulevard
Arlington, VA 22229
1-800-872-0001
www.usatoday.com

The Value Line
220 East 42nd Street
New York, NY 10017-5891
1-800-833-0046
www.valueline.com

The Wall Street Journal
(Part of Dow Jones)
200 Liberty Street
New York, NY 10281
1-800-568-7625
www.wsj.com (fee-based service); 1-800-369-2834 to order the online version

Worth
575 Lexington Avenue
New York, NY 10022
1-800-777-1851
www.worth.com

CABLE TV NETWORKS

CNBC Cable Network
2200 Fletcher Avenue
Fort Lee, NJ 07024-5005
1-201-585-2622

CNBC provides business information, featuring a number of programs including *Today's Business, Squawk Box* (a hot business talk show), *Business Center, The Edge* (focusing on personal finance and tips on marketing and saving money), *Market Watch, Power Lunch, Street Signs, and Market Wrap Up I and II.*

CNN Cable News Network
P.O. Box 105366
100 International Boulevard
Atlanta, GA 30348
1-404-827-1500

Business shows include *Business Day, Managing with Lou Dobbs, Moneyweek, Pinacle,* and *Your Money.*

CNN Financial News Network
5 Penn Plaza, 20th Floor
New York, NY 10001-1810
1-212-714-7848

Shows include *Before Hours* (which features the market activity from Europe and Asia), *Biz Buzz, Digital Jam* (concerning technology and money), *Family Values* (about family financial matters), *In the Game, It's Only Money,* and *Moneyline.*

FNC/Fox News Channel
The Cavuto Business Report
1211 Avenue of the Americas
New York, NY 10036-8701
1-212-301-3228

Daily business finance program featuring interviews and a late look at the Wall Street news of the day.

Syndicated financial shows to look for include *Adam Smith's Money World, Bloomberg Business News, Financial Freedom,* and *Talk about Money.* You can also watch *The Wall Street Journal Report* Sunday mornings on CBS television.

FINANCIAL WEB SITES

There are numerous financial Web sites available to anyone who has access to the Internet. Besides the sites offered by financial institutions and mutual fund families are Web sites set up by the leading financial magazines. Most of the magazine sites offer information on retirement planning, investing, home buying, and other significant areas of personal finance. Naturally, many sites give advice and suggestions on the latest stocks and funds to buy. Read advice tips carefully and look for second opinions before jumping to buy or sell. Some sites require you to pay to be hooked up with the latest daily stock quotes. This service is usually for the more advanced investors.

Here are just a few of the leading financial Web sites:

Equity Analytics, Ltd. at www.e-analytics.com
Invest-o-rama at www.investorama.com
Microsoft Investor at www.investor.com
Morningstar at www.morningstar.com
Motley Fool at www.fool.com
Personal Finance Magazine at www.pfonline.com
Quicken at www.quicken.com
Thompson Investors Network at www.moneynet.com
Zacks investment research at www.ultra.zacks.com

AMERICAN ASSOCIATION OF INDIVIDUAL INVESTORS

The American Association of Individual Investors (AAII) is an independent not-for-profit organization. For the past twenty years it has been helping individuals to invest their own money.

Through various publications, videos, and seminars, the various chapters of AAII help over 175,000 current members by focusing on investing and investment techniques. Their guidance helps both new and seasoned investors and is not limited to those with large sums of money. They are, essentially, a professional association for non-professionals.

The $49 membership entitles you to their journal, which is published ten times annually and offers how-to articles and information on investing. Perhaps the best feature of the journal is its objectivity; it is not sponsored by investment companies and does not recommend specific investments.

Also included in membership is an annual guide to mutual funds, annual reports, educational material, and other publications. There are seventy local chapters and several ways to contact AAII: 1-312-280-0170 (membership services); 1-800-428-2244 (seminar registration and product information); www.aaii.com or AAII@AOL.com (Keyword AAII).

There are also several books available from AAII, for members and nonmembers, including *The Individual Investor's Guide to Low Load Mutual Funds, Investing Basics and Beyond, Stock Investing Basics, Portfolio Building Basics*, and others.

NATIONAL ASSOCIATION OF PERSONAL FINANCE ADVISORS

The National Association of Personal Finance Advisors (NAPFA) is a fifteen-year-old membership association dedicated to helping the public receive impartial fee-based financial advise from qualified experts in the field. Members must submit a financial plan, meet educational requirements (including strict continuing education requirements), and work on a fee-only basis. NAPFA members should provide comprehensive information on a broad cross section of issues. The only organization of its kind, NAPFA has nearly six hundred members throughout the United States. You can contact NAPFA to meet with a financial planner by calling 1-888-FEE-ONLY or 1-800-366-2732.

INDEX

We Have
EVERYTHING

More bestselling Everything titles
available from your local bookseller:

Everything **After College Book**
Everything **Astrology Book**
Everything **Baby Names Book**
Everything® **Bartender's Book**
Everything **Bedtime Story Book**
Everything **Beer Book**
Everything **Bicycle Book**
Everything **Bird Book**
Everything **Casino Gambling Book**
Everything **Cat Book**
Everything® **Christmas Book**
Everything **College Survival Book**
Everything **Crossword and Puzzle Book**
Everything **Dessert Book**
Everything **Dog Book**
Everything **Dreams Book**
Everything **Etiquette Book**
Everything **Family Tree Book**
Everything **Fly-Fishing Book**
Everything **Games Book**

Everything **Get Ready For Baby Book**
Everything **Golf Book**
Everything **Guide to Walt Disney World®,**
    Universal Studios®, and Greater Orlando
Everything **Home Buying Book**
Everything **Home Improvement Book**
Everything **Internet Book**
Everything **Jewish Wedding Book**
Everything **Low-Fat High-Flavor Cookbook**
Everything **Money Book**
Everything **Pasta Book**
Everything **Pregnancy Book**
Everything **Study Book**
Everything **Trivia Book**
Everything® **Wedding Book**
Everything® **Wedding Checklist**
Everything® **Wedding Etiquette Book**
Everything® **Wedding Organizer**
Everything® **Wedding Vows Book**
Everything **Wine Book**